STEPHEN HEATHORN

For Home, Country, and Race: Constructing Gender, Class, and Englishness in the Elementary School, 1880–1914

UNIVERSITY OF TORONTO PRESS
Toronto Buffalo London

Printed in Canada

ISBN 0-8020-4436-0

Printed on acid-free paper

Canadian Cataloguing in Publication Data

Heathorn, Stephen J., 1965–
    For home, country, and race : constructing gender, class, and Englishness
    in the elementary school, 1880–1914

    (Studies in gender and history series)
    Includes bibliographical references and index.
    ISBN 0-8020-4436-0

    1. Nationalism and education – England – History.   2. Nationalism –
    Study and teaching (Elementary) – England – History.   3. Working class –
    Education – England – History.   4. Education, Elementary – England –
    History.   I. Title.   II. Series.

    LC93.E5H42 2000   372.942   C99-932478-0

University of Toronto Press acknowledges the financial assistance to its
publishing program of the Canada Council for the Arts and the Ontario Arts
Council.

This book has been published with the help of a grant from the Humanities
and Social Sciences Federation of Canada, using funds provided by the Social
Sciences and Humanities Research Council of Canada.

University of Toronto Press acknowledges the financial support for its
publishing activities of the Government of Canada through the Book Publishing Industry Development Program (BPIDP).

Contents

Preface

How the Nation?

Nationalism is sometimes seen solely as a political ideology, one used only by individuals with a definite political agenda. But national identity is ultimately a social concept: people who have a developed sense of national identity share what appears to be an intuitive sense of their own collective experience and community – no matter how tenuous this sense may be – and believe that there are meaningful differences between this community and others.[1] Now, while this suggests that national identities have definite political implications, they are not necessarily of a 'party political' nature. Indeed, it is only the process of building national identity that allows for the mobilization of people for political purposes on the basis of nationalist claims. This process of defining the meaning of the nation and of national identity might be referred to as the 'how' of nationalism. It was my interest in the 'how' rather than the 'why' of nationalism that prompted me to undertake this study of the means by which the English masses were taught their national identity.

People today who experience their formal education in only one country rarely (if ever) think about how much of their early schooling was devoted to the construction and maintenance of their national identity. Although I did not completely understand this at the time, my own experience illustrates the point. In 1979, in my early teenage years, my family moved from England to Canada. On the very first day at my new school, I experienced near terror when confronted by the subtle but nonetheless alien exercises of building national identity in the classroom. I had expected there to be some differences in my new school, but I was initially reassured. Canadian science and math seemed to me sufficiently similar to what I had been taught in Britain (despite the slightly different terminology of the 'new math,' which had still not made its way to my English school in the late 1970s), and by lunchtime my initial nervousness had gone. I looked forward to the afternoon, for which I had scheduled my favourite subjects, geography and history.

But it was in these classes that my earlier confidence evaporated. The first exercise in my geography class was to sketch, from memory, a map of Canada. This caused me tremendous consternation. Not having had any Canadian schooling, I pleaded to the teacher that I was unable to do this. My pleas fell on deaf ears, however, and I struggled through my cartography exercise in quiet panic. It was not the mediocre results of my efforts, nor the fear of unfamiliar subject matter that caused my agitation. Rather it was a dread, brought on by a sense of helplessness and of not belonging, and by my realization that my non-Canadian background put me at a disadvantage in this rather simple exercise. Similarly, in my first history class I felt completely lost and overwhelmed: not because the material was new, but because it was presented with the assumption that I possessed a base of common 'national' knowledge.

Clearly, I faced far fewer problems of acculturation than immigrants from totally different cultures, especially those who also had to learn a new language. But this merely highlights my point. In providing what appears to be common cultural knowledge, schooling is explicitly engaged in a process of national-identity construction, part of which is establishing in the minds of students not just the place of their country in world affairs, but – more importantly – their own 'place' in the complex abstraction called a nation. By itself, the contention that state-supported schooling is engaged in the construction of a shared national culture may not appear to be particularly surprising or controversial. However, the process of building national identity is infused with ideas about social roles, political participation, and gender and ethnic differences. In examining the construction of national identity, we find that prescriptions about how the world and the people within it *should* relate to one another are increasingly taken for granted.

The origin of this book was a dissertation analysing nationalism in English school books at the end of the nineteenth and beginning of the twentieth century. My reading of the books and teaching materials used in elementary schools was initially premised on the assumption that we can learn a great deal about the construction of identity from what that society's professional delegates – its chosen educators – try to teach their children. Unsurprisingly, the choice of suitable school materials and ideas was found to reflect the educators' own values and beliefs rather than those of the parents or children in the elementary system. But this book has evolved somewhat beyond a study of the ideology contained within reading materials produced for the late-Victorian and Edwardian elementary education. The analysis here demonstrates that a near-systematic process of national-identity construction was initiated between 1880 and 1914. However unconsciously, professional educators and school-book writers were engaged in a process of secular 'nation building' among the working classes.

While it has become common for historians of continental Europe to point to the importance of secularization and nationalism in the overall development of nineteenth-century mass education, there has been some reluctance to ascribe a similar process in the English case.[2] Partly because large-scale state intervention in education came later to England than it did to France or Germany, and partly because English education throughout the nineteenth century was organized explicitly along class lines, many educational historians have seen nationalist and imperialist ideologies as merely the surf thrown up by the more momentous tidal movements of class and gender formation. Thus, while acknowledging the existence of nationalist rhetoric, social historians have tended to look 'beyond' or 'below' the rhetoric evident in teaching materials in an effort to examine the 'hidden social content' of elementary schooling, usually seeking to uncover the workings of capitalist socio-economic relationships in the organization of the school system and in the discipline of the classroom and the structure of the curriculum. Moreover, despite excellent curriculum histories that indicate when, how, and why specific subjects came to be included in classroom instruction, educational historians have rarely provided analyses of the actual discursive content of these subjects. Historians of 'popular imperialism,' on the other hand, have consistently pointed to the role of education in the justification of the imperial enterprise. Yet their investigations into the imperialist content of mass elementary schooling have so far been limited in scope by a position that generally divorces imperialism from wider expressions of cultural nationalism and conflates elite education with the schooling provided the masses, thereby underplaying the intimate connections among nationalism, imperialist sentiment, and domestic social concerns.

The interpretation offered here bridges these divergent historiographies. Primarily, this is a book about the formation of national identity. More specifically, it is a study of how working-class individuals were directed to understand themselves as part of a social whole, defined through the gendered abstraction of the nation; about how the inherent disorder, disjunction, and chaotic nature of life experience was framed through a constructed social formation. It is a work of history, rather than of sociology or cultural studies, because the processes of identity formation have been radically different at different times and in different places. And yet, this study's focus on the period that simultaneously marked the apex of the British Empire and also the substantially increased professional middle-class concern about the education of the working masses (not a coincident convergence) is quite deliberate. Arguably, the cultural changes that manifested themselves in Britain in this period provided a legacy that survived and influenced many other developments throughout the rest of the century. The cultural changes of this period cannot be dismissed as merely 'past history'; their influences are with us still.

Acknowledgments

Many friends and colleagues helped me turn my doctoral dissertation into this book, offering both advice and encouragement, and also in some cases by reading chapter drafts (or parts thereof). To Adam Crerar, Paul Deslandes, Simon Devereaux, Margot Finn, Jane Harrison, Richard Helmstadter, Matthew Hendley, Franca Iacovetta, Trevor Lloyd, Gerry Lorentz, John McCormick, Ian Radforth, Greg Smith, Eric Rauchway, Ellen Ross, Richard Rempel, Deborah van Seters, and all my colleagues at Indiana University–Purdue University Indianapolis, I offer my heartfelt appreciation. A very special thank you to Russell McCutcheon, whose critical perspective has been key in the evolution of this project in its current form, and to Keith Surridge in London, who helped me wrangle with publishers and libraries for illustrations. I would also like to thank Gerry Hallowell, Emily Andrew, Jill McConkey, Wayne Herrington, and the staff at the University of Toronto Press, along with the manuscript review committee and the several anonymous reviewers of the manuscript, for all their suggestions and advice. I am grateful to *Victorian Studies* and Indiana University Press for permission to include in this book passages from my article '"Let Us Remember That We, Too, Are English": Constructions of Citizenship and National Identity in English Elementary School Reading Books,' which appeared in *Victorian Studies* 38, no. 3 (1995), 395–427. This book has been published with the help of a grant from the Humanities and Social Sciences Federation of Canada's Aid to Scholarly Publications Program, using funds provided by the Social Sciences and Humanities Research Council of Canada. This support is greatly appreciated.

Of course, to thank is not to deflect criticism: any deficiencies or errors that remain are wholly mine. Lastly, special thanks are due to all my family, and especially my wife, Sherisse Webb, who along with excellent suggestions for its improvement, provided encouragement and support throughout the long germination of this project.

FOR HOME, COUNTRY, AND RACE:
CONSTRUCTING GENDER, CLASS, AND
ENGLISHNESS IN THE ELEMENTARY SCHOOL,
1880–1914

Introduction:

Reading the Nation – Elementary School Culture and National Identity

National culture is impossible without books.

R.E. Hughes, *The Making of Citizens: A Study in Comparative Education* (1907)

At the turn of the twentieth century, English elementary school class-rooms – the primary and often only location of working-class formal schooling – were workshops of a reformulated English nationalism. It was here that the children of the working masses first forged personal and collective identities within the context of systematic, state-sanctioned, academically constructed, nationalist aims. This was the period of the bellicose, self-aggrandizing, militarist, and overtly political forms of British nationalism commonly associated with the Edwardian conservative leagues.[1] But while these self-conscious propagandists and clearly defined political, organized movements were certainly an important part of the national landscape, it was elementary classroom nationalism that manufactured the shared national 'culture' and implied social roles of working-class national identity.[2] Arguably, the latter had first to be present for the former to have any real meaning: before political claims about the need of the nation for a larger navy, or an aggressive forward policy in the empire, or a call to arms in defence of the homeland could be effective, the idea of the nation itself ('our homeland') and one's place within it ('our duties and responsibilities') had to be defined and explained to all the working-class children whose early lives were mostly local and limited, framed primarily by their neighbourhood and family. In other words, before these children could begin to process, interpret, accept, mediate, reject, and/

or act on the images, symbols, values, and ideals of nationalist and imperialist rhetoric that were paraded before them on a daily basis, a framework of understandings and meanings was necessary – a vocabulary and syntax of national identity.

Of course, nationalism in Britain generally, and the role of education in the building of national identities specifically, pre-dates the later nineteenth century. What was new to this period, however, was both the perceived need to encourage a sense of national identity among the masses through schooling (imperialist ideologues being but one group to do this, albeit with the most transparently nationalist agenda) and a somewhat reconfigured vision of what was deemed appropriate for the masses. By the 1880s it no longer seemed sufficient that just the middle classes and the highest ranks of the artisanal classes be instructed in their 'national' responsibilities. Between the eighteenth and mid-nineteenth centuries, the experience of war against France, popular anti-Catholic prejudice, economic expansion, evangelicalism, liberal 'populism,' and the ideals of progress were all ingredients in the diffusion of nationalist ideals beyond the middle classes.[3] But during the last third of the nineteenth century, middle-class anxieties began to emerge, first about the active role of the masses in the social and political functioning of the 'nation,' and second about the continued effectiveness of the ad hoc nature by which the masses to that point had come to understand their national identity, if at all. With the heightened apprehension about Britain's economic situation that accompanied the perceived arrival of economic depression and successive extensions of the franchise, schooling came to be seen by many middle-class writers as a necessary mechanism for moulding a 'responsible' and self-aware citizenry.

At the very same time, graduates from the new schools of education, civic universities, and teacher training colleges were championing the pedagogical ideas being embraced by their counterparts on the continent and in the United States. But their calls for pedagogical change were contextualized by claims far broader than the demands of the new educational theory. Deploying the rhetoric of contemporary social and political commentators, the new educationalists pointed to the connection between the health and wealth of the state and the need for 'national' schooling; to education being 'the battlefield' of the 'new warfare' between states; and to education being fundamental to the future retention of the empire.[4] The new education's methods and proposed subjects in Britain were thus formulated within the context of concerns about social unrest, economic decline, and political volatility rather than questions of the content of child-development and education alone. Ultimately, the aim of the new education was to help each individual contribute something to a social whole defined within the parameters of 'the nation.'[5] As one leading educationalist, F.H. Hayward, noted in 1909, 'the fact that the vast majority of the English nation pass through the primary schools on their road to the full rights and responsibilities of citizenship' positively required more care and effort to be expended on the 'incalculable' value of 'sound views of education' for all children, regardless of their social status and position.[6] Similarly, J.G. Fitch, a renowned school inspector, argued as early as 1880:

In the development of individual character and intelligence, the more room we leave for spontaneous action the better; but when we are members of a community, the healthy corporate life of that community requires of us an abnegation of self. The soldier in the army must act *qua* that machine, which is working towards some greater end than could possibly be achieved if he retained complete autonomy. And every one amongst us is called, as citizen, as member of a council of municipality, or public company, to work with others towards ends which require unity of action, and which are incompatible with the assertion of our individual rights. It is then for this class of duties that school should in some measure prepare every child.[7]

Fitch's comments neatly summarize the context in which elementary education was being considered at this time; the schooling of working-class children was preparation for their corporate, community-oriented duties and responsibilities. The fact that Fitch uses military, commercial, and municipal metaphors further highlights the socio-political nature of the debates about elementary schooling.

Later, in his chapter of the 1908 government report on the state of moral instruction in schools, J.J. Findlay wrote, 'People are asking on every hand, What are the schools really doing to promote the nation's well-being?' To M.E. Sadler, respected professor of history and administration of education, and the editor of the report, it was no mere coincidence that this question was being asked during a period of tremendous socio-economic, political, and cultural challenges to the moral certainties and tranquil social order of the previous epoch. 'A great change in the intellectual outlook of a people is quickly and inevitably followed by education upheaval and unrest,' he explained.

'Through such a period of readjustment and disquietude, hopeful yet harassing, the schools of all nations are now passing.' For Sadler and the others who prepared the report, 'it is felt that a systematic effort should be made to foster a stronger sense of our national obligation, including ... a stronger sense of our obligation towards those who are our fellow subjects in different parts of the empire.'[8] Thus, by the turn of the century, the necessities of energetically moulding the social whole into a dutiful citizenry and of the state in actively performing this function for the nation came to be increasingly articulated by educationalists. As R.E. Hughes astutely summed up this attitude in 1907: 'The school is a political institution maintained by the state for the cultivation and propagation of national ideals.' Thus, every school, by its very nature, was 'a machine deliberately contrived for the manufacture of citizens.'[9]

Even those educationalists who deplored the rise of what they considered to be the jingoistic excesses of contemporary patriotism, and who viewed the school as a means to widespread social reform, still saw the 'long neglected' encouragement of a shared national culture as an essential task in education. From within the educationally liberal London School Board, E. Lyulph Stanley suggested in 1899 that it was vital that the working man and woman be more than just subjected to the 'civilizing' influence of school. They now had to be actively *taught* the responsibilities of citizenship and national loyalty as well.[10] Another liberal educationalist, Thomas Raymont, argued that the goal of making complete citizens required each student to understand 'that the spiritual inheritance of a British or an American or a German child is predominantly British or American or German, and that in that inheritance he must on the whole find salvation.' National ideas, Raymont continued, 'are a governing factor in the direct fashioning of character, no less are they operative in the determination of curricula.' For Raymont and others, it was axiomatic that the 'national culture should form the basis of instruction,' and changes were necessary so that the national culture could become 'the *basis* of all school instruction.'[11] Among those educational reformers who sought to alleviate the appalling social conditions of the inner cities – and even to generate enthusiasm for socialism under the guise of educational reform – the use of this rhetoric, especially that of 'national efficiency,' must be considered highly ambiguous.[12] But despite their genuine attempts to ameliorate social problems, organizations such as the Fabians, H.M. Hyndman's Social Democratic Party, Robert Blatchford's Clarion movement, and the Toynbee Hall and University Settlement schemes could not avoid framing their activities within the general vocabulary of the reconfigured 'national culture' discourse. And this demonstrative need to impart a vocabulary of identity – the 'national culture' – regardless of its political origin, was in fact one of the most persistent subtexts in the form and content of elementary education provision in the three decades prior to the First World War. The promotion of an accepted 'national culture' – or more accurately, a 'nationalist culture' – throughout English society was the self-appointed task not only of the ideologues associated with the conservative leagues, but also of the liberal mainstream of late-Victorian and Edwardian educationalists. The emphases might differ, but the projected end point was essentially the same.

The Changing Content of Working-Class Schooling

Knowing the aims of school instruction and finding out what the content of this instruction actually entailed are, of course, two different things. Without the ability to interrogate teachers directly about what they taught, we are left with the scattered accounts they left in memoirs and school records, the straying memories of their students, the varied observers of the time, and the books and other materials used in the classroom. These last sources have seemed to many scholars to have the most potential for analysis of the content of schooling, but the claims made on their basis have also been among the most problematic. To date, historical analyses of British school books have focused mostly on formal subject textbooks, especially history texts.[13] This has been the case because these books were often written by recognizable, sometimes famous authors whom librarians thought worthy of collecting. As a result, certain formal texts – a particular favourite being Fletcher and Kipling's extremely jingoistic *History of England* (first published in 1911, but still in print in the 1980s) – are cited by some historians as if they enjoyed a wide influence in mass educational culture at a time when, in fact, few if any children in the elementary school system would have had direct access to them. Indeed, the reliance on formal subject texts for evidence of what elementary school students were reading is extremely problematic. The vast majority of formal subject textbooks, like the expensive Fletcher and Kipling text, were written for the higher grade, and secondary schools or even the upper-middle-class Public Schools, all of which were attended by only a small minority of the population. Moreover, between 1870 and 1914, the amount of time devoted to formal class subjects, especially history, was severely limited. Until 1900 less than one in four elementary students received any formal history instruction at all, and those who did were frequently subjected to only a few lessons a year. The purchase of such books for elementary students was therefore impracticable. Even after 1900, when some history instruction was made compulsory by the Education Code, the minimum requirement entailed only about a dozen history lessons a year, which meant that in many schools the purchase of specialized history textbooks was thought entirely unnecessary.[14]

Although history and other subject textbooks were rare phenomena in the elementary classroom, students did have books to read. The staples of the elementary classroom throughout the Victorian and Edwardian periods were the cheap reading books used to teach and practise reading skills. Indeed, besides the verbal instruction provided by their teachers, the way in which most elementary schoolchildren 'learned their letters' throughout the nineteenth century was through exposure to these primers, commonly called 'readers.' During the first half of Queen Victoria's reign, these readers used catechisms, rhymes, 'general knowledge' conversations, and short passages taken from other works for reading practice and to convey their messages. These dry, often list-oriented books meshed perfectly with the requirements of the 'three R' (reading, writing, and arithmetic) curriculum of in-class reading aloud and rote memorization that dominated mid-Victorian pedagogical practice. Institutional and administrative pressures, as well as demands of parents, reinforced this 'three R' curriculum and the use of these simple books.[15] This was particularly reflected in the passing of Robert Lowe's revised Education Code in 1862, which instituted the notorious 'payment by results' method of applying the government grant to schools. After the passing of this code, school funding from the government was dependent on the reports of inspectors, who examined students in the three Rs (and needlework for girls) and observed the maintenance of classroom discipline. Since subjects such as history, geography, science, and the like were not examined by the inspectors in this rigid system, the use of general-purpose readers was administratively enshrined to the detriment of subject-oriented books. This remained the case even after the passing of the 1870 Education Act, which created a system of school boards empowered to finance, from the local rates, the building and running of non-denominational schools in areas where there was an insufficient number of existing Anglican, or other denominational, 'voluntary' schools.

The general readers used in all schools from the 1840s into the school board period, like the formal subject texts used in secondary and elite schools, were also depositories of ideological messages. Readers were often the first books that most working-class children read, and so they formed the basis of all their future reading: these books not only provided basic literacy, but also a lexicon for the development of personal and collective identity. J.M. Goldstrom's classic study, *The Social Content of Education, 1808–1870*, demonstrates that, for the first two-thirds of the century, readers moved from providing overtly religious messages to also supplying the dictates of political economy. They admonished their working-class readership about the necessity of acquiescence to the social order and deference to their social superiors. Numerous examples of social identity prescriptions can be found in these books. Dunn and Crossley's *Daily Lesson Books*, readers produced for the British and Foreign School Society during the 1840s and 1850s, provided lessons on the habits of diligence, forethought, temperance, and frugality, and included explanatory notes for the teacher on how to inculcate these traits in their young charges. A sample of this can be seen in the third volume, which explained 'the folly of thinking it unjust that one man should receive more than another in his labour,' the 'impossibility of regulating wages by law,' and the ways in which the 'labourer can improve his lot' through 'increased skill' and 'knowledge of best markets for labour.' Such lessons actually began early in the first and simplest of these readers, with the most basic of prescriptions: 'We must all work,' for 'God did not mean man to live without work.'[16] Similar lessons could be found in the stories and passages of the National Society's readers, used in Anglican schools, which were based on the same organization and principles.[17]

The passing of Lowe's 1862 Education Code increased reader use and did not much change the social tenor of the content.[18] For instance, the 1864 *Revised Lesson Book for Standard II* intoned, 'Capital is the result of labour and savings. Nothing is more certain than that, taking the working classes in the entire mass, they get a fair share of the proceeds of the national industry.'[19] This lesson was hammered home with a simple, if improbable, 'autobiography' in which a working-class lad leaves school, enters a cotton factory, saves assiduously, moves around the country and abroad to find better paying employment, marries late, and at the age of fifty is able to retire on his accumulated capital of £50,000. In his own words the hero then proudly proclaims, 'I am now richer, and have many advantages over many men of my age, who lived and worked with me in early life.' He goes on to explain the moral of his life, that his advantages were 'purchased' through sacrifices: extra studying, moving to unfamiliar places, hard labour, and the abnegation of leisure and luxuries. 'Having made these sacrifices of leisure, of ease, and of enjoyment; having laboured so hard and risked health, my all, and even my life, have I not a just claim to all that I possess?'[20] The telling of popular folk tales, such as Robin Hood, was similarly prefaced or recast with social prescriptions in mind. In *Nelson's School Series*, the author warned: 'We must not regard Robin as a common robber, although his example is not one that can be held up for imitation these days. He must be looked upon rather as one of those proud nobles, whom the grinding oppression of Norman rulers had driven to a lawless life.'[21] Popular teaching manuals of the day, like the one by the reader author Henry Dunn, explained to teachers how best to use readers; they were deliberately organized so that in-class reading and discussion of a single volume could last for months, and in some cases every day of a student's school life.[22] Each passage in the reader would be read and reread aloud in class by the students, and every word, synonym, and idea encompassed would be thoroughly dissected and discussed by the teacher and students together. The use of readers thus corresponded to the suggested aim of the secular elements of the mid-century curriculum for elementary students: the three Rs, temperance, political economy, money matters, biographies of 'good men,' preservation of health, geography, history, and 'why laws should be obeyed.'[23] While learning to read, elementary students were simultaneously being initiated into the ethos of mid-century liberal culture. The literacy being built was double-edged: both linguistic and socio-political.

While reader use remained at the core of classroom instruction in the 1870s and after, the readers themselves transformed markedly from the books published over the previous fifty years. This was due to the changing education codes and the emerging debate on the aims and methods of working-class literacy.[24] The Revised Code of 1862 had stated that working-class children ought to receive sufficient instruction in reading for their 'business in life.'[25] In subsequent codes, however, the required attainment for each standard was modified and a higher level of proficiency was expected. The most far-reaching changes were made to the codes set out between 1875 and 1882, in which 'intelligent' and 'expressive' reading was required at all standards (the levels of educational attainment dictated by examinations: most elementary students received instruction in Standards I through IV, but a decreasing number went on to the highest levels allowed in the elementary school, Standard VI and, later, Standard VII), and evidence of complete fluency was demanded in the higher levels.[26] Equally significant was the special interest put on the reading of English history and/or literature in the stated requirements of the 1882 code.[27] With the exception of a few minor changes in 1890, these remained the requirements of reading until the demise of the examination system in 1896 and continued to be the de facto bases for judging reading performance until after the Great War. Significantly, examination of literacy was to be conducted through the reading of passages from English history and English literature rather than from the lines of simple 'poetry,' 'modern narratives,' or 'newspapers' of the earlier code. To accommodate these changes, the 1880 and 1882 codes officially mandated the use of historical, geographical, and literary readers in the elementary school system. Instruction in the basics of geography, history, and English literature thus was reinserted into the curriculum through the 'back door' of the basic requirements for reading proficiency.

The ideological prescriptions contained within the new reader sets produced after 1880 indicate an even more significant change. As will be fully detailed in later chapters, rather than merely stressing the dictates of political economy, moral improvement, or spiritual salvation, reading books provided more involved narratives about national origins, character, and culture. Increasingly, elementary students were encouraged to read simple stories and biographies that elucidated from 'where' and 'whence' they came. A few examples here will suffice to demonstrate the tenor of this change. From the 1880s, reading books took pains to explain to elementary students their genealogical origins: 'Now in the north of Germany there lived a very strong race of men, tall and fair, and very handsome. They had blue eyes and yellow hair ... These people were our forefathers, just as Englishmen were the forefathers of our relations who live in the colonies and America.'[28] Such stories were supplemented with messages about England's particular, and special, 'place' in the world. As another reader from the 1880s noted: 'It is not the size of a country nor the amount of its gold and silver and other riches that makes a nation great and powerful, but the number of men and women and children in it that have kind hearts and wise heads and healthy bodies.'[29] Alongside these characterizations of who the English were, were illustrations and descriptions about who were *not* English, about who else inhabited the world and their relationship to the English: 'You have wondered what kind of people you would meet with if you went all over the world. You would find some very strange looking people, as you will see by these little pictures. You would meet with yellow faces, some copper-colour, some black. Most of them with very funny clothes, some with scarcely any at all.'[30] Furthermore, these characterizations also included the supposed relationships between Englishmen and women, and between the rulers and the ruled:

Her Majesty the queen was very anxious about her wounded soldiers. Wishing to hear how they were being cared for, the Queen wrote a letter in which she said – 'Would you tell Mrs Herbert that I beg she would let me see frequently the account she receives from Miss Nightingale or Mrs Bracebridge, as I hear no details of the wounded, though I see so many from officers, etc., about the battlefield, and naturally the former must interest *me* more than any one.

'Let Mrs Herbert know that I wish Miss Nightingale and the ladies would tell those poor noble, wounded, and sick men, that no one takes a warmer interest or feels more for their sufferings or admires their courage and heroism more than their Queen. Day and night she thinks of her beloved troops.'[31]

A passage such as this conveyed prescriptive ideas about 'appropriate' gender roles (through the image of the caring, supportive Nightingale and her nurses contrasted with the heroic, noble soldiers) and about the presumed place and role of the monarchy in the national community (the queen as 'mother' figure to the nation, taking an interest in *all* her subjects).

In short, the ideological subtext about social roles in readers moved from the mid-century dictates of spiritual salvation and political economy to include the far more encompassing scope of the nature of national identity, and the social roles of men and women within this imagined national community. It is to decoding the meaning of these messages, within the highly specific context of their production and transmission, that the greater part of this book is devoted.

School Books for the Masses

Clearly, the context of the production and consumption of elementary school reading books must first be understood before any analysis of their significance can be attempted. We certainly need to be sure that the materials to be examined played a consequential part in the work-ing-class child's acquisition of 'literacy.' There is a variety of evidence which does suggest that readers played a vital part in the schooling of the vast majority of working-class children in the period 1880 to 1914. First, publication and purchasing figures indicate that elementary schools across the country invested heavily in readers for in-class use. The purchase and use of the more substantial formal subject textbooks (the books that have most often been studied) pales in comparison. For instance, taking the figures for only the volume intended for Stan-dard III in each case, Longman published 480,000 *New Reading Books* between 1885 and 1902, 205,000 *New Geography Readers* between 1880 and 1900, 115,000 *Ship Historical Readers* between 1891 and 1902, and 120,000 *Ship Literary Readers* between 1894 and 1904. This compares with a grand total of only 34,000 copies of Oscar Browning's *Modern England* and 26,000 of Mandell Creighton's *Age of Elizabeth* published between 1879 and 1905, and yet these were two of the more popular formal history textbooks of the period. Even allowing for the possibil-ity that some books printed were not sold, and that some books sold were not read, the ten to one ratio of readers to formal texts indicates the markets for each group. The vast majority of the formal texts, such as Oman's famous *History of England* (only 6,000 copies published by Edward Arnold between 1897 and 1902), were more likely used for schools servicing the middle and upper classes, and for children who had already mastered reading.[32]

Second, the records of the Manchester School Board indicate that, at best, formal texts might have been purchased only for school libraries, head teachers, and pupil-teachers studying for their certification ex-ams.[33] Given the assessed rates of the Manchester board and the size of the city it served, its resources were probably somewhere near the average for England as a whole.[34] If so, then few elementary schools could have afforded to spend more than a few shillings a year per student on new books. The clerk of the Manchester board noted that, over the year 1894–5, the average attendance of the board's schools had been 37,189 and the amount spent on books £4,938. This resulted in a net per head expenditure of 2s 7d. The clerk also noted that £895 had been collected from students via 'book money,' leaving a net of 2s 2d per head of book expenses paid by the board out of the rates for the year.[35] Such a budget precluded the purchasing of expensive texts for in-class use, even had they been desirable.

Third, a breakdown of reader use showing the number of books that students were exposed to in the elementary classroom can be obtained through the requisition records for urban school boards and the book-use surveys initiated by educational authorities. Between 1897 and 1900, some 95,520 history readers (in twenty-six distinct sets), 83,018 geography readers (sixteen sets), and slightly more than 500,000 general-purpose readers (sixty-five sets) were bought for distribution in London schools.[36] Meanwhile, a 1912 Board of Education report on the availability of books in one hundred typical London-area elementary schools noted that, in the upper standards (Standards V, VI, and VII), 70 per cent of the children read seven or more readers in-class per year (average, 7.5 books per year); in the middle standards (III, IV), 55 per cent read six or more per year (average, 5.8); and in the lower standards (I, II), 70 per cent read five or more per year (average, 5.5).[37] London was a prosperous school board, and in many smaller towns and rural areas the number of books available would likely have been less. However, as similar numbers of readers regularly appear in school-logbook 'lists of books to be used in the coming year' in other localities,[38] we can be reasonably certain that all children schooled in English elementary schools read from at least a couple of readers in their classrooms every year.

The Commercialization and Professionalization of School-Book Production

Understandably, the huge market for school books caused by the expansion of elementary education in the 1870s drew tremendous interest from a variety of commercial publishers, whose educational sales and profits subsequently soared.[39] Firms such as A. & C. Black, Blackie, Cassell, Chambers, Collins, Longman, Macmillan, Nelson, Pitman, and later Edward Arnold came to dominate this highly competitive market. Longman and Cassell early on produced innovative series that won acclaim from school boards and educationalists alike and provided the basic formula for many other houses. By the 1890s Longman was publishing simultaneously more than a dozen different elementary reader series, many of which had total publication runs of between 50,000 and 115,000 books per standard per year.[40] The large Scottish firms also applied themselves to producing for the English market. The firm of Thomas Nelson and Sons sold an astounding 5,065,184 *Royal Readers* – a series widely used throughout England – in the four years 1878–81, producing a net profit for the company of £49,543.[41] This single series amounted to some 45 per cent of Nelson's profits in its educational publishing category during this period. The *Royal Readers* series was reissued in frequently modified form until after the First World War. Blackie, another Scottish firm, turned out its innovative *Comprehensive Readers* in 1879 and went on to produce some of the most successful series of general, history, and geography readers of this period.[42] The house of Collins, meanwhile, reduced its total title list after 1875 and concentrated on a few standardized sets. The most positive result was the *Graphic Readers*, which sold in the several hundreds of thousands in the 1890s, and to which were then added the even more spectacularly successful *New Graphic Readers*, the first of their kind to be illustrated with three-colour pictures. At the behest of the London County Council, in 1904–5 Collins redesigned its geographic *Wide-World Readers* in quarto (a new size for school books), set in bold type with reproductions of historical paintings from British galleries.[43] This created a new standard for reader production values that was to be emulated well into the middle of the twentieth century.

While not the leader in sales or profits, a striking example of the successful mass-educational market suppliers was the new firm of Edward Arnold, which began publishing in 1890. Arnold built up his concern almost entirely through mass-education market sales. Starting with arithmetic books and J.H. Yoxall's edited adaptations of stories from Dickens in *Arnold's English Literature Series*, Arnold added over 200 titles to his cheap reader series (covering literature, geography, history, domestic science, drawing, and Bible study) in ten years.[44] Few of these books exceeded one shilling in price, and many cost as little as eight pence, a feat made possible by the practice of paying their authors a flat fee. Arnold depended entirely on board school publishing for its very existence prior to 1900, but its tremendous success in this field allowed it to expand quickly into other areas.

In addition to the commercial publishers, the National Society and the Educational Supply Company continued to publish texts for the new elementary school market, and the ancient university presses also began to publish in this area. The National Society enlisted the help of the popular children's book writer C.M. Yonge for both its historical and literature readers. Most significantly, Yonge was responsible for the *Westminster Reading Books* (1890) and *The English History Reading Books* (1881), which together became among the most widely used of all sets in Anglican schools.[45] Moreover, at the Oxford University Press, a school-book committee was formed in 1863 and began publishing the Clarendon Press Series in 1866. First directed at Public Schools, many were later intended for a wider school audience.[46] Cambridge's press entered this market somewhat later, with a focus more on secondary rather than elementary education; the Pitt Press series, for instance, was aimed at providing texts useful for candidates for Cambridge local exams. However, as with Oxford's Clarendon Press, some local education authorities did make use of Cambridge reading books for their elementary schools.[47]

The vast increase in sales and the large potential profits to be made in the publishing of school readers meant that great attention was paid to the demands of the school codes, the dictates of the inspectorship, and the perceived desires of the educational authorities.[48] Commercial publishers were regularly censured by the school boards and local education authorities for attempting to bypass formal selection procedures and peddle their wares directly to the teachers.[49] Indeed, the content of classroom texts tended to be strictly monitored by the boards and local education authorities. In most districts in England, publishers had to submit their texts to municipal or county education officials or to a standing textbook committee of a school board or voluntary school who would sanction books by placing them on an approved requisition list.[50] In the 1880s publishers regularly complained that the use of approved requisition lists damaged their trade. The school boards countered that the market was flooded with inferior products, that teachers had no time to properly examine the merits of the masses of cheap readers being produced, and that teachers sometimes chose books for the wrong reasons: 'that they were apt to choose those that only helped children pass exams without training their minds.'[51]

By the end of the century, the close monitoring of titles by requisition committees resulted in the publishers stressing the professional nature of their products' authorship: stressing, that is, the credibility of their authors and editors. Accordingly, authors of the books used in the elementary school increasingly came from the ranks of professional academics and educationalists.[52] As the following chapters will demonstrate, a symbiotic relationship developed, wherein the publishers wanted academics to write their school books because it helped get them onto approved selection lists, while academics wanted to write these books because this activity helped to justify their aspirations for professional status and the establishment of new academic disciplines. Indeed, the bulk of reader authors at the end of the century seemed to have belonged to three broad but overlapping groups, all with professional pretensions. The first cohort was that of university-trained academics in the disciplines of history, geography, and English literature. The second group was the equally recently established academic educationalists and their instructor colleagues in teacher training colleges. The third group was one of headmasters, grammar school teachers, and officials in the secondary and elementary school systems. As this study will detail, by the turn of the century nearly all individuals in these cohorts had received some form of university education, and despite the pre-eminence of women as teachers in the elementary school system, the majority of the authors of school readers were men. The end result was that a cadre of professional middle-class men came to dominate reader authorship, and it was their views that came to dominate the content of the books used to teach literacy to working-class children.

The commercialization of reader production and the professionalization of authorship, moreover, led to a homogenization of the views expressed; differences of opinion, as we shall see, were slight, and variations in content were limited. To suggest that the new reading books for mass education drew from the professionalizing academic trio of geography, history, and English literature does not mean that elementary school readers were simply carbon-copy proofs of major academic works with all the big words taken out. While it is true that the professionalization of reader authorship meant that the same or similar authors were responsible for writing books for university, secondary, and elementary school systems, school readers were written, edited, and packaged with the dual purpose of developing reading skills and imparting 'useful' and 'proper' knowledge to their intended working-class audience.[53]

Reading School Books, Reading the Nation

As should already be evident, school texts are useful in the study of the dominant culture of a particular time precisely because they signify 'particular constructions of reality, particular ways of selecting and organizing that vast universe of possible knowledge.'[54] Such texts necessarily embody what Raymond Williams has called a 'selective tradition': they reflect someone's selection, someone's vision of legitimate knowledge and culture.[55] Publishers and authors clearly intended their work to be read by a specific audience and no doubt were concerned that their works have specific effects. However, much of what is analysed in this study concerns the veiled and partially veiled dictates of ideological assertions that were often internally inconsistent: we should not assume that these assertions were always explicit to their espousers. Indeed, the vast majority of writers, editors, and teachers connected to turn-of-the-century schooling would not have seen their views as in any sense 'ideological.' Reading-book authors were as immersed in a constructed national culture, an imagined national character, and an unfolding national story as they wanted their audience to be. It would also, thus, be misleading to attribute the ideological prescriptions discussed in later chapters to entirely conscious, cynical attempts at 'social control' by hypocritical, propagandistic manipulators who preached one thing while believing something else. Social-identity construction is far more complicated than the terms propaganda and indoctrination imply. The authors of these texts were certainly not innocent of social prescription, but the ultimate result of their labour was rarely as clearly foreseen or as wilful as the term propaganda suggests.

This is not to say that school texts were therefore expressions of a pre-existent 'national culture' or 'character.' To suggest that the books used in schools simply reflected an already existing national culture is to reify this concept of national culture or character into a tangible, objective existence. That is the very aim of nationalist ideology: to naturalize and essentialize the nation, to suggest that the meaning of human existence can only be understood through the focused lens of 'the nation.' What is being argued here, therefore, is that the authors of the nationalist prescription found in elementary schooling were both sincere – in the sense that these authors no doubt believed in these ideas themselves: they were, after all, the product of nearly a century of academic inquiry and sustained belief – and also socially manipulative. The largely middle-class authors of school books saw as their mission the replacement, or the reduction of the appeal, of other potentially divisive collectivities such as class. The growth of elementary schooling for the masses coincided with the rise of mass labour movements, such as the London Dockers and match-girl strikes of the late 1880s. It should come as no surprise, then, that educators and academics, the suppliers of 'approved knowledge,' would use this opportunity to direct their subjects' attention away from what they saw as disruptive communities of interest and towards the more 'natural' unifying collectivity of the nation.

Some cautions need to be made, however, about presuming a one-to-one relationship between text and identity. For a start, the books considered here were not read in a vacuum. The role of the teacher in relation to the texts was an important part of the learning process. Clearly we should not assume that all teachers necessarily accepted everything that was presented in school books. As Dina Copelman has powerfully argued, the elementary school system as a whole and the classroom in particular were arenas of contestation between the national framers of educational policy, local school officials, teachers, parents, and students. And it was within this complicated social whole that identities were forged through schooling. However, while a social drama was enacted within elementary schooling, it has to be remembered that when it came to the actual content of instruction, many elementary teachers in this period were inadequately trained (although standards were certainly rising), and the majority of them were women who were often closer, socially, to their pupils than to their superiors. The women teachers in particular were thus in an ambiguous, often awkward socio-political position in the hierarchy of educational provision.[56] Some teachers, no doubt, attempted to subvert or offer alternative interpretations to the textual content of elementary schooling. Most, however, were either oblivious to the deep ideological dictate of the materials they relied on or, because of their own struggles to attain respectable and professional status, were not in a position to actively subvert it.

Moreover, there are epistemological arguments for privileging a contextualized reading of elementary reading books as a path to understanding how schooling helped construct the identities of schoolchildren. These books were instrumental in providing the most basic instruction in literacy: once ideologically unpacked, their form, use, and content can provide us with a glimpse of the lexicon of identity as it was deployed in schools. These texts were not the basis of isolated reading experiences by already literate individuals, but rather tools used to promote literacy among children still in the early stages of their formal schooling. The reading of specially prepared school books was thus the very nexus of the power/knowledge dialectic in the elementary classroom. They provided root meanings for abstract concepts of identification (or what I have repeatedly called the 'vocabulary of identity') such as the 'nation,' 'home,' and 'race,' and structured those meanings in a system of images and connected symbols (a 'syntax of identity') through historical, geographical, and literary narratives. Because it was the readers that were used to teach children how to read and use language in a (more) sophisticated way, the readers provided the conceptual apparatus needed to process information presented to them both in other aspects of their school experience and after. And thus, children were not only learning the alphabet of the English language, they were also learning the alphabet of their presumed identity. The actual identity of each child was, of course, 'written,' 'built,' or 'mapped' differently according to the matrix of conditions both before, during, and after school (parental guidance or lack thereof, pre-school learning, teacher mediation, workplace 'experience,' and so on) that was unique to her or him. As a result, no absolutely definitive conclusions can (or ever could) be made about the effects of these school books on the formation of the working-class child's subjectivity.

The claim that is made in this study about the effects of exposure to these books is that the boundaries of student subjectivity were circumscribed by the vocabulary and syntax of identity presented to them in the process of becoming reading-literate. And, as we shall see, the dominant language of the readers was that of the liberal nation-state. Learning to read the alphabet and learning to read the nation, therefore, went hand-in-glove. If, as individuals got older, their 'experience' of the world did not accord with the language – the vocabulary and syntax – of their elementary education, then they had to 'overcome' their primary instruction. This perhaps explains the evident 'conversion' experiences of many working-class individuals who, in later life, embraced oppositional positions to the liberal nation, such as socialism. Some children may have even rejected or unconsciously mediated their elementary education at the point of contact, but the very exposure to the language of the nation explains why even those that embraced an anti-liberal position rarely escaped the entire pull of nationalism. Even a radical-populist vision of England required an understanding of certain shared symbols of the nation. This also explains, at least in part, why so large a percentage of the population, regardless of their personal politics, never thought to question or oppose the claims made upon them by their nation-state, and why so many actively supported the 'nation' in times of crisis – most particularly, of course, the call to arms in 1914.

Plan of the Study

To accomplish its task, this book proceeds as follows. The first two chapters explore the promoted concept of the nation – 'our country' – through the prism of the language of 'citizenship' and the discipline of history. Chapter 1 sets out the context of educational claims about citizenship, the belief in the power of history to teach citizenship in the elementary school, the practical limits of its incorporation into the curriculum, and considers the authorship of the books that were supposed to impart citizenship through instruction in history. Chapter 2 examines the liberal/Whig master narrative of English history that was presented in most school reading books in light of this concern about 'citizenship.' Through exploring the subtext of gender- and class-identity construction, this chapter demonstrates how the history presented to working-class children as a basis of their identity was largely emptied of any radical or 'populist' alternatives to a socially inclusive, yet functionalist and statist, view of the nation.

Chapters 3 and 4 delineate the promotion of English ethnicity – 'our race' – through the language of racial inclusion and exclusion. These chapters amplify, but also challenge, recent work on racial stereotypes in British colonialism by suggesting that, at the turn of the century, the vocabulary of race was actually integral to English national identity *rather than simply* legitimating an imperialist world-view. Chapter 3 focuses on claims about Englishness, about an inclusive identity that was constructed through ideas of genealogical and cultural inheritance. Chapter 4 examines how the excluded 'racial other' was both a necessary correlative to the categories of inclusion – the 'them' that had to be distinguished from 'us' (both geographically and socio-economically) – and also a reflection of contemporary fears about domestic racial degeneration. Race was a slippery concept in nineteenth-century usage and could denote not only biological but also social and cultural difference. Indeed, the authors of books for the elementary school system frequently invoked the language of race in their discussions of English ethnicity and national origins in a manner that easily traversed the term's biological connotations and social-cultural meanings.

Chapter 5 examines the familial language of identity, of 'our home.' Working-class girls were taught to think of their own national duty in terms of their roles as wives and mothers to the English race. As both mothers and wives, English women were also tied symbolically to the English nation as the keepers of the home, a position that placed them at the core of patriotic sentiments and emotions. Moreover, the working mother's duties were also extended to conceiving and raising 'worthy' specimens of the English race. Educational effort was therefore expended in ensuring that working women knew as much about hygiene and 'efficient' domestic management as possible. However, the dictates of the prevailing social hierarchy in England at this time frustrated much of this effort, for undercutting this ideology of racial motherhood and the support of the domestic ideal for the working-class home was the need for the upper classes to have a surplus of well-trained domestic servants.

Chapter 6 rounds out the analysis with an exploration of three short case studies on how the vocabulary of identity connected together and with other school practices to form a comprehensive syntax of identity construction. The first part of Chapter 6 demonstrates the influence of one pervasive theme – the importance of the navy and of English seafaring – and how this theme included many of the discrete issues, narratives, and symbols presented throughout school books. The second part of the chapter details how the readers interacted with some of the wider culture of the elementary classroom, through an examination of the narratives, rituals, and practices concerned with the national flag. Last is an overview of one of the other socially specific processes of nationalist significance in the elementary school – the use of physical exercise and drill – and how these physical activities paralleled, and interrelated with, the textual content of the classroom experience.

Lastly, the Conclusion of this study explores the impact of the vocabulary and syntax of identity found in elementary school materials and details some of the general implications of the specific arguments presented, particularly as they relate to the issues of authorial intentionality, questions of 'propaganda' and 'social control,' and assessments of the effectiveness of school culture in moulding nationalist subjectivities. Ultimately, this study will demonstrate that instruction in basic literacy was, for the great majority of the English population between 1880 and 1914, the means by which an understanding of the 'nation' and one's 'place' within in it, as well as one's place in the world, was first discursively formed. 'Experience' of the idea of the nation and of national identity through whatever other media and circumstance – comics, juvenile and adult literature, newspapers, advertisements, the music hall and theatre, museums, parades, the workplace, memorials, and state spectacles, for example – all relied to a lesser or greater degree on the minimum 'national literacy' provided by early schooling. The point of this work is to discover how the 'experience of the nation' became possible: the conditions, that is, which made that experience possible in the first place, rather than dwell on the quality of that experience. For as Joan Scott has recently reminded us, 'experience is at once always already an interpretation *and* something that needs to be interpreted.' It is to the task of understanding the discursive nature of 'experience' and the politics of its construction, that critical task for any examination of the processes of identity production,[57] that we now turn in this study of the nationalist content of elementary education in the period 1880 to 1914.

1

Citizen Authors and the Language of Citizenship

It has been their endeavour to show that our national education in England, with all its variety and heterogeneity, its divisions and its cross-currents, is yet one and indivisible – one in its common aim of furthering the highest welfare of every section of our people, and indivisible in its set purpose of providing for each and all alike the training of the mind, development of faculties, and moulding of character which shall best fit each and all for effectively playing his or her part as a citizen of our Empire and a loyal subject of the Queen.

Opening Address of the English Education Exhibition by the Duke of Devonshire, *School Board Chronicle*, 13 January 1900

Since the French Revolution, the term 'citizenship' has been used to describe political and social relationships among individuals, the civic community (variously defined), and the state. Specifically, 'citizenship' differs from prior notions of 'subjecthood' in that it embraces some form of popular and/or electoral sovereignty. While the exact implications, forms, and connotations of the concept have changed significantly over time,[1] it is important to keep these basic points in mind when examining the educational prescriptions of turn-of-the-twentieth-century English elementary schooling. For as expressed in school reading books from the 1880s onward, 'good citizenship' was increasingly prescribed as an important element of the working-class schoolchild's identity. The prefaces of readers and discussions of their use found in manuals of teaching method were replete with state-ments on the need to inculcate in students the fundamentals of citizenship and its perceived corollary, patriotism. That the term 'citizen' and not 'subject' was used in these texts, intended as they were for the mass of the population, is significant. Technically, all members of the population were (and still are) British 'subjects' of the crown. Moreover, these authors were well aware of the still considerable franchise limitations before 1918: after the franchise enlargement of the Third Reform Act of 1884 and the Redistribution Acts of 1885, still only about half of the male students and none of the female students in elementary schools were expected to attain voting rights in later life.[2] One author, Osman Newland, cautioned students to this effect in his 1907 reader *The Model Citizen*. Subjects of the crown in Britain were called citizens, he noted, because they had certain rights and duties in common, but in reality only those with the vote had what could be called full citizenship. However, Newland was rare in his explicit explanation to his prospective audience of the social rather than political expectations of citizenship.[3] Other authors of English elementary school readers almost invariably pointed to the benefits and duties of English citizenship in their discussion of past and present peoples and events in a manner that simply elided discussion of political rights. Indeed, over the next two chapters it will be demonstrated that in the seemingly inclusive language of citizenship presented to elementary schoolchildren there was a subtext of social prescription about class and gender identities.

The general debate about citizenship through education was marked by both masculinist and socially statist assumptions. The good 'citizen' was presumed to be male, and in large part 'good citizenship' was the civic code of an approved form of masculinity. While women were also encouraged to be good citizens, and some aspects of good citizenship were held to be universal, women were expected to enjoy the benefits of citizenship through their association with men, either as daughters or wives, and to fulfil their civic and national duty in their domestic roles and by being mothers to future citizens. Doing one's duty, being loyal and 'patriotic,' but in a modest and self-sacrificing manner, was thus both worthy of citizenship and 'manly.' James Welton, professor of education at the University of Leeds, noted in 1906 that good citizenship entailed emulating the 'noblest ideas which have been operative in the national life' and that the 'true patriot is he who does his duty manfully in both public and private relations of life, not he who most persistently blows the trumpet of self-glorifica-

tion or beats the drum of ostentatious advertisement.' When elucidated from the position of an avid imperialist such as the Earl of
Meath, 'manly' values and those of 'good citizenship' – 'love of hard
work, thrift, self-denial, endurance, and indomitable pluck' – were
enjoined as the 'hall-marks of an imperial race.'[4]

Duty, discipline, reserve, obedience to superiors – values integral to
the later-Victorian middle- and upper-class masculine code – were
projected through the concept of citizenship for working-class boys.
However, while in the schooling of the elite the masculine code was
clearly intended to produce men worthy of leadership roles in the
nation and empire,[5] in the radically different social conditions of the
elementary school this intention was less certain. Arguably the basic
intention of the elementary system in this period was to reward the
very small number deemed 'of talent' with scholarships, and merely
to produce loyal, obedient, and disciplined followers among the rest.
Indeed, the social conditions and context of elementary schooling mediated the content of their education about English citizenship, the
meaning of their supposed national inclusion, and of their masculinity. Thus, we find that school reading books frequently implored their
working-class audience to view their independence and liberties
through the lenses of national duty and social obligation. As the 1895
Standard IV *Whitehall Literary Readers*, after explaining how John Stuart
Mill defined the good as the useful, asked, 'Who are the useful members of the community? We fearlessly reply – Those who do their duty
... without doubt, devotion to duty has always distinguished our greatest public men.'[6] Civic inclusion, social value, and duty were all enjoined. Moreover, readers intoned on the necessity of each 'boy' to be
'wiser, better educated, and more tolerant' and to be 'as brave, honest,' and 'true' as his forefathers and 'as much a *man*' as they had
been.[7] Book VI of *The King Alfred Readers* further commented that the
'true man' must be independent, and that schoolboys should 'lay the
foundation of a manliness which will be independent in the truest
sense.'[8] For the authors of these books, duties, responsibilities, and
entreaties to 'manly' loyalty and social deference, rather than rights or
the possibilities of social opportunities, formed the basic meanings
encoded in the vocabulary of citizenship aimed at working-class youth.
Before examining how the language of citizenship functioned in elementary school culture, and how a key element of citizenship was
presented in school books, the changing context of teaching 'citizenship' in the national culture first needs to be briefly delineated.

The Meaning of Citizenship in the Context of Education, 1880–1914

From the 1880s onward there emerged a spate of comparative reports and recommendations from educationalists and political commentators on the importance of providing some form of in-class instruction on the 'duties of citizenship.' While the term 'preparation for citizenship' had been used by political commentators in the debates leading up to the passing of Forster's Education Act in 1870, public debate on what this actually entailed peaked only in the 1890s, which was when the content of education became part of the more general concern about national efficiency. Spurred on by the 1895 Bryce Report on Secondary Education and the 1896 'Made in Germany' scare that had been whipped up as a result of E.E. Williams's book of the same name, great pressure was applied to the government by various groups over the questions of the administration and content of state-aided education.[9] Reform was urged, as it was alleged that the rise in economic competition, especially from Germany, was due to its superior state-run education machinery. The dismal physical condition of working-class recruits during the Anglo–Boer War only added further fuel to the debate as liberal and conservative imperialists joined the ranks of the national efficiency advocates in demanding that something be done about the state of 'national' education. The administrative overhaul of the Board of Education and of the entire elementary school system during the years 1899 to 1902 was one of the results of this wide-ranging debate.[10]

Not only the administration of elementary education was in question at this time, however. Content and curricula became the focuses of much debate as well. Scientific and technical training were usually the most prominent demands of the national efficiency movement, but these were often tempered with calls for better civic training as well. Sir Norman Lockyer, a lifelong advocate of science and technical training and a scientist himself, noted in 1905 that 'it is generally accepted both in this country and others, that whether the citizens of a State are educated or not is a matter of absolutely supreme importance.' And this necessary education was not merely of the intellect, but also of morals and physique. Education was 'no longer merely the concern of the child or the child's parent. It is acknowledged to be the only true foundation for a State's welfare and continued progress under conditions of peace or under condition of war.' Other 'scientifically predisposed' national efficiency advocates, such as Laurie Magnus, evinced similar concerns that technical and manual training should proceed hand-in-hand with more overt concern for elucidating the values of citizenship.[11] Meanwhile, avowed imperialist propagandists, such as the Earl of Meath, while sometimes endorsing the suggestions made by national efficiency advocates, were usually more prone to pointing out the failings of the schools with regard to the inculcation of citizenship and patriotism. Meath himself pointed to the importance of citizenship as an imperial virtue, since 'it is not the British Isles, but the British Empire that has to be reckoned as the state.' Good citizenship in this view was the 'bond of empire,' as indispensable as patriotism as a source of 'untold strength' to the national well-being. In fact, as early as 1893 Meath had been lecturing about the 'ideal citizen' and how best to produce more of them in schools.[12]

Indeed, conservative commentators tended to lay heavy emphasis on loyalty, duty, and obedience to authority. The Right Reverend Bishop Welldon, former headmaster of Harrow, noted in 1908 that the citizen was indebted to the 'ordered community' of the nation-state, 'for nearly all the safety and comfort of his life, for his personal liberty, for his security in the acquisition and the transmission of his property, for his means of communication, for the supply of food, for trade, for culture, for the world-wide dignity which attaches to the membership of the British Empire.' Welldon suggested that education for good citizenship was essential for the boys of all classes and walks of life, because it was necessary to instil in them 'the God-given mission of their race' and a sense of their 'own personal responsibility' to the past, present, and future welfare of the British Empire. Hence, 'the citizen of the future must be prepared to sacrifice himself for the State,' and 'the citizen of the British empire must in future do his duty, and he must do it for its own sake rather than for any recognition or reward which it might bring.'[13] Conservative and social imperialists, such as Welldon and Meath, Lord Roberts and Lord Milner, all commented on the implicit connections between the necessary tasks of national citizenship and the qualities demanded of an 'imperial race.'[14] Indeed, a large variety of nationalist organizations sprang up in this period advocating elements of this conservative vision of citizenship that would override class divisions and unite the nation. Although these groups and the publicity they generated were directed at the entire population, they mainly found their audience among the middle and upper classes. Nevertheless, the resonance of their arguments permeated the world-view of elementary educators, who presumed that a 'filtration effect' would eventually occur whereby the lower classes would get caught up in the political and moral concerns of the social elite.[15]

Meanwhile, the writings of James Bryce, given his prominent position in British politics and educational policy making, provide perhaps the most relevant summary of the mainstream liberal view of citizenship at this time. In a lecture given at Columbia University in New York City in 1908, Bryce prefaced a discussion of citizenship with his contention that 'everywhere in human society' there were two principles that were antagonistic to one another, and yet each was both equally 'essential to the well-being of civil society.' These were the 'principle of Obedience and the principle of Independence, the submission of the individual will to other wills and the assertion of that will against other wills.' Asserting that a reasonable English compromise between the two had created 'Free or Popular government,' Bryce then suggested that citizenship within such a free, democratic state required three qualities – intelligence, self-control, and conscience. 'The citizen must be able to understand the interests of the community, must be able to subordinate his own will to the general will, must feel his responsibility to the community and be prepared to serve it by voting, working, or (if need be) fighting.' In such a community, power and responsibility went together, and thus 'Duty [was] the correlative of Right.' Bryce, therefore, put extreme emphasis on early education in developing the future citizen's proper 'sense of loyalty,' and in fostering the correlation between responsibilities and rights, duties and privileges.[16] It should be noted here that citizenship in Bryce's explanation was only partially to do with political participation. Voting was only one way in which a citizen might demonstrate 'his' civic responsibilities, and it was in no way a necessary condition of being a good citizen. While the exercise of nationally defined duties – voting, working, fighting – and the healthy development of loyalty to state and nation were here held to be the key components of a citizen's identity, the definition of citizenship was held by another commentator to be the 'right ordering of our several loyalties.'[17]

L.H. Hobhouse provided a 'new liberal' view of citizenship. Accepting Bryce's conventional liberal concern with individual liberty, Hobhouse and the progressive left-liberals of this period contended that citizenship also referred to the political, civic, and social responsibilities of the state for the well-being of the individual. This was the beginning of the idea of 'social citizenship,' which was to have a fundamental impact on welfare policy in the middle part of the twentieth century. For Hobhouse and the early 'new liberals,' social democrats, and Fabians, citizenship rights were still derived from property rights – a view that had been essential to the moral and political ascendancy of the property-owning middle class throughout the nineteenth century, and which was entirely harmonious with the class inequalities of British society and its competitive market economy.[18] The difference between the mid-nineteenth-century liberal view and that of the progressives at the end of the century was that property rights were extended to persons in non-property classes through the argument that labour could be regarded as the property of the labourer. This redefinition was an attempt to make the concept of citizenship more socially inclusive without denying the importance of private property or resorting to overtly socialist models of social membership through changing the ownership of production.

The basic contours of this general debate regarding the meaning of citizenship were echoed in the discussions among professional educationalists, educational reformers, teachers, and members of the educational authorities about the connection between schools and citizenship between 1880 and 1914. Recommendations came from a variety of different political and pedagogical positions, but the common frame to nearly all the arguments and suggestions was that some understanding of 'good citizenship' ought to be a legacy of elementary schooling. Probably the most common view was summed up by S.S. Laurie on the opening page of his 1892 treatise on education, where he advised that 'education wisely directed can form men into good citizens if we begin the process of formation early.' Indeed, the state should 'guarantee' for all working men enough stimulation of their intelligence and virtues so that they could 'discharge well the ordinary duties of men in all their political, industrial, and personal relationships.' The preparation of the citizen for *ordinary* duties was the central point here. Laurie's vision was essentially one in which the male child was taught to appreciate his 'personal life' through the experience of the work 'best suited to him' and through the inculcation of the proper perception of his civic duties, which would thereby enliven his existence. There was no suggestion that the child could ever advance beyond his already assigned social station – he would likely always remain an 'industrial worker' – but this fact could be made palatable to him through the recognition of his importance to society, his place in the nation, and through the exercise of his various rights and responsibilities.[19] This was a vision that was simultaneously socially inclusive (although with regard to women only through association with men) and socially deferential.

This vision echoed the teaching of earlier in the century when 'manly self-respect and independence' of the working classes was thought to lie in the enforcing of 'immediate obedience and submission to authority, deference to others, courtesy to equals, respect to superiors' through rigid discipline in the classroom.[20] Strict discipline, order, and unquestioning obedience to authority – the main precepts of mid-century elementary schooling – were all retained at the turn of the twentieth century, but these alone were no longer thought sufficient to the task of creating good citizens. As an inspector lamented in 1901, 'the discipline may be excellent in a school, but the moral tone sadly defective, if not almost absent.' Thus, he agreed that there should be more emphasis 'in every school to teach and inculcate manners as apart from knowledge of things' and that 'lessons in the small courtesies of life' will aid the promotion of 'good citizenship.'[21] The equation of moral tone and manners with citizenship indicates that the 'new' language of citizenship might be akin to putting old wine in new bottles: that the language of citizenship was merely a reworking of the older imperative to 'civilize' the working classes. But this obscures the evident new concern with the content rather than structure of schooling, and with the concern to promote feelings of national community and of communal obligation.

At mid-century merely getting working-class children to school was seen by many as the best means to 'civilize' them. This was because, in general, the aims of mid-century schooling were formulated according to the same values that characterized the liberal-nationalist premises of English middle-class culture. Protestant religious and moral values were central, as were emphases on the refinement of the individual character and the inculcation of ideas about liberty, responsibility, and the 'immutable laws' of political economy. Although denominational disputes fractured the administrative landscape, and there was some minor variation in methods, the actual secular content of most elementary schooling from the 1840s was virtually the same. Pedagogic theory was constructed around the doctrines of instrumental learning and faculty psychology. These doctrines had evolved into a loose tissue of ideas about general method, which combined notions of original sin – that children had naturally bad characters which had to be reformed – with a tabula rasa view of intelligence and learning that envisioned children developing the individual 'faculties' of their minds (the reasoning faculty, the observational faculty, etc.) through the introduction of basic concepts that had to be learned and relearned by constant repetition.[22] These ideas about children's intellectual and moral development meshed perfectly with the theological and social role of the teacher and of formal schooling itself. Throughout the first half of the century, middle-class evangelical thought shared with liberal political economy an atomistic view of society in which the individual was responsible for his or her own decisions and actions. Only through tireless effort, 'self-help,' and the development of a moral conscience could one steer clear of sin and thereby hope to attain deliverance.[23] The education of the working classes by the churches and non-conformist religious organizations therefore tended to be seen in terms of individual salvation rather than as charity providing the means to better their lives. Even High Church Anglicans 'saw the poor as individual souls to be saved and not as members of society to be transformed.'[24] The role of church-run schooling for the working classes was fundamentally moral and religious with a social subtext; it was intent mainly on directing the individual towards pious 'contentment in the station of life to which God had assigned them.'[25]

In the new language of civic training used by educationalists at the end of the century, the deferential social aims of elementary education remained, but now a new rhetoric of national inclusion was inserted into arguments about curricula reform and the content of teaching. Education reformers, radicals, liberals, socialists, conventional and reactionary conservatives all used the language of citizenship in their suggestions for curricula reform. One of the more distinct voices calling for educational change in the period immediately following the turn of the century was R.E. Hughes. A proponent of political and educational decentralization, and a vigorous critic of the national efficiency movement, Hughes wrote a trio of widely reviewed books between 1902 and 1905 that all stressed the need for education in 'democratic citizenship.'[26] Although his reasoning transversed many ideological divisions, Hughes's views are representative of a broad spectrum of educational reformers in the way in which he constructed his reformatory arguments. Hughes poured scorn on those reformers that wanted to remake the English system in the mould of other more 'successful' and 'efficient' European ones. His critique relied on pervasive assumptions about the English national 'character' and the 'national idiosyncrasies' that had to be protected. Hughes proclaimed that adopting German standards or methods of 'making' citizens would be disastrous, since it would 'kill those characteristics which make the Anglo-Saxon what he is today, a wanderer on the face of the earth, practical, resourceful, and self-reliant.' For Hughes, the English educational system, after it had been freed from the fetters of payment by results, was the system most in tune with national life and the system that was most 'characteristic of the people.' Thus, to quarrel with the system was 'to quarrel with the national character,' and paradoxically, 'to Germanise the English school' would undermine its 'Saxon' genius. Hughes laid great stress on the importance of the teaching of citizenship, but it should be a type of citizenship and a type of teaching that was unique to the English character.[27]

Like most other commentators on citizenship, Hughes emphasized the reciprocal nature of civic rights and duties, but he also suggested, in line with the 'new liberalism' and some of the social-imperialists, that if national duties were expected of the citizen then the national community had 'a duty to give its citizens of its best – to give to every future citizen within its borders a full measure of opportunity for development.'[28] He stridently rejected the idea, frequently advanced by some national efficiency proponents, that national elementary schooling should be vocationally based.[29] Instead, Hughes sought to further entrench a liberal curriculum that fully developed the child into a complete, loyal citizen, and which would destroy the corrosive differences between people, thereby unifying 'national life.' In his educational vision, the school owed a political duty to the national community. This was to 'inculcate in its pupils true loyalty and spirit' and to develop a 'constant readiness of self-sacrifice to the common weal.' This was to be achieved not by scrapping the existing system and replacing it with a 'Prussian' one, but by using established English tradition and emphasizing to the Englishman the 'mission of their race,' the 'imperial character of their heritage,' and the 'glorious nature' of English heroes, history, and literature. Furthermore, this task – the developing of 'pride of race' – could and should be accomplished 'without appealing to jingoism or insular prejudices.'

This was all possible only if 'loyalty and patriotism' and the maturation of good citizenship were taught 'indirectly' through using 'every lesson' and 'every opportunity for filling our children with great examples' of 'their country's literature,' the 'nobility of their country's national duties and privileges,' and the 'splendour of the past and the glorious possibilities of the future.' Only through these indirect means

could a genuine patriotic attitude develop based on a sound understanding of each citizen's obligations and privileges. Thus, Hughes in
his practical proposals specifically advocated physical, intellectual, and
moral content in teaching. Games, drill, and gymnastics were necessary to encourage physical growth and to instil self-control, discipline,
loyalty, and *esprit de corps*.[30] The encouragement of reading was essential for the development of thinking, since reading allowed the 'thoughts
of the race' to be made available to the student, but perhaps even
more important was the teaching of history, since through the study
of 'history the child acquires the experience of the race, learns his
place in society and his duties and privileges as citizen.'[31] Indeed,
history offered the moral lessons by which pupils would come to
understand their heritage and thus their place in the nation. Such an
understanding would then naturally lead to the reconciliation of differences among all members of the nation, resulting in a national community fully alive to its members' responsibilities to one another.[32]

Hughes's proposal that the elementary school should engage in 'character building for citizenship' – as opposed to the mid-century conception of moral reformation and spiritual salvation – was echoed in
many educational quarters during the 1890s and throughout the
Edwardian period. Indeed, much of what Hughes promoted in his
books about training for citizenship could justly be said to have been
operative in elementary education long before 1914. Even an educationalist such as Thomas Raymont, who held very different views
from those of Hughes, agreed that the primary aims of education were
'the formation of the character' and 'the making of good citizens.' The
underlying assumption in such successful 'character building' was that
the elementary schools would restrain the mass of the citizenry from
radical action and socialize them into an acceptance of the 'norm' of
differential access to social status and political power. Some educationalists worried aloud that this particular connotation of 'good citizenship' was being promoted too successfully and in too narrow a
fashion. Raymont, for instance, warned against the 'the inculcation of
a narrow and selfish patriotism.' For the 'waving of national flags and
the singing of national anthems, though quite proper in their way,
stand for a very small part of what we mean by trying to make good
citizens.' Indeed, Raymont suggested that the 'national greatness'
should be 'understood and appreciated, but there must be no exploitation of the people by the privileged classes, who identify their own
interests with those of the state.'[33]

Sophie Bryant, headmistress of North London Collegiate School, was more in tune with mainstream views in her summation that 'the duty of the citizen was to be loyally obedient. This obedience is the auxiliary of reason, and almost a part of reason, in securing social peace [and] the true citizen's acceptance of the social will.'[34] A section entitled 'The Purpose of the Elementary School' in the 1909 Board of Education's *Suggestions to Teachers* makes clear how the 'official view' of the meaning of citizenship had crystallized to one that echoed this kind of position, where 'flag-waving' and the national culture went hand-in-glove: 'The high function of the teacher is to prepare the child for the life of the good citizen, to create and foster the aptitude for work and for the intelligent use of leisure, and to develop those features of character which are most readily influenced by school life, such as loyalty to comrades, loyalty to institutions, unselfishness and an orderly and disciplined habit of mind.' Clearly, by this point 'good citizenship' was being viewed in terms of loyalty to the social whole rather than simply as improvement of the individual. 'Patriotism' in this mainstream view was as connected to the celebration of the national character as it was to taking pride in the institutions and traditions of the state. And history lessons – 'Thirty-five lessons on citizenship, local and national'[35] – were intended as the principal vehicle for the instruction of these values.

Formal 'civics' classes were also proposed and adopted in some schools from the late 1880s. First in evening continuation schools, and later in the higher classes of some elementary schools, the embracing of instruction in 'civics' spurred the production of numerous 'citizenship' reading books.[36] W.E. Forster claimed the impulse behind this movement was to be found in the contemporary recognition that the Reform and Redistribution Acts of 1884–5 had created a vast new pool of potential voters who needed to be properly instructed in democratic ideals. But Forster also noted that the purpose of instruction in 'civics' was 'to tell children what ought to be the principles which should actuate them as patriotic citizens.'[37] Forster conceded that beyond explaining the basic mechanics of government, 'civics' ought to be used to instil certain values, such as loyalty, duty, and obedience: in essence, he was suggesting that these books should shape a deferential 'civic' social identity. Indeed, those reading books that were actually produced after 1885 dealt with the parameters of citizenship by describing the relationship of the individual to the national collectivity in terms of social rather than strictly political obligations and privileges, and devoted only a nominal amount of space to the actual mechanics of political participation.

For the most part, the authors of these 'civics' readers tended to be amateur historians, journalists, and politicians. The prime example of this group was H.O. Arnold-Forster (1855–1909), who was simultaneously the grandson of Thomas Arnold of Rugby, the nephew of Matthew Arnold, and the adopted son of W.E. Forster. Schooled at Exmouth and Rugby, he attended University College, Oxford, and earned his BA in 1877 and his MA in 1900. After being called to the Bar at Lincoln's Inn in 1879, he grew interested in publishing and became secretary of Cassell's publishing house in 1885. He took over from Lyttelton Gell as director of the Education Department at Cassell and joined the Board of Directors in 1890. Arnold-Forster entered national party politics in the early 1880s, and was secretary of the Imperial Federation League in 1884. An avid supporter of Joseph Chamberlain, in 1886 he became a Liberal-Unionist. He sat as an MP for West Belfast from 1892, and he was later sent to South Africa at the behest of Chamberlain to report on the state of colonial affairs. Arnold-Forster wrote extensively on military matters and was a strong advocate of army and naval efficiency. As director of the Education Department at the Cassell publishing firm, Arnold-Forster pushed for the publication of 'civics' instruction and authored the immensely successful *Citizen Reader*, which went through twenty-four editions and sold more than 500,000 copies between 1886 and 1910.[38] Exploiting his knowledge and his connections at both Cassell and his cousin's firm (Edward Arnold), Arnold-Forster authored several other reader sets as well, including *Laws of Everyday Life* (1889); a five-volume set of geography readers, *This World of Ours* (1891); a seven-volume set of history readers, *Things New and Old* (1893); and a songbook for elementary schools entitled *Scarlet and Blue: or, Songs for Soldiers and Sailors*.

Other successful 'civics' readers were penned by the likes of J. St Loe Strachey (1860–1927), W. Beach Thomas (1868–1957), and H.E. Malden (1849–1931). Strachey was the second son of the Third Baronet of Sutton Court. Privately educated, he then attended Balliol, Oxford, where he received his BA in 1882. In 1884 he settled in London, was called to the Inner Temple in 1885, but decided on a journalistic rather than a law career in 1886. Strachey worked as the editor of the *Cornhill* magazine, 1896–8, and the *Spectator*, 1895–1925. Strongly Unionist and an ardent militarist, he was vigorously opposed to socialism and tariff reform and took up the minority position of the Unionist–free traders.

Among his works was Macmillan's reader, *The Citizen and the State*, published in 1913. Meanwhile, W. Beach Thomas, the editor and author of the *Citizen Books* (1908), was the son of a clergyman and was schooled at Shrewsbury. He matriculated to Christ Church, Oxford, where he received a BA in 1891. In later life he developed a passionate love of the outdoors and the English countryside. Between 1891 and 1898 he taught at Bradford and Dulwich schools, but in 1898 he turned to full-time journalism. Finally, H.E. Malden, the author of *The Life and Duties of a Citizen*, was the son of a professor of Greek at University College, London, and was schooled at Ipswich. He attended Trinity Hall, Cambridge, where he received his BA in 1872 and his MA in 1875. A local amateur historian, Malden was a prominent member of the Surrey Archaeological Society, the editor of the *Victoria County History* for Surrey, and was later made honorary secretary of the Royal Historical Society.

The 'civics' readers penned by these authors offer some of the clearest evidence that the terms 'citizenship' and 'citizen' were used in the elementary classroom as a concrete way of linking a sense of community with the abstraction of nationality. W.B. Thomas noted that 'we use the word citizen of every man who can claim nationality,' and Malden further counselled that the 'duty of every citizen certainly is not to be a Conservative, nor a Unionist, nor a Liberal, nor a Radical, but to be an Englishman.' And while the individual 'may think that he can perform the duties of an Englishman best in conjunction with one or other of these parties, the duty of which he has to be reminded is a duty which is common to all.' Good citizenship thus came to be closely associated with those qualities deemed essential to Englishness, and the qualities of the Englishman with that of the good citizen.[39] Much of the discourse on citizenship in these readers echoed the common refrain that, along with rights and freedoms, the citizen was bound by duties and responsibilities.[40] This was demonstrated through examples from history and the various degrees of public participation in government and society. Civics readers tended to present the structure of central and local governments in a mechanical, legalistic, and procedural manner. This approach emphasized consensus rather than conflict, and the individual as part of the nation rather than as belonging to social segments, classes, and interest groups. For the most part, even party conflict was ignored. Loyalty to the sovereign, the glories of the empire, the welcome necessity of the armed services, taxes, education, and the police, and above all, the duties of the individual citizen to his nation and race dominated these books. The overarching effect was to constitutionalize British politics, and present rights and duties, and the constitution itself, as an inert body of tradition and rigid rules that needed to be learned, accepted, and obeyed. The rules of the game were set out and made unassailable through reference to the lessons of history. Citizenship readers were, in fact, intended to be used in conjunction with other history books and lessons, and indeed, despite the growing concern about the need to inculcate good citizenship, the use of these formal civics readers was not the most favoured method for its instruction. Rather, it was history teaching that came to be seen as the proper vehicle for this instruction. As, in the words of the London School Board's curriculum adviser, 'without history, Citizenship has no root; without Citizenship, history has no fruit.'[41] It is to this renewed interest in the social possibilities of history teaching that we now turn.

History Instruction and the Making of Good Citizens

The teaching of history in elementary schools between 1850 and 1914 presents somewhat of a paradox. Formal in-class instruction of history (that is, as a special subject given a regular place on the timetable) declined rapidly after the implementation of Lowe's 1862 Revised Education Code, reaching a low point in the early 1890s. Meanwhile, the actual exposure of students to history and history books increased quite remarkably from the 1880s and was matched by a modest increase in formal class instruction after 1900 as well.[42] This trend roughly reflects the impact of changed attitudes regarding the purposes of history education over this same time frame. The collapse in the popularity of history instruction after the passing of Lowe's 1862 code was caused by a number of interlocking factors. A wide-ranging curriculum that included subjects other than the grant-receiving three Rs was thought by educationalists and school managers to be too costly, and likely wasted on children whose later lives would be consumed in manual labour. Many teachers' manuals of method did not spend much time on the particular virtues of history instruction because it was not seen as particularly useful in instilling individual discipline and obedience. Gill's comments in his introduction to teaching were typical of the mid-nineteenth-century view of what history instruction might possibly demonstrate to working-class children. 'History,' he claimed, 'will make them prize our advantages in liberty, employment, food, clothing, dwellings, and instruction, compared with former periods.'[43] Apart from this traditional liberal demonstration of material progress and the fortunate state of contemporary affairs, history was nevertheless seen by some educationalists as useful in its practical lessons on the importance of piety, individual freedom, social respect, and self-help. History was viewed as a guide to those liberal universal values to which each worthy individual should aspire. James Currie's *Principles and Practice of Common School Education* (1861), for example, warned the teacher to be wary of textbooks glorifying war, excepting those conducted for the high moral purposes of 'liberty and independence.' In fact, war was to be regarded 'as a divergence from the true course of a nation's history, both on moral and on social grounds,' and 'wars of aggression, or wars undertaken on insufficient grounds, are not to be palliated, much less to be boasted in, however favourably they may display military prowess.'[44] Of course, it was not explained exactly which conflicts should be considered legitimate attempts to gain liberty and independence.

This evident desire to impart sound morals, social deference, and liberal socio-economic values was a key part of the rationale behind the whole process of mid-century elementary schooling. History instruction did not therefore have any special or necessary place within it. Indeed, in those cases where history was actually taught in the 1860s, 1870s, and early 1880s, contemporary observers suggest that classroom emphasis was placed on lists of information that could be simply memorized and reproduced at an inspector's examination. Even the inspectors despairingly commented on the fact that learning by rote long lists of kings and battles was the dominant technique. Indeed, most of the history textbooks of this period were organized as catechisms or merely lists of names and dates with the barest of connecting narrative.[45] Joshua Fitch bitterly complained in 1878 that books were still being written that contained lists of 'important and unimportant facts with but little attempt to distinguish between them.' A typical example from the 1870s noted, for instance, 'Ethelwulf reigned from 836 to 856, and his reign was remarkable for the ravages of the Danes who at first had troubled our coasts in 787. Ethelbald his son reigned from 856 to 860. Ethelbert, his brother, reigned from 860 to 866, and during his reign the Danes stormed Winchester, but were twice defeated in 860.'[46] Those educationalists and observers who were keen on promoting the moral value of history consequently despaired that its teaching in the 1870s seemed 'to combine the respective disadvantages of the multiplication table and the Newgate Calendar.'[47]

Given the general disregard for the particular usefulness of history – its tendency to be despised by both students and teachers alike for its 'tedious' and 'mind-numbing' attributes – it is really no wonder that the subject was not offered in many schools.[48] A further problem after the furore generated by the institution of school boards was that subjects such as history raised political and religious difficulties as well. The London School Board, clearly a trendsetter in the new state-aided system, had initially disallowed any history to be taught in its schools, partly on the grounds of economy and partly because its teaching raised religious difficulties. In fact, objections to the purchase of history texts thought to be biased towards one particular religion or denomination or another were raised in school board meetings all over the country by a variety of groups representing Anglicans, Catholics, and Dissenters throughout the early 1870s.[49] Even when the Education Code was modified to allow a grant to be given for the teaching of history or geography in 1876, most school boards elided possible religious objections to the teaching of history by offering the less-controversial geography.

From the early 1880s, however, history was increasingly reinserted into the curriculum in a less formal way. This was done through the use of the historical readers to teach reading. Historical readers were mandated by the Education Code to make up at least a third of reading texts after 1880 and, with their geographical and literary counterparts, quickly came to be the most important and widely used of all the texts available in elementary schools. While the perceived importance of having some history taught to working-class schoolchildren steadily increased between 1880 and 1900, the antiquated system of education grants and lingering concerns about the biases of the school boards, particularly as they increasingly came under attack for their 'extravagance' in the 1890s, meant that neither the Board of Education nor the school boards themselves were very willing to embrace formal history instruction until after the demise of the 'payment by results' system in 1896. Thereafter, arguments about the importance of history prevailed and the Education Code of 1900 made a limited course of history mandatory in all schools. What was particularly striking about this increased recognition of the importance of some form of history

instruction within the curriculum was that it echoed the growing public debate about the role of the schools in producing 'good citizens.'

As was noted earlier, patriotism and the teaching of history had
long been associated. Valerie Chancellor has pointed to the wide-ranging debate that took place on the issue of history and patriotism in
1900 amid the opening acts of the Anglo–Boer War, but much earlier,
in May 1887, the *Educational Times* had noted that history was often
considered 'the nursery of patriotism and public virtue.'[50] The connection between patriotism and citizenship was marked out in public and
educational debate before the explosion of interest and concern over
national education in the early 1890s. Fitch, in his 1885 *Lectures on
Teaching*, had pointed to 'the necessity for so teaching as to inspire our
scholars with a love and admiration of the country we live in and for
the institutions by which we are governed.'[51] In fact, by the 1890s a
whole spate of new teachers' manuals had been produced that revised
substantially the teaching aims and methods of mid-century. In all of
them the new concerns about the active teaching of citizenship and its
corollary, patriotism, found a prominent place. The three Rs still retained pride of place in these books, but other subjects, especially
history and geography, were now given special attention and import.
'History fosters patriotism,' David Salmon noted. 'It fills the student
with admiration for his forefathers' wisdom, heroism, and devotion to
duty, which have made the nation what it is; with longings for a
chance of emulating their glorious deeds; and failing that, with a firm
resolve to do nothing that shall tarnish the fair fame of their common
country, and to pay the debt which he owes his ancestors, by transmitting down entire those sacred rights to which he himself was born.'[52]

The more cautious 1894 text by John Landon suggested that students should come to realize what 'a glorious inheritance' had been
handed down to them from their forefathers.[53] A.H. Garlick's 1896
manual agreed that history teaching should be used to this end, because history inevitably 'calls forth feelings of *patriotism*. It stimulates
the *national* pride, promotes a love of virtue, gives powerful object
lessons against vice, and tends, rightly taught, to make *good citizens*.
This ought to be its prime aim.'[54] History instruction was thus specifically invested with the role of training the patriotic and loyal citizen.
The 'glorious deeds' of past ancestors, and the 'sacred rights' won in
the past, now became the material with which to instil the appropriate
values of duty and loyalty.[55] Clearly, patriotism and the duties of citi-

zenship were closely connected in the study of history, as numerous other teachers' manuals also observed.[56] But it was not just any history that could serve these purposes. 'If we wish our scholars to be patriotic, and at the same time to become worthy citizens,' the Anglican National Society's manual for instructing teachers explained, the type of history taught had to be carefully chosen. It was 'necessary to place in the background the conflicts, the plots, and the intrigues which centre about a few individuals, and bring into far greater prominence the efforts of those who have laboured successfully for the moral, the social, the intellectual, and the material progress of the nation.'[57]

In 1905, five years after history lessons were made a compulsory part of the elementary curriculum, the Board of Education produced a series of suggestions for its teaching that echoed many of these statements.[58] In general, it was suggested:

All boys and girls in Great Britain have, by the mere fact of Birth, certain rights and duties which some day or other they will exercise, and it is the province of history to trace how those rights and duties arise.

From geography they learn how Great Britain is but one country among many. It is therefore important that from the history lessons they should learn something about the nationality which distinguishes them from the people of other countries. They cannot understand this, however, unless they are taught how the British nation grew up and how the mother country in her turn has founded daughter countries beyond the seas. The broad facts of this growth when properly handled ought to form a stirring theme full of interest to even young citizens of the British Empire.[59]

It was thought imperative that, by the age of twelve, children 'should have some idea of the nature of the great nations and stages in civilization.' The scheme thereby proposed that by the time they left school, students would have acquired 'a tolerably connected view of the main outlines of British history,' including 'the growth of free institutions, the expansion of empire, the establishment of our position amongst nations.' A wise choice of reading material was indispensable for this task, since it was claimed that 'no book is read so often and remembered with such verbal accuracy as the history Text-book.' Given the limitations of time, and supposed student interest, it was thought appropriate to gear teaching to 'what children can understand,' which was thought to be 'personal character and prowess, adventure, discovery, invention, war,' whereas the covering of political and religious conflict was advisable only so far as it promoted an understanding of 'national life and the rights and duties of a citizen.' For these reasons it was particularly necessary to 'pass over' periods of which the history was merely 'a record of bad government.' The most appropriate subjects and events were, instead, 'the Crusades, the Civil War, the reign of Elizabeth, the great wars for Colonial Supremacy, and the war of American Independence.'[60] Clearly passing over 'bad government' also meant passing over episodes that might be of interest to radicalism and systematic criticism of the socio-political order.

In seeking to impart this understanding and, moreover, to strengthen the values of duty and loyalty, the Board of Education thought it desirable that history be a stirring and enjoyable subject. This was to be accomplished through the use of lively stories and biographies and the reading of historical romances. By 1914 it was advocated the 'younger the child, the stronger the romantic element in the narrative should be.'[61] Many of the new history readers written in this period were intended to function through romance in much the same way.[62] Indeed, this was a particularly useful approach with regards to the aim of promoting patriotic feeling and national sentiment, for as one educator remarked at the turn of the century, 'patriotism rests partly on carefully restrained appeals to imagination; and I know of no reason why this may not form a definite end of the teaching of History almost from the beginning.' If patriotism was developed from an early age then, citizenship – 'one concrete side of Patriotism' – would be 'slowly won at a much later period.' However, this could only happen if the 'germs of patriotic feeling' were 'planted by the agency of the imaginative faculty.'[63] E.H. Godwin of Durham, at the Northern England Education Conference in 1908, concurred with his colleagues that the study of civics could not be disregarded but should form the essence of the history lesson, which in elementary schools 'should be romantic, as full of life as possible, [as] full of colour and activity' as possible.[64] Textbook writers and publishers saw definite advantages in making their products more readable and enjoyable, and the introduction of net pricing after 1890 brought about vastly increased output and sales of the new readers.[65] Publishers also sought out a new type of reader author to produce the new books, and at this point it would seem appropriate to discuss the general nature of the new reader authorship, primarily through the example of history reader authors.

Authoring Citizenship through History

In the first two-thirds of the nineteenth century the most prolific writers of school books had been clergymen and the amateur generalist writers.[66] Some of the most famous of these writers were women of the gentry or upper middle class and/or the wives or daughters of clergymen. Charlotte Yonge (1823–1901), for instance, was the daughter of a Devon magistrate who devoted herself to writing books for children and teaching scripture daily at a local village school. She published 160 different books, including three widely used reader sets for the National Society. Elizabeth M. Sewell (b. 1815), a writer of many children's reading books and other didactic works, was the daughter of Mary Sewell, the prominent anti-slavery activist and writer of religious prose and poetry, and a clergyman from Yarmouth. Elizabeth Penrose, the author of the widely distributed and reissued *History of England* (1823), was also the daughter of a well-to-do clergyman. Meanwhile, the author of perhaps the most reprinted and widely known of children's histories, *Little Arthur's History of England* (1834), was Lady Maria Callcott, the daughter of a rear admiral and the wife of two naval officers, her second husband being himself a rear admiral. Reading books specifically prepared for elementary schools during the first three-quarters of the century tended to be written by women such as these and by churchmen operating under the auspices of specific denominational organizations, such as the National Society, the British and Foreign Schools Society, and the Society for Promoting Christian Knowledge. Their authors, like the women noted above, tended by and large to be amateur generalists and/or individuals with a denominational connection, many of whom had neither specialized educational qualifications nor 'professional' educationalist status.

Towards the end of the century publishers seemed to have deemed professional credentials and the reputations of established educational scholars and academics as key to getting their books noticed by school authorities and teachers. Professional and specialist status allowed publishers to make pretences about the more 'objective,' 'unbiased,' and 'scientifically' based nature of their new products compared with the older efforts, while still expecting a strong narrative storyline.[67] Many history readers used in elementary schools were actually written by some of the leading academics of the day. Samuel Rawlinson Gardiner (1829–1902), John Holland Rose (1855–1942), and T.F. Tout (1855–1929), for example, wrote both influential academic histories and widely used elementary school reading books. Gardiner, the son of a career civil servant in Bengal, was variously fellow and professor of history at colleges in both Cambridge and Oxford. Along with his seminal academic work on seventeenth-century England, he was the author or co-author of numerous reader sets, including the *English History Reading Books* (1881–4), *Illustrated English History* (1887), and *Longman's New Historical Series* (1887–8). Tout, an academic of a later generation than Gardiner, was the son of a wine-merchant who matriculated by scholarship to Balliol College, Oxford, in 1874. He rose to be professor of medieval and modern history at the University of Manchester from 1890 to 1925 and, along with his academic works on Edward I and other medieval subjects, was also an author in the *Longman's Historical Series for Schools* (1903).

Other history reading-book authors such as Frederick York Powell (1850–1902), Francis B. Kirkman (b. 1869), and Oscar Browning (1837–1923), while not producing major academic works, nevertheless had lifelong attachments to Oxford and Cambridge universities, sometimes exerting great influence. Indeed, Powell was Regius Professor of History at Oxford from 1894 until his death in 1902, and yet, besides an edition of Icelandic sagas, his most influential works were perhaps his elementary school books, including volumes in *Longman's English History Reading Books* (1881–2) and *Longman's New Historical Readers* (1888). Kirkman was a lecturer at Lincoln College, Oxford, and author of Blackie's *Raleigh History Readers* (1898) as well as editor and author of books in Longman's 'Ship' reader series. But an even more striking figure was Browning. A lifelong fellow of King's College, Cambridge, and lecturer there between 1880 and 1908, he was also editor of Pitman's *King Edward Readers* (1902–5) as well as author of a variety of other school books, mainly for use in secondary schools, but also including a widely used elementary civics reader, *The Citizen: His Rights and Responsibilities* (1893). Reba Soffer notes that Browning was a figure of great influence among historians at Cambridge, founding the King's College Politics Society, which included among it members many of the more important historians to come out of Cambridge between 1880 and 1930.[68] Among this group was W.F. Reddway, another fellow of King's College, Cambridge, and author of readers and school texts, including sections on politics and the history of Parliament in the *King Edward History Readers*.

These historians – like their counterparts in the disciplines of geography and English literature – were carving out new academic disciplinary boundaries at the end of the nineteenth century, and much of this was being done through their self-suggested role of 'public' teachers as through their actual academic research.[69] Following J.R. Seeley, many of these professional academic authors, particularly the historians, extolled the implicit connection between their own discipline and the moulding of an effective imperial-national citizenship.[70] And yet these authors had to present their historical material in a form that could be easily digested by their young audience. Thus, history reader authors, even many of those written by academics, increasingly turned their volumes into collections of historical stories and biographies, and melodrama and romance were deliberately plotted into their longer historical narratives. A review of the *Marcus Ward History Readers* in the *School Board Chronicle* in 1883 noted that while it might not be desirable 'to commit ourselves absolutely to the principle of teaching history only through reading lessons ... there cannot be a doubt of the improvement that this system has introduced into our school histories.'[71] S.C. Bryant noted in 1910 that 'a good historical story vitalises the conception of past events and brings their characters into relation with the present.' This was believed to be 'especially true of stories of things and persons in the history of our own race' since these particular stories fostered 'race-consciousness, the feeling of kinship and community of blood.' Such race-consciousness and kinship were the essential building blocks of national pride in children, which could be further developed through stories that dwelt on the 'instinct of hero-worship which is quick in the healthy child.'[72] Accounts of battles, military heroes, and great adventurers, cast in melodramatic language, were often accompanied by romanticized illustrations. Many series began to incorporate colour plates of a similar style in their books as well.

No doubt such romanticization made the readers – and not just the history readers, but all types that included historical and/or adventure narratives – more readable, but it also structured the presentation of the historical and contemporary events in a particular way, imparting to them a discursive force that reinforced their didactic message.[73] The dry list- and event-centred narratives of the mid-century texts did little to evoke the imagination of the child reader. But by reading romance children could pass into the realm of semi-historical fantasy, into the imaginative enactment of possibilities beyond the restraints of their direct experience.[74] Romance has always been a favoured narrative genre: it is the prototypical storytelling structure. A child presented with a set of practical imperatives – civic duty and loyalty to the nation, for instance – might more easily understand their importance and the purpose that may be served by conforming to them if these imperatives are presented, not as dry abstract concepts, but as part of an ongoing quest-story in which the child identifies with the heroes and plot. In such a structure, a national community is more easily imagined, since the narrative of history might be seen as part of an inevitable pattern and an identification made with past members of the national community. The Board of Education was perhaps alluding to this in its comment in 1905 that 'English History should be an inheritance of childhood; its characters and incidents should have the charm of a story which is not only interesting and true, but is also personal to the child, and should thus grow into his thoughts. History thus treated would not be a task, for the child would always be anxious to know more of it.'[75]

The manner by which the social dictates of 'good citizenship,' Englishness, and gender ideology worked together in the content of school readers is perhaps most clearly seen in the Whig/liberal trajectory of the growth of English liberties that was the master narrative of virtually all history readers, and its logic and substance will be examined in some detail in the next chapter. But for the remainder of this present chapter, one key theme that was ubiquitous in history readers will be examined independently from that narrative.

Citizenship and Nationality in Reading-Book Historical Narratives

In history readers, love of liberty was figured as an 'innate' English characteristic that could not long be suppressed – 'It is from our Anglo-Saxon forefathers that we inherit the love of liberty which is so marked a feature of the British race'[76] – and the realization of this attribute was frequently found in the language of military honour and sacrifice. This was evident in the self-denial and self-sacrifice of those national heroes whose efforts, suffering, and/or death were represented as the basis of the freedom, prosperity, and honour that all good citizens now enjoyed. *Cassell's Historical Course for Schools* (1884) asserted:

In the past our country has grown stronger and better the more its rulers and people have striven to act rightly. It is the duty of Englishmen and Englishwomen to do their best to make England great in the future also. The first thing necessary is that they should live worthy and honourable lives themselves; for a country can only be great when its people are temperate, truthful, orderly, reverent, industrious, merciful and courageous. It may happen, as it has happened to Englishmen before, that we shall be called on to make great sacrifices, and overcome great difficulties, in doing our duty to our country and our fellow-men; but we have to bear them patiently and courageously, remembering that it is through the toils and the sacrifices of our forefathers in days gone by that England had become the noble and prosperous country in which it is our happiness to live.[77]

Although both men and women were thus encouraged to be good citizens in their everyday lives, sacrifice was virtually always connected to martial heroes in school books at this time: men gave their lives for their peers and descendants, while women gave up their sons and husbands to the glory of the nation. Indeed, military themes – comprising a veritable cult of martial figures and values – saturated elementary school books, especially those of the 1890s and early 1900s, just as they did in books and magazines intended for lower-middle, middle- and upper-class children.[78] Overwhelmingly in these texts it is the soldier or sailor that is represented as the paradigmatic English hero, as a figure, that is, after whom elementary schoolboys should model their own citizen identity.

By imagining the soldier or sailor as a hero, and narrating stories about his dangerous and daring exploits in times of war or adventure, the authors of historical and literary readers used the typical tropes of the romantic genre.[79] The past was depicted as a world more exciting and dangerous than the present, rendering the actions of the hero, indeed, the hero himself, superior to other people and to the environment within which he moved. In romance the whole of the narrative is subordinated to the central figure of the hero, and it is presented exclusively from his perspective as a series of obstacles to be overcome in the accomplishment of his quest and the fulfilment of his search for identity. Unhindered by fears, scruples, doubts, ambivalence, conflicting needs or loyalties, the male hero fully triumphs by the end of the narrative or, in the tragic-romance mould, unthinkingly sacrifices himself for his comrades and country. As such, the hero functions as a figure of desirable and virtuous masculinity: a self to aspire to. A close imaginative relationship existed in British fiction between romantic adventure narratives and the British Empire. Martin Green has identified a British tradition of 'adventure tales' located on the imperial frontier, which, he argues, constituted an 'energizing myth of imperialism.'[80] These stories celebrated the empire as 'a place where adventures took place and men became heroes.' The historical narratives found within reading books were replete with 'real' heroes who were represented in equally romanticized and idealized terms. Representations of heroic masculinity in these books thus had the added authority of 'history.' Since a 'real man' was being implicitly defined at the end of the century as he who was prepared to venture, fight, and sacrifice for his home, country, and race, the example of authentic English heroes became fused, in a potent ideological configuration, with representations of imperial-national identity.

Glorified and romanticized as heroic 'forefathers,' historical martial figures provided role models for the sort of masculine patriotism that was held to be the natural outgrowth of good citizenship. Favoured examples were taken from the period of the Anglo-Saxons, particularly Alfred the Great and Harold; the English 'sea dogs' of the Elizabethan period; Wellington and Nelson; the English heroes of the 1857 Indian Mutiny; and the long list of adventuring, imperial generals such as Clive, Wolfe, Wolesley, Roberts, and Baden-Powell. Teachers' class outlines and other sources indicate that these figures were also the favoured topics in oral history lessons, and that reading-book lessons on the great soldiers and sailors of the past were integral to history instruction.[81] History seemed to confirm the godlike power of the Englishman to conquer and enjoy influence over indigenous populations in far-off lands. Robert MacDonald has shown that by the turn of the century popular history was often written as an imperial adventure tale in which the world of home was separated from the world of action. Mother England, Britannia, and Victoria herself came to 'symbolize the maternal mistress served by the knights of the empire, who, with the feminine bracketed-off to a safe, symbolic role,' were free to become more assertively masculine.[82] The imperial backdrop was crucial to the figuring of martial heroes as 'romantic' adventurers, and hence to the building of a vital masculinity.

But descriptions of the historical Englishman acting vigorously in the colonial wilds also highlighted the degree to which the empire was integral to the reading books' discussion of citizenship and patriotism. For as many authors noted, the 'duties of the English citizen are not bounded by the narrow shores of these islands,' but were explicitly connected to the present and future welfare of an empire that was 'a consequence of our constitution and of our national character, and is bound up with them.'[83] English citizens were encouraged to identify actively with the wider community that their 'forefathers' had gained for them. 'It is right that every man and woman should love the country in which they live,' Arnold-Forster explained, and those 'who really love their country, and are truly proud of its great history, will be particularly careful not to do anything by which it may be dishonoured.' Every schoolchild could accomplish this, for 'as long as you do your best to make the British Empire the first among *nations* in all that is right and just, so long will you do well to honour and to love the flag which, by the bravery and the wisdom of our forefathers, has become so famous.'[84] Since the empire was so frequently equated with the nation itself, it required little justification in the texts to extend the 'civic' duties of the citizen to the wider empire. While this extended community was a sacred trust and an honourable inheritance, it necessitated the shouldering of great responsibilities to sustain it. This might even be an onerous, unrewarding burden, yet the clear message in these texts was that the very future of the nation was at stake, and the responsibility for its maintenance ought to be borne by all those who resided within the civic community, standing united 'shoulder to shoulder,' regardless of their social class, demonstrating their willingness to share 'the obligations as well as the dignity of empire.'[85]

Perhaps the epitome of the English military imperial-patriot was General 'Chinese' Gordon, the story of whom featured in practically every history reader published after 1885 and was noted as a subject of verbal instruction in many elementary school logbooks.[86] Gordon's death at the 'Mahdi's savage hands' at Khartoum in 1885 was depicted as a martyrdom to the glorious destiny of the English people. He had lived an exemplary Englishman's life; he was noted for his bravery, steadfastness, dignity, charity, kindliness, and attention to duty.[87] After having lived such a 'worthy' life, his death 'in the line of duty' was especially revered. As the Standard IV volume of the *Chambers's Alternative History Readers*, published in 1898, observed: 'Thus did this great and good man die, after having endured a siege of over three hundred days. His loss was greatly mourned in England; for in him, bravery, courage, and sincerity were combined with true goodness, gentleness, and charity. Many monuments were erected to his memory, and probably no other man ever won the love of his countrymen so entirely as did the great hero, General Gordon.'[88] Gordon's example was consistently extolled as an appropriate model for the male youth of the country, regardless of their social background. Not only had his been the ultimate sacrifice for his nation, his example also demonstrated the prime dictum of good citizenship and patriotism: 'Every citizen ought to remember one very important thing about the patriotism which has made our country what it is. Those who love their country best are content to serve it without the hope of immediate reward, or even the encouragement of praise.'[89] That Gordon 'did not die in vain' and stood as a wholesome example for all to follow, as 'humbly and truly' as possible, was a point made with tedious repetition in historical readers.

Another figure of immense symbolic stature was the British Admiral Lord Nelson. Only Gordon rivalled his status as a national hero in the later nineteenth century, and he certainly received a great deal of attention in the late-nineteenth and early twentieth-century classroom.[90] Logbooks and other school records attest that for many elementary schoolteachers Nelson clearly served as an important role model for their working-class students to emulate.[91] In reading books he was represented as all that was worthy in an Englishman: born to parents of modest means, and suffering from a weak constitution, he nevertheless overcame many difficulties through the strength of his character, eventually sacrificing his life for his nation in its time of need.[92] The *King Alfred Readers* proclaimed that students should never forget that Nelson's 'strength was in his heart and in his will, not in his body,' and that this proved 'what great deeds may be done by those who are weak in body but strong in mind.'[93] Nelson was, in fact, consistently pointed to as an inspirational leader in history readers, but while the fact that he was 'a self-made' man might have been read into his biography and had appeal for students and teachers, in the readers themselves his rise in social status did not receive much attention. Rather, it was his personal strength and sacrifice for the nation that tended to be stressed.[94]

This association of Nelson's greatness with his will rather than with his natural physical (dis)abilities offered a particularly suitable masculine identity to working-class boys that did not have to rely on the dictates of athleticism and muscular Christianity common to the elite Public Schools. Instead, Nelson was heroic and worthy of emulation primarily because of his attention to duty. 'The history of the Navy of England has been a very glorious one,' Arnold-Forster's *The Citizen Reader* explained, because '"Duty" had been the great watchword of the navy, and it was because he knew how great a power this simple word would have over the minds of his men that Admiral Nelson chose for his message to the fleet at the great victory of Trafalgar, the famous words – "England expects every man to do his duty."'[95] This last phrase (often with illustrations of it in naval signal flags), and also Nelson's (erroneously) reported last words – 'thank God I have done my duty' – featured in the pages and on the covers of countless readers. Attention to national duty sometimes seems to have been regarded as something uniquely English by some. In a general comparison of the English and French, one text reported that 'English sailors were brave and skillful, and they had one admiral – Horatio Nelson – who was as great a commander by sea as Napoleon was by land, and was, beside, a much better man; for while Napoleon was always thinking of himself and his own glory, Nelson thought only how he might best do his duty to England.'[96] Duty, and its corollary, discipline, of course, had multiple meanings in the classroom: obedience to teachers and figures of authority was here combined with the militarist and nationalist resonance of civic responsibilities.

The fact was that only a small minority of working-class boys, and certainly no girls, would actually go into military or naval service, and working-class children really had little hope of becoming a great military leader like Gordon or Nelson. While some readers acknowledged this, one, John Finnemore's *Famous Englishmen* (1901), devoted a considerable number of pages to the explanation of why the 'average' boy and girl *should still* care about such heroic figures. 'A hero needs heroes to follow him,' Finnemore observed, 'a great man must be greatly supported.' As he further explained, 'in every age we may call the great man the statue, and the people who supported him the pedestal. Few people in our time will become statues, but we can all take our share in forming a firm pedestal in support of a great leader and a great cause.' The concept of a 'pedestal' was ambiguous enough to be useful in promoting both the desire to fight under a great leader (here always assumed to be male) for the boys and a supportive role for the girls as well. To provide a practical example of this principle, Finnemore turned to the recent experience of the Anglo–Boer War, extolling the collective triumph of famous generals, common soldiers, and the population at home. After explaining how the men bravely volunteered to fight, leaving their homes and families, and describing how the loyal non-combatants in the population all pulled together behind the government's aims, Finnemore concluded that men and women who follow and support 'great men' through wisely obeying the laws of the land 'are just as necessary as the famous leader himself.' Everyone was capable of doing this, but without such obedience and support the future, claimed Finnemore, would 'contain very few Famous Englishmen.' Finnemore never explained to his young readers how they were supposed to distinguish and recognize great aims and great men from lesser causes and individuals; it was simply implied that the patriotism and selflessness of the Englishmen who 'fought so stoutly in the trenches,' and of the women and children who 'murmured "no surrender" with lips that trembled with hunger,' qualified the occasion as one in which the actions were worthy and just.[97] The absence of moral judgments in Finnemore's account was a distinct change from the approach taken in mid-century texts, when no leader or act of war was above moral reproach.[98] By the end of the century, however, it seems that the actions of the 'true patriot' were justified solely by his or her devotion to duty, nation, and empire.

Indeed, even in those books that stressed the purely civil aspects of citizenship, martial themes remained prominent. In one fictionalized didactic tale of good citizenship, *The Model Citizen* reader described how a passer-by saved some children from a house fire, something that 'every good citizen should do.' What is especially significant about this minor tale of heroism is that the hero is a soldier, 'whose chief duty is to fight for his country, to protect us all from foreign enemies who would take away from us our liberties and our citizen rights.' Yet the actions of this 'brave soldier' in this case were 'no part of his duty as a soldier,' for he was 'not paid to do it.' Rather, he demonstrated that good citizenship required courage and self-sacrifice, not for personal gain, but for the benefit of the nation as a whole.[99] This tale clearly does not require a martial figure to get across its essential message, thus it is significant that a soldier is employed in this narrative of appropriate citizen behaviour. Clearly, martial figures were presumed to convey, innately, some of the most important aspects of citizenship as it was conceived by school-book writers at this time.

The prevalence of military themes – suggesting worthy masculine role models within suitably patriotic narratives – could probably be found in the schooling of all English youth. However, the very specific social context of elementary education gave this martial metaphor of citizenship a socially specific function. For instance, Arnold-Forster ended his discussion of the British Army and Navy by suggesting: 'When boys and girls go out of school in order, one by one, class by class, they show that they have learnt the use of discipline. When they do their drill, moving their hands or feet together at the word of command, they show that they have learnt the use of discipline.'[100]

The discipline of the national hero was thus projected into the class-room in an effort to create social deference. Another text was even more direct in making the analogy between school and the military. Under the heading 'little soldiers,' the *King Alfred Readers* suggested:

Little boys like to play at soldiers. They make paper caps and wooden swords. Then they march together like little men. Some play on their toy trumpets.

Now let us think we are soldiers in school. Here we are sitting all in a very straight row. Heads up! Eyes Straight!

Who is the officer? Why, the teacher, of course. He calls, 'Fold arms!' We must obey at once like the soldiers.

Then he says, 'Look at me!' Every eye is turned to our officer, just like the real soldiers in the street.

We are little soldiers. We have learnt to obey at once, and with happy smiling faces. This makes the school hours pass very pleasantly.[101]

Here the students were the willing soldiers, learning to obey orders from their officer, and suggesting that their classroom discipline was as important, as necessary, and as enjoyable as that of the 'real' soldiers the children were taught to admire. Social obedience to figures of authority – in this case the teacher as officer – was thus figured into the everyday practices of the classroom; as we shall see in Chapter 6, this was reinforced in physical education as well. Given the problems of disorder in large classrooms of rambunctious students, teachers no doubt looked for any help in retaining some semblance of control. But in passages like those above, the prestige that was heaped on military themes infused such exercises in classroom discipline with social pre-scription, all the while cloaked in 'national' indispensability.

Martial themes in the historical narratives in elementary school read-ing books – intended, as they were, to demonstrate to working-class children their place in the great 'national tradition' – amalgamated ideas about English nationality with that of appropriate social and gender roles. Overwhelmingly, historical national heroes were the brave and daring men who had built up the nation and helped secure the empire. For boys, the upholding of masculine behaviour, as the legacy of the heroes of the past demonstrated, was integral to a national identity that was constructed as being socially inclusive. The lesson of the past was that great men were Englishmen and therefore true 'citi-zens' not through voting or other civic responsibilities, but because they had been active defenders of the nation. They had 'done their duty,' whether it was by following Nelson or Gordon into battle, or by saving a fellow citizen from a burning building. And while it was not expected that all future Englishmen would become soldiers, they ought to try to emulate their forebears' examples and become part of the loyal pedestal: supporters of those Englishmen who were striving to defend the nation and its ideal of liberty. This will become more evident as we explore in detail both the structuring framework of history as it was presented in reading books and the specific content encoded into these books. It is to this task – unravelling the meanings inherent in the liberal master narrative found in history readers – that we now turn.

2

The Syntax of National Identity: The Liberal Master Narrative

Historical teaching should leave behind a sense of time, a feeling of reverence for the past; a sense of nationality, membership of a nation, a feeling of the responsibilities of citizenship. (hear, hear) The historical lesson should have been to the pupil a source of inspiration ... If he had got a feeling of membership of a great community, a feeling of pride in his nationality, if he was inspired by what he had learnt, the historical lesson to him had been of immense value.

Professor Green, discussion of papers on the purpose of history instruction in elementary schools, North of England Education Conference, *School Government Chronicle* 79 (11 January 1908)

In the specific stories of elementary school reading books, duty to the nation – defined as manly activity in the public realm and womanly devotion in the domestic sphere – was the major responsibility demanded of the 'good' English citizen. School readers also outlined for children the supposed benefits of citizenship. The idea of progress was, of course, the key element of this narrative. National history unfolded from the humble beginnings of the first Anglo-Saxons, through centuries of growth, to the benefits and privileges of the present and the expected glorious destiny of the future.[1] This general trajectory of an ascending movement towards greater perfection was evident in just about every kind of history, geography, and civics reader, and many literature readers as well. A typical summation of this historical progress was presented in the conclusion of the first book of the 1884 *Cassell's Historical Course for Schools*:

Thus has Britain been changed into modern England, and the great English nation formed out of the German and British barbarians of the past, by the manliness, the wisdom, and the piety of our forefathers. At every moment of our lives, in the food we eat, in the clothes we wear, in the towns and the villages we inhabit, in the books we read, in the laws we live under, in the very thoughts and principles which guide us onwards, each one of us reaps the fruit of their labours. Them we cannot repay, but we reverence them, and in return we must labour for the good of those who will come after us. Every new discovery, every improvement in the laws, every change for the better in our own habits and our principles, works toward this end.[2]

While the significance of the 'British' changing 'into modern England' will be explored in the next chapter, the other elements of this passage can be seen to aptly sum up the gendered basics of the liberal master narrative as it was presented to working-class students. Progress had been achieved, not through struggle, but through the wisdom, piety, and 'manliness' of the Englishman – the 'English citizen' – going back through time to the ancient, barbaric 'forefathers.' What comprised this progress was clearly spelt out: 'the food we eat, the clothes we wear,' the places in which 'we' live, the books, laws, and ideas that 'we' value. Children were thus encouraged to view their material situation, humble though it may be, as somehow the product of the labours and achievements of the Englishmen who had come before them. But, of course, the very nature of this story of progress was such that it was without end. Children ought to work within the boundaries of the values of their forefathers: boys to continue to labour with diligence, girls to support their future husbands' efforts. In this we see the figuring of 'national time': the positing of vital continuities between a nation's ancient past and the present, which are then used to legitimate calls for collective effort of the nation's population in the future.

As Anne McClintock and others have suggested, the construction of nationalist chronologies through constructions such as national time frequently mirrored a gendered division in national symbols in which the female was set up as the embodiment of the nation, as the atavistic, apolitical, authentic, and inert 'body' of national tradition, while the male was depicted as the agent of national change – forward-looking, potent, and historic.[3] Such a gendered division is apparent in many of the illustrations that accompanied readers providing the national-progress historical narrative. Gracing the covers of many readers, for instance, was the image of Britannia, a symbol that evoked antiquity and quiet strength – dressed in armour, and placed in a pose that removed her from real time and place, her gaze directed vigilantly out to sea – and who was, clearly, above the nitty-gritty of social life and politics.[4] Very few history readers had any other images of women, the clear exceptions being illustrations of Queen Victoria and Elizabeth I (considered below) and very occasionally Florence Nightingale or Boadicea. In contrast, most of the illustrations that accompanied history narratives were of famous English*men*. They were depicted as the historical agents of the nation's progress – as soldiers and sailors (usually in battle), monarchs, reformers, and occasionally, inventors and politicians.[5] It was not merely the illustrations of the nation's history of progress, however, that were gendered in this manner. The narratives of readers themselves, as we shall see, were frequently gendered in a similar fashion. Moreover, another feature of this historical master narrative requiring analysis was the emptying of its radical progressive potential with a statist social message.

Victorian Liberalism: The People and 'National Culture'

When the 'political classes' of mid-Victorian England thought about their nation and their nationality, they did so through the lens of a diffuse cultural and political ideology which held that individual freedom and the establishment of free institutions within a national framework of the laws of political economy would result in prosperity and 'progress' for all within society. The advocates of this liberal vision were Protestant, mostly middle-class men, who claimed to speak on behalf of all of England.[6] Bolstered by the 'Whig' interpretation of history, which legitimated the views held by the politically active middle classes about their nation, its origins, and its destiny, the political liberalism and cultural nationalism of mid-Victorian England were very much intertwined.[7] A sense of common nationality was an integral part of the cultural hegemony of liberal society, and citizenship in the nation was conceived in a variety of liberal political, moral, religious, and economic terms. Indeed, within mid-century liberalism, national identity and liberal freedoms had remarkable consanguinity; specific freedoms – the freedom of subjects, freedom of speech, freedom of ideas, freedom of religion, freedom of contract, freedom to conduct enterprise, freedom of markets, freedom of trade – were all represented as being part of the middle-class ideal of Englishness.[8]

Although the boundaries of this liberal nation were largely determined by the male middle classes, its appeal could transcend social
divisions. The unquestionable popularity of continental liberal-nationalist leaders such as Mazzini and Kossuth among both middle- and
working-class radicals testifies to the persuasiveness of liberal-nationalist political ideals at various times in Victorian Britain.[9] Similarly,
recent work on nineteenth-century liberal radicalism has demonstrated
that the liberal rhetoric of 'the people' had a powerful appeal to both
working- and middle-class activists. Chartism, for instance, was as
much focused on the democratization of citizenship and the bringing
of working men into the national community politically as it was directed by the exigencies of socio-economic divisions. And much liberal rhetoric drew on the radical patriotism that had long celebrated
England as the birthright of the 'freeborn Englishman.'[10] Nevertheless,
as Margot Finn has ably detailed, fractures existed between the proponents of the liberal nation and the radical patriotic culture of Chartist
and trade unionist leaders, especially after the collapse of Chartism as
a mass movement. Indeed, although a sense of national identity was
integral to both radical and mainstream liberal politics and culture,
this fact did not militate against either the existence or the further
development of mobilized class feeling.[11] In fact, far from being inimi-
cal to the development of class-consciousness, divergent appeals to
the 'nation' may even have reinforced the development of class or
other feelings of social difference. In the mélange of competing liberal,
radical, Christian, and democratic socialist claims to the rights of the
'free born Englishman,' the 'nation,' and 'the people,' quite different
conceptions of national identity could be posited by deploying the
same or similar symbols and historical narratives. Patrick Joyce has
suggested that most claims to speak on behalf of the nation – 'the
people' – fell under a distinctly English 'populist' tradition: a combined working- and middle-class radical opposition to entrenched and
hereditary privilege.[12] And Joyce argues that this radical populism
was more significant than any nascent class identities. By the end of
the century, however, such a populist reading of 'the people' was
under attack from within the ranks of the professionalizing middle
class.[13] Citizenship, as it was promoted in elementary education at
least, invoked the language of inclusion – the language of 'the people'
– but emptied the concept of any 'populist,' combative, or transforma-
tive aims. A radical 'populist' reading of some of these books was

certainly still possible. However, the liberal master narrative – as it was presented in elementary school reading – led in a more statist and state-patriotic direction than what Patrick Joyce has suggested obtained in working-class culture in general during the second half of the century.[14]

For the remainder of this chapter, the master narrative of English history as it was presented in history and other reading books will be deconstructed, in an effort to demonstrate how, in 'learning their letters,' working-class children were also drawn into identifying with supposed innate gender divisions and socio-political hierarchy.

The History Reader and the Liberal Master Narrative

Historical readers conformed to contemporary pedagogical ideas about how both reading and the acquiring of information could and should be instructed. They were written with the foreknowledge that to be successful they had to get the tacit approval of school board officials and government inspectors. Unlike the formal history textbooks used in secondary and elite schools, which typically contained a straightforward historical narrative covering, usually, the 'whole' of English history,[15] reader sets tended to be broken down with the practical needs of the elementary classroom teacher in mind.[16] The first two or three history readers in a series were usually comprised of simple 'romantic' stories taken from English history, as it was a commonly vocalized precept that 'romance was ever attractive to the young.'[17] The later volumes would be arranged either in the 'concentric method' – texts that each told the story of English history in an ascending degree of detail and textual difficulty – or using a chronological method, with books starting with ancient and medieval history and each successive one progressing through the remaining centuries with the difficulty increasing in the books as they approached the contemporary period. The pedagogical principle behind this arrangement was explained by E.H. Spalding, the lecturer in history at Goldsmiths' College and later principal of Bingley, who noted in the preface to her widely influential series, the *Piers Plowman Histories*, that history was a 'story' of how 'society has slowly developed out of primitive beginnings in a remote past.' In order to help children comprehend this, reading books ought to focus on different aspects of that evolution at different stages of the child's life. 'For example, children of Standards I & II in an elementary school, and to a large extent children of Standard III, are mainly inter-

ested in individuals.' Thus, the early readers in the series were devoted to simple biographical accounts. 'Later on children begin to be
interested in the life of society,' which required the mid-series readers
to explore the differences in English society over time, while the last
books in the series were devoted mainly to political developments as
the older children were able 'to grasp the idea of national life and
government.'[18]

Such a structure of presentation fit well with the fundamental trajectory of most historical readers, which put forward in increasing
detail over successive years the idea of the 'story of England's history'
as one of 'steady and advancing growth.'[19] Sometimes such expressions of positivist optimism were tempered with reflections about the
fortunate nature of the English 'race,' which 'with many grievous failings and mistakes, has nevertheless succeeded in producing and con-
tinuing the best example of liberty and order in its government which
the world has ever seen.'[20] Confident of the superiority of its civilization, the English story was one of sure and upward progression.[21]
These affirmations of the progressive evolution of English liberty and
good government contained a healthy dose of 'aren't we all so lucky'
to be living in such an enlightened state. After explaining the logic of
the patience, suffering, and sacrifice of 'our' English forefathers – that
along with the attainment of English-style liberty had come, 'inevitably,' an 'orderly' and just society – it was proudly concluded by Oscar
Browning that 'it [had been] the genius of England to gain by reform
what other nations attempt by revolution.'[22]

Specific freedoms and general liberty were thus held up as both the
reward for centuries of national sacrifice and patience and an inducement to the schoolchild to honour and respect these values and all
those individuals who strove to uphold them in the present and future. For, as another reading book reasoned, 'our country has grown
stronger and better the more its rulers and peoples have striven to act
rightly. It is the duty of Englishmen and Englishwomen to do their
best to make England great in the future also.' For this to happen, it
was necessary that all children should strive to 'live worthy and
honourable lives themselves; for a country can only be great when its
people are temperate, truthful, orderly, reverent, industrious, merciful, and courageous.'[23] This reference to 'rulers and peoples' striving
to act rightly, and others to the great suffering, patience, and indomitable will of the people, represented both the heart and substance, and
also the inherent contradiction, of the liberal master narrative as it was

presented to schoolchildren. This was because the 'struggle for the freedom of the people' sat uneasily alongside the supposedly peaceful evolution of English rights and freedoms as embodied in the unwritten constitution. There was an unresolved tension, in other words, within the liberal narrative between the notion of an evolutionary growth of freedoms and the necessarily violent historical struggles against tyranny and oppression.

As it did in many later-Victorian histories intended for an adult readership, English history in elementary reading books tended to start with the Anglo-Saxons and move through subsequent eras in a more or less positivist fashion, pointing to the reclamation of the original freedoms of the Anglo-Saxons in the modern constitutional framework.[24] Certain events and periods had more prominence than others: for instance, the signing of Magna Carta and Simon de Montfort's subsequent parliamentary efforts, the 'state making' of Edward I, Henry VIII's break with Rome, the Elizabethan expansion of England, the seventeenth-century Civil War and the constitutional settlement of the Glorious Revolution, and the various political reforms of the nineteenth century all claimed prime importance. The 'racial' aspect of this English narrative will be explored in the following chapters. Here we shall examine the post-Conquest narrative as it was presented to working-class children, stressing those fracture points at which this construction of 'national time' was forced into contradiction.

The National Logic of English Progress: The Medieval Period

Magna Carta, the agreement between King John and his major vassals signed in 1215, received a generous amount of attention in both historical and civics readers and was frequently alluded to in geographical and literary readers as well. Magna Carta's prevalence in classroom instruction was such that, in 1908, an educational reformer used the practice of elementary schoolchildren being made to memorize all of the Charter's individual clauses as an example of poor teaching method. The importance of knowledge about the Charter was not derided, but it was suggested instead that children ought to learn about its importance through an appeal to their 'romantic sense,' and by connecting the 'periods of the growth of the nation' with the corresponding 'stages of the growth of the child.'[25] Even this suggestion made Magna Carta into the civic equivalent of the letters of the alphabet; the most basic of building blocks on which all other English constitutional developments were based. S.R. Gardiner repeatedly referred to the Charter as the most basic and significant foundation of both the common law and the English constitution in his elementary school history readers.[26] Many reading books extolled the significance of Magna Carta through references to the 'brown and shrivelled copy of the Great Charter in the British Museum,' a document so revered that 'all Englishmen who love their country should try to see it at least once in their lives.' Magna Carta was 'dear to the hearts of all Britons,' and its placement in the British Museum made that location a shrine to English nationhood.[27]

Discussions of Magna Carta in school readers inevitably started with descriptions of the wickedness of King John, 'the worst king that has ever ruled England.' John was, in fact, the most reviled of all domestic monarchs in school readers.[28] As the *Raleigh History Readers* suggested, the signing of Magna Carta was 'an event which Englishmen look back upon as one of the most important events in their History. The chief figure in the scene was a king – a king so bad that no other king of England has borne his name.'[29] John was clearly depicted as the villain that set about the process leading to Magna Carta: he had offended the entirety of 'the people.' The Great Charter was rarely characterized as a compromise between a king and his major vassals; rather, it was portrayed both as the triumph of the virtues of the Anglo-Saxon constitutional tradition and, simultaneously, as the first example of a voluntary banding together of the entire 'English' population for a common cause since the Conquest. As one reader noted, 'the English had become a united nation ... [t]he Great Charter was not meant to contain anything new, but only to say exactly what the old liberties of England were, and how the king was bound to treat his subjects.' Indeed, the Charter was only possible because 'all classes [had] joined together against the king, and he had none to help him but some foreign soldiers whom he had hired and brought to England.'[30] Significantly, this example of rebellion against the monarch was not simply phrased as 'the people' rising against their lawful but corrupt ruler, but was also tempered with John's singular 'treachery' – he was singled out in English history as being so extraordinarily wicked that no other monarch would dare use his name – and for his reliance on 'foreign' troops to aid his oppression. A later volume in the same series further explained the full significance of John's actions with regards to the relationship of the Normans and Saxons and their co-support of the Great Charter, from which 'all later constitutional liberty is but a development.' The Charter was the 'first great act of the Anglo-Norman nation' and 'under the guidance of the Church and the Barons, gradually infused into the masterly administration of the Normans the antique spirit of English equality and freedom.'[31]

This message was propounded with remarkable consistency in these texts throughout this period. *Chambers's Historical Readers* noted that, from the signing of Magna Carta, 'Normans and Englishmen' began to be more friendly, and the love of their common country of England increased steadily. Somehow, with the signing of Magna Carta all men within England were now 'ruled by the same laws and spoke the same language,' and all the laws and traditions that had characterized the English before the Norman Conquest had been returned to their proper prominence.[32] According to the history readers, the consensus of the English nation seems to have been nearly unanimous in the signing of this document. The 1895 *Warwick Readers* referred to it as the 'charter which made Englishmen for ever free' and which, 'it must be remembered, [indicated] that the best of the English clergy were on the side of the barons.'[33] The popular struggle was here portrayed as the entire nation against the one man who defied it. Through the 'King's wickedness,' the *Tower History Readers* of 1911 explained, all the barons combined for the common good, 'and the Normans grew proud of their name as "Englishmen."' New bonds of friendship and community were forged in opposition to the king's tyranny, resulting in 'the great charter of freedom and justice, which is the source of all the liberties we Englishmen enjoy today.'[34]

The resurgence of the 'English' political tradition via Magna Carta was posited as a struggle against a common tyrant sufficient to encourage a reconciliation between Anglo-Saxons and Normans. Clearly this could be read in the 'populist' tradition of the 'people' banding together against the oppression of corrupt, entrenched privilege. Being devoted to the struggle against any sort of tyranny was a common claim made for the English; in a very real sense it was posited as one of the defining 'essences' of Englishness. Sometimes this was praised as an 'innate' or 'racial' virtue. At other times it was presented as part of the evolutionary heritage of the English, as 'some of the greatest victories for English liberty have sprung from the sufferings caused by the rule of weak, or even wicked kings.' From misery, the 'people' learned to 'make a stand for their freedom and their rights.'[35] Indeed, the Anglo-Saxon struggle against the tyranny of Norman rule was itself pointed to as a prime example of the English character. But in most readers it was the hyperbolic claims about the *scale* of John's tyranny that permitted the remarkable reconciliation between the two erstwhile 'racial' foes. John's 'evil rule had turned the whole nation against him,' and the Charter that was drawn up was to 'put in a definite form' all the historic English rights and liberties 'for which Englishmen were ever afterwards prepared to fight if necessary.'[36] None of the texts commented on the apparent incongruity of the claim that it was ancient Anglo-Saxon liberties that the Norman nobles enshrined in the Charter with John. Such inconsistencies and contradictions were simply ignored or lightly papered over.

There was, indeed, an effort to 'Anglicize' the development of English constitutional arrangements, which is most apparent in the usual treatment of the 'English' hero Simon de Montfort. De Montfort's efforts to have Henry III honour the wishes of 'Parliament' were noted time and again in general elementary school books as another of the foundations of the English constitution. As a hero fighting against the evil of a cosmopolitan, 'foreign-dominated' court after Magna Carta had supposedly returned England to the proper course of reinstating the ancient English liberties, de Montfort was depicted as the 'leader of the patriotic party, [who] laid down his life for the cause, dying before the object of his hopes – namely the just government of the people – was realized.' He represented the 'will of the people' for parliamentary government: that 'only Englishmen might hold great English offices.'[37] This conjunction of the 'will of the people' with ridding England of a foreign (French) element and returning governance to 'the English' is suggestive. It was not the nature of the freedoms that were at issue, but that they were being denied to Englishmen by foreigners. *The Warwick Readers* proclaimed that de Montfort – 'Simon the Righteous' – was 'a good and a great man' who, sober and simple in his life, and a lover of books and good conversation, 'worked hard to secure freedom for Englishmen.'[38] His actions at the Oxford Parliament in 1265 were described as a 'heroic struggle against the foreigners.' He 'cleansed England from the foreigners' and removed the power of the 'French vultures that preyed around Henry's Court.'[39] The Oxford Parliament was by this deed acclaimed as the foundation of truly popular representation for all England and all Englishmen.[40]

De Montfort's Norman French heritage was clearly a minor difficulty for reader authors when it came to retelling this particular story. Texts from the early 1880s made exceptions for his 'Frenchness,' or took pains to downplay his background and stress his understanding of the potential greatness of England when he made the choice to 'adopt' England as his nation. Over the course of the period 1890 to 1914 texts stressed that he became an 'Englishman at heart' whose 'greatest wish was to see England well governed' and of whom there was 'no doubt that he had a real love for his adopted country.'[41] In fact, in many explanations, he both adopted England and was himself adopted by the grateful English, because after leaving France he 'threw off all French feeling, and became heart and soul an Englishman.'[42] Other accounts stressed how he learned the wisdom of the English ways, 'the hidden genius of the old English institutions,' and was, after a time, readily accepted by the English, who adored him as 'a saint and martyr.'[43] In some of the later readers, de Montfort's Norman origins were used as an explanation for the same process that Magna Carta was credited with, namely 'the wedding together of all the people in England into one nation in one common cause.'[44] By embracing English ideals, de Montfort's Frenchness was thus transcended. In other later texts, however, de Montfort lost his French background, language, and name entirely. He became Earl Simon of Montfort, 'a good Englishman,' or simply Simon the 'brave and good man' responsible for the 'first real parliament in our History.'[45] Regardless of whether the reader author chose to see de Montfort as a Frenchman who became an honorary Englishman, or to never mention his French heritage, the suggestion remained that this early struggle to resurrect ancient English liberties was based not on class or other social distinction, but on 'national' difference. The oppressive group, those that denied the Englishman his rights, was not really English at all.

Connected explicitly to Magna Carta and de Montfort's founding of Parliament, the reign of Edward I formed the third of the three heralded constitutional building blocks of the English state and nation in the late medieval period. Edward and his reign's depiction tended to resume the narration of the implicit struggle between the Saxons and Normans after the Conquest and, once again, signalled its resolution. Edward himself was often represented as the first truly English king since Harold, and was characterized as the manifestation of long-suppressed English values in the person of an individual monarch. The full significance of the flowering of these traits and values in the nation at large would not occur until the reigns of the Tudors and Elizabeth, but it was suggested that it was in Edward's reign that the path of English national greatness, conceived in terms of both constitutional-state development and national-race characteristics, was thought to have been firmly and finally set.

With Edward I, monarchs were again the friends of the people, very much part of the nation and not its enemy: he was often referred to as the 'friend of the people' and the 'noblest of our English Kings.' Edward's 'English' pedigree and 'typically English' physical characteristics were especially revered, for 'he had the golden hair and the tall and stalwart figure which the English people loved to recall in connection with their ancient kings.'[46] The Reverend Morris paid special attention to Edward's appearance, which was 'tall and commanding,' and to his character, which was said to be 'open, manly, and royal.' While his 'severity sometimes reached the point of cruelty,' Edward I had many worthy English traits: his 'prudence, foresight, vigilance, energy, and industry, made him a wise statesman and a successful soldier.' Furthermore, his efforts to improve the English common laws were so distinguished as to deservedly bestow upon him the nickname 'the English Justinian.'[47] When Edward's personality traits were discussed in these books, they were often correlated with either his innate 'Englishness' and English sensibility, or his prowess as an English statesman. This was a distinct change from mid-century school books, which were mostly concerned with praising or condemning Edward's personal moral attributes and failings, particularly his hot temper.[48] By 1895 reader authors were often praising Edward's English sympathies and state-making expertise. This can be seen in one of the few accounts that did not simply refer to Edward *as* English, but rather described him as the 'first king since the conquest who bore an old English name.' His English name was somehow indicative of his whole English character, for he 'was also the first who showed a real desire to understand Englishmen, and to make England, by the aid of the English, a great power in Europe. The work he did, and the wisdom he showed, make him one of the greatest of English sovereigns.'[49]

Most other accounts pointed to how, politically, militarily, and administratively, Edward had proved himself to be 'thoroughly English.' It was suggested, for instance, that Edward had learned much from his old foe de Montfort, and that '[w]hen he came to be king, he upheld the principle that what was for the good of all should be consulted on by all. He gathered around him Parliaments even more complete than that which Simon had summoned, and there strove to do justice to all.' Indeed, for the English at least, the reign of Edward was seemingly near idyllic, as he 'allowed no foreigners to thrust Englishmen out of places of authority on the soil of England,' and he made no promises he could not keep. 'In his hands England prospered as it had never done before. Edward kept the peace well, and in his days the barons did not dare either to oppress the freeholder and the citizen, or to resist the authority of the king.'[50] Again, Edward was seen as a friend of the people, mostly because he favoured the English, as opposed, for instance, to John.

The focus on the persona of Edward I as a distinctly English law-bringer in the development of the English law and constitution was the result of two interrelated factors. First, the emphasis on providing a continuous narrative of things English – on stressing the continuity of Englishness from the present back to the founding myth of the Anglo-Saxons – required fastening onto any reasonable facet of the events or time in question that could reasonably be represented as a product of Englishness. This was particularly so for the late medieval period. Much of Edward's personal character, and that of his regime, was anything but English – at least as the late Victorians would like to have defined it. But in his apparent character Edward seemed to offer a trace of those values held dear as English in the imagination of professional reader writers. Second, emphasizing the role of the 'great' individual, although hardly a new approach to the understanding of history, was nevertheless believed by many pedagogical experts to be the most appropriate method of conveying both the scope and feel of historical events to young children. This approach was particularly favoured when dealing with the constitution and law, necessarily abstract concepts whose complexity could only be alluded to in the elementary classroom.[51] In their attempts to make history more lively, exciting, and romantic, reader authors often reverted to simple character descriptions as their explanation for the iconic events of English history, particularly as they went further back in time. But unlike the moralizing on the perceived virtues and faults of past figures that characterized the school histories of mid-century, these character depictions romanticized those early English heroes who were perceived to be advancing the forward progress of English freedom and greatness, and demonized those who seemed to stand in the way of this progression.[52]

History and Gender Identity: The Case of Elizabeth I

The Elizabethan age occupied a special place in the late-Victorian and Edwardian construction of the national historical narrative. In both a chronological and figurative sense, Elizabeth's reign was the connection between the medieval period and the late-Victorian present: it was in this period that the foundations of the Victorian empire were thought to have been laid and the nation-state and Protestantism consolidated; in this era that English values and greatness had triumphantly asserted themselves after a period of relative dormancy; in this period that seafarers, explorers, merchants, poets, and writers had all flourished; and, consequently, here that the 'true' core values of Englishness – the moulding of the Saxon 'spirit' to the changed circumstances of the modern world – had first emerged. The standard history readers allocated large amounts of space to elucidating these themes and extolling the glories of the period. Elizabeth's accession was portrayed as universally welcomed and accepted, and her reign proved to be the 'most glorious reign in the history of our country.' The tenor of her reign was depicted as being new, exciting, and socially inclusive, wherein 'a new spirit seemed to inspire all classes' and the 'whole nation awakened suddenly to a knowledge of its strength and freedom.'[53] And due to the glory of this 'Merrie England,' the Elizabethan age was represented as being very much a part of the contemporary national culture. 'Much that constitutes the glory and greatness of England today' was traced back to Elizabeth's reign, in which the patriotic Englishman 'can find the roots of our national life and character.'[54] Elizabeth's reign was accorded such a special place in the 'story of the nation' that entire readers were devoted to it, since 'no period in our history is of more absorbing interest to the student than the reign of Queen Elizabeth.'[55]

In reader after reader, the Elizabethan age was central to the entire trajectory of imperial expansion and was depicted as the revitalization of the English 'greatness' in which 'all classes' were united and 'inspired.' Innate racial traits were also operative in this narrative, as the 'natural' seafaring talents of the privateering 'sea dogs' were depicted as merely the resurgence of 'those characteristics of the race' that had been the stimulus of the original sea-roving Anglo-Saxons.[56] This was, in essence, a symbolic relocating of the 'foundations of modern English greatness' to the late sixteenth century from its previous locus in the late-seventeenth-century Glorious Revolution – as the constitutional 'Whig' interpretations prevalent in the earlier part of the nineteenth century had trumpeted. The implication being that the divisive events of the seventeenth century were less important to the English character and to notions of citizenship than the radical 'populist' narrative of the revolution and civil war. Indeed, not only was the Elizabethan period depicted as that of the inception of empire, to it was also attributed the rebirth and growth of those libertarian characteristics, 'that love of freedom,' that was to distinguish the English 'during the next century, [and that] was to prove once and for all that English people would never endure the yoke of a tyrant.'[57] The 'gloriousness' of the Elizabethan age was thus assured for a number of reasons, and yet for the purposes of promoting 'good citizenship' within the confines of the ideological specifications that we have noted, this period also presented some ironic difficulties for reading-book authors. This was largely because of the nature and character of Elizabeth herself.

Elizabeth was both a strong public woman and a national icon: a figure whose real as opposed to merely symbolic role in the nation's story was undeniable, but whose gender identity made aspects of this role highly problematic. The 'proper' depiction of Elizabeth was a quandary that preceded the efforts of the late Victorians. After all, in the historical master narrative, citizenship was represented as falling within the public arena in which the Englishman resided, acted, and ruled. It was placed within the socially constructed boundaries of separate spheres: men had their place, women theirs. Moreover, in the figuring of the nationalist narrative – national time – it was men who had been the agents of national change: women's place was in the nation's iconography, they were symbols of the nation's continuity, tradition, and timelessness. The narratives and images offered to children at school about the responsibilities that membership in the public realm entailed reflected the inherently precarious, and sometimes contradictory, nature of the ideologically differentiated male and female role models written into school materials. Fredric Jameson has argued that the double-binds and dilemmas of socially constructed categories, such as, in this case, public/private and change/continuity, have to be solved or papered over through narrative.[58] Indeed, it is at those points in the nationalist narratives found in classroom culture where the reader comes to a figure or event that does not fit into the appropriate roles 'normally' assigned to men and women that we see the work of gender ideology most clearly, in either masking or trying to explain away the apparent contradiction.

Throughout the nineteenth century, history texts struggled to represent the importance of Elizabeth, a figure who, as a strong-willed female active in public affairs, presented a dilemma from the perspective of Victorian gender ideology. The remoulding of nationalist culture at the end of the nineteenth century, with its placement of the

Elizabethan age squarely at the centre of the overarching historical narrative of the English, added somewhat to this difficulty. A comparison between the depiction of Elizabeth in a typical mid-nineteenth-century school text and the way her persona was characterized at the end of the century should demonstrate the continuities, deviations, and ironies of her representation in a wider historical perspective.

In a popular 1864 elementary history text written by the Reverend Brewer, Elizabeth's reign was described in the following manner:

Elizabeth was a great and excellent Queen, but neither a great nor excellent woman. This may seem strange, but I think I can make it plain.

A man may be a good man of business, but not a good man. He may attend to his shop, buy and sell well, make money, and grow rich; but may be ill-natured, neglect his children, and neither read his Bible nor say his prayers. So a queen may rule the nation wisely, make good laws, do all she can to make her people rich and happy, and be a capital queen; but in private life she may be fretful, vain, envious, and passionate. Queen Elizabeth, as a queen, is worthy of all praise; but as a woman she had many faults which deserve blame.[59]

It is significant that this explanation of the dichotomy between Elizabeth's public virtues and her private failings drew upon an analogy of the stereotyped mid-Victorian 'Man of Business,' for it demonstrates that different root metaphors were at work in conceptions of the nation in the mid-Victorian and later periods. In this example, the attempt to place Elizabeth within the confines of 'separate spheres' ideology was done through reference to easily recognizable mid-century liberal values. The role of the queen within the nation was doubly framed within a liberal-nationalist framework. Her 'public' role of enacting wise laws and promoting the prosperity of the nation at large was praised; neglect of her 'private' responsibilities and her distinctly undesirable female qualities – vanity, jealousy, fecklessness, passion – were sharply criticized. Elizabeth's morality was found wanting, and worse, her personal failings had an impact on affairs of state. Regarding Elizabeth's treatment of Mary Queen of Scots, for instance, Brewer's text noted, 'It is my opinion that Elizabeth disliked her, not because she was naughty but because she was beautiful. She thought that the gentlemen of her court would admire her cousin the most and Elizabeth was too fond of admiration to allow others to be admired more than herself.'[60] As an unmarried queen, Elizabeth was unavoidably active in the public sphere, and for the most part praised for actions, but she was judged flawed because her 'womanly' nature was not up to Victorian standards, or more precisely, she could not be depicted as Queen Victoria herself was – as both a noble sovereign and a paragon of domestic virtue, morals, and manners. The irony is, of course, that Elizabeth when judged in her male role was considered a great national 'success,' and yet when judged as a woman she was a 'failure.'

The ironies of Elizabeth's depiction were not to be resolved in later accounts, but her representation did alter. The liberal-nationalist emphasis on political and material progress, morality, and the importance of private conduct diminished (though never vanished) from the accounts in the later readers: new elements were added while older ones were reconfigured. Generally, Elizabeth's public reputation increased in school books towards the end of the century, but heightened emphasis was placed on the greatness of her reign as opposed to her person.[61] The weaknesses of her personal character still received mention, but they were, in many accounts, de-emphasized; in others, Elizabeth's personal failings were hived off into the realm of 'the court,' which was held to have little impact on the actual 'progress' of the nation. Furthermore, unlike the metaphor of the personally irresponsible but successful man of business used in the mid-century text, the metaphors and rhetorical devices used at the end of the century tended to revolve around determinate factors beyond Elizabeth's own agency: namely, her 'race,' the commanding influence of her council advisers, or sometimes her position as a cipher for the English 'spirit.' Moreover, the dynamic of those accounts in which her gender role was emphasized tended to be as the loving, supportive, home-bound patron of the brave English adventurer.

The two episodes of Elizabeth's reign that received most attention in the school readers were the defeat of the Spanish Armada in 1588 and the careers and 'heroic' deeds of Drake, Raleigh, Hawkins, and the other 'sea dogs.' Significantly, the most repeated passage concerns Elizabeth's speech to her troops and sailors at Tilbury on the eve of their engagement with the Armada in the English Channel. Many texts faithfully reported that she had declared: '"I come amongst you, as you see, at this time – to lay down my life for my God, and for my kingdom, and for my people, my honour and my blood, even in the dust. I know I have the body but of a weak and feeble woman; but I have the heart of a king, and a king of England too, and think foul scorn that Parma or Spain, or any prince of Europe, should dare to

invade the borders of my realm.'"[62] The commentaries that followed
the presentation of this passage are interesting and significant in that
they were disposed to stress the patriotic Englishness of her character
that this speech revealed. *The English History Reading Books* (1881) proclaimed, 'Was it strange that when Elizabeth spoke such words as
these thousands of her subjects were ready to die in her cause, which
was their own as well as hers?' and that she 'kept her popularity to
the end, because she was above all an Englishwoman. She never
thought of sacrificing the interests of her country to please a king of
Spain or any other foreigner.'[63] Another set of books from 1898 suggested these words proved 'that she would not let any one persuade
her to act in a way that was not the best for England,' while yet
another from 1895 suggested 'the queen was quite right, when she
spoke these brave words, for there was not a man in England who
was not ready and willing to die for her and for his country.'[64]

The presentation of the Tilbury speech, and the commentaries that
accompanied it, implicitly set up a gendered meaning system in which
loyalty and patriotism were figured within a complementary relationship between the female sovereign and her people. Unlike the depiction of, say, Edward I, Henry V, Richard I, Cromwell, or William III,
whose military conduct in school readers was detailed by staging them
as active leaders/heroes, leading their men into battle and gaining
their loyalty by example, Elizabeth was depicted not so much as the
leader of the nation-in-arms, but as a symbol of what was being fought
for. The people were ready to fight and die for her, because she was a
true English monarch, 'with the heart of a King,' but who nevertheless
as a 'feeble woman' could not actually lead them into the fight (and
this despite the fact that she reportedly gave the Tilbury speech from
horseback and partially cloaked in armour). The reciprocal nature of
this relationship between female monarch and people was highlighted
by the frequency with which it was reported that Elizabeth 'liked to
talk of her "good husbands, the people,"' or her 'good husband, England,' and that although she had a 'strong will of her own, she liked to
exercise it in such a way as to please those whom she called her
husbands.'[65] And even if she could not be said to be leading the defence of England, all 'Englishmen felt that [Elizabeth] was with them
and for them against the world. She was English to the backbone.'[66]

Thus, while the symbolic role of Elizabeth gained prominence (as
did that of the monarch generally, as will be detailed later in this
chapter), her leadership role in the running of the state and her per-

sonal responsibility for the glories of the age declined, although she was still credited for bringing together a wise and competent group of advisers.[67] Revealingly, *The Royal Standard Series* contained one of the few texts of this period that pointed directly to Elizabeth's prominent leadership in the affairs of state. But in this case a somewhat modified version of the mid-Victorian dichotomy between public and private conduct was invoked, since in 'the council chamber her keen, vigorous intellect and the instinct of command, characteristic of her race, dominated perhaps the most famous group of statesmen in our history.' But in 'her court she was a very woman, with all a woman's vanity – coquettish, emotional, swayed hither and thither by the merest caprice of pride or spite, or personal inclination.'[68] The principal difference here from the mid-century accounts is that Elizabeth's 'race' was used to mark off her positive attributes, and this, along with the fact that she had available to her a group of wise and competent statesmen, was what fundamentally made her reign 'great.' The 'problem' of Elizabeth's gender was here countered by indicating that her race identity in some way compensated for the deficiencies of her being a woman. Indeed, the mere fact of her gender was used as a means to discount what was considered the negative side of her character: her womanly faults were made entirely natural. She was depicted as having as little control over her personal conduct as over the positively determined fact of her 'race,' which allowed her to properly conduct her public duties.

Critically, however, in most accounts Elizabeth was routinely praised for sustaining the 'great English captains,' the 'sea dogs,' with money and honours; for encouraging their adventures, and revelling in their brave deeds. Ultimately it was they, rather than she, who were portrayed as the very essence of all that was virtuous in the English at this time. Elizabeth's reign was foreordained as one in which great things could happen, but the dictates of the romantic genre ultimately decreed that it was the great men of her day who would be responsible for the great deeds, done in the name of England and showering honour on their queen. It was thus Drake, Raleigh, Hawkins, Howard, Frobisher, Grenville, and Sidney, rather than Elizabeth, who provided the chivalric, adventurous role models for the new generation of 'manly good citizens.' Consequently, descriptions of their deeds took up far more space in the readers than did discussions of Elizabeth's policies or of Elizabeth herself: a feature that was both the reverse of the mid-century approach and one that was almost unique in the extremely sovereign-centric approach to history instruction pursued at the end of the century.

Collectively, it was the great captains 'who gave England the proud title of Mistress of the Seas,' a suggestively gendered description of their relationship to the nation. They were attributed with doing much for the glory of England in the present: 'Our hearts still beat faster as we read of their exploits. No enterprise was too bold or too dangerous for them. Under such men as Drake and Hawkins, they carried the English flag into seas where it had never been seen before, fought and won against the greatest odds, and made their name a terror through all the colonies of Spain.'[69] The Reverend Dawe in a curious and ambiguous mixture of historical narration and contemporary observation, explained that the innate English spirit of adventure was unleashed by Elizabeth, and that this spirit drove Englishmen 'to seek a more varied and fuller life,' and further, that they had succeeded because the Englishman in general was 'gifted with great pluck, where fighting has to be done, with good staying power under stress and storm, with self-reliance when cut off from friends, and above all, with a spirit of justice and fair play.'[70]

Individually, the great Elizabethan captains were each praised for a variety of specific deeds and talents. Drake and Raleigh tended to be given pride of place, as they embodied the innate curiosity, seamanship, courage, and basic restlessness of the English captains – factors necessary for England's conquest and expansion. Raleigh was given praise for his learning and chivalric conduct, for his explorations, and for his founding of a new home for the English 'race.'[71] Drake meanwhile was acclaimed for his boldness, 'pluck,' seamanship, and those more inestimable values of 'Englishness.'[72] He was credited with doing much 'for the strength and glory of England,' his chivalry was praised, and his loyalty to England deemed unquenchable. Indeed, it was suggested that Philip of Spain 'offered to take him into his service,' which indicated both his admiration for the 'great admiral, and how little he knew the spirit of a true-born Englishman.'[73]

The specific deeds of other figures, especially Grenville and Sidney, were also prominent in these texts. The tale of Grenville's ship *The Revenge* fighting against fifty-three Spanish vessels and being destroyed rather than surrendering was included in many readers either through tragic-romantic narration, or through the inclusion of Tennyson's 1878 poem, 'The Revenge.'[74] Indeed, the reports of government investigations and the lesson plans in numerous school logbooks indicate that this story and Tennyson's poem were particular favourites in the elementary school classroom.[75] Moreover, Grenville's reported last words provided the implicit lesson: 'Here die I, Richard Grenville, with a joyful and quiet mind, for I have ended my life as a good sailor ought. I have fought for my country and my queen, for honour and for God.'[76] Similarly, the chivalric last action of Sir Philip Sidney, mortally wounded but forgoing a taste of water so that a 'common' soldier might drink, was also referred to repeatedly.[77] Indeed, Sidney's death was said to have caused 'mourning throughout the army, as if every man had lost a brother or a son; and there was mourning for him also throughout all England amongst soldiers and poets, and scholars and women who had loved him for his gentle manliness.'[78] Many educationalists wholeheartedly endorsed the use of such stories, although F.H. Hayward was critical of the lesson that was being conveyed: 'Tennyson's *Revenge* is a favourite school piece. The teacher may ask ... whether the sailors of any other country than England would have fought as bravely as Grenville's men. The class unanimously answers "no."'[79] Haywood's cosmopolitan and anti-jingo perspective caused him here to rebel against the nationalist masculinity that he believed was understood by the children exposed to these stories.

The 'common English' seaman and soldier was also included for praise and reverence, both for his loyalty to his superiors – the captains – 'through thick and thin,' and for his own 'brave and hardy' actions.[80] The authors of these texts were especially careful to include lowly mariners in their hyperbolic descriptions of English pluck: 'England was fortunate in her captains, men of splendid daring and courage, who had fought and beaten the Spaniards on the sea in all parts of the world. The common seamen were worthy of their commanders. They loved their country, and would have died for their commanders. They cheerfully put up with the bad and scanty food.'[81] Officers and men were locked together in these stories. Finnemore, in a practical example of his concept of the 'pedestal,' noted that the famous Drake, 'the first Englishman to sail around the world,' did not sail alone: 'Every sea-dog of his crew had as stout a heart as the great commander, or that wonderful voyage could never have been carried through.'[82] Character traits common to *all* Englishmen were thus proposed as the initiators of English imperial growth: obviously, when it came to fighting the nation's battles against foreign foes there was something inherent in the Englishman that led to English success, just as it was the whole nation's efforts that would lead to English dominance in world-imperial affairs. But their actions, their daring and bold deeds, were accomplished *for* queen and country. Elizabeth, as a symbol of England the nation and of English women that resided within, was protected from invasion, and the spoils of overseas adventure were brought back to honour her, precisely because 'she was loved by her people' as an English monarch, and because 'this feeling so inspired many a gallant Englishman to do her honour and win her smile by deeds of daring.'[83] But if Englishmen were willing to band together to defend the nation, what about the social and political conflicts within the nation that mark the period after the Elizabethan golden age?

A Revolution of the People or the Despotism of One Man?

The seventeenth century was, of course, one of the key sites for a 'populist' reading of English history: in such a reading the middle classes with the aid of all the lower ranks of society banded together to fight against the tyranny of the king and the entrenched power of the aristocracy and conservative church. In some history readers published in these years such a reading was still quite possible, and as Dina Copelman has suggested, those board schoolteachers of a sceptical disposition may have mediated the messages of the books they used in the direction of populist liberalism.[84] Reading books written in the 1880s especially inclined towards framing their discussion of the Civil War, Restoration, and Glorious Revolution as a popular struggle to return to the balance of the ancient constitution. For although the early Tudor and especially the Elizabethan periods were depicted in positive terms, and the passing of the Act of Supremacy making Henry VIII head of the Church of England justly noted as a key event, the religious and political troubles that had been sparked and which eventually resulted in the strife of the Civil War tended to be reported only as a sidetrack, or even a setback, to the growth of English freedom and liberties. This was especially signalled by the palpable sense of relief evident in many texts when they came to explaining the 'Glorious' revolutionary settlement of 1688. Morris's *Historical Readers* from 1883, for example, noted:

The revolution ... gave a decisive answer to the question, 'Whence do English Sovereigns obtain their right to rule the nation?' Since the days of Henry VII a notion had grown up that the king, like a father, had his authority direct from

heaven, and therefore ruled by divine right. He was consequently not responsible to the nation for the exercise of this right, and had a sacred claim to the
obedience of his subjects. The Stuart kings especially maintained this view of
their power.

In early English history the popular belief was that the Sovereign obtained
his power from the people. The Kingship then was elective, and based upon
contract.

While a father's authority was, in this account, unquestionable – suggesting another level of gendered meaning – the king's right to abso-
lute authority was suggested to be a usurpation of the former, correct
belief system, namely the ancient Anglo-Saxon constitution. 'The leaders of the English Revolution sought to remedy these things in their
famous "Declaration," in which the claims of the people in accordance
with the ancient principles of the English Constitution, were clearly
expressed.' Morris proved his point with reference to the tradition of
the coronation ceremony, in which 'the people' were called upon to
acknowledge the new sovereign as their ruler: 'it should not be forgotten that the ancient practice has always been recognized in the ceremony of coronation.'[85]

If the 'people' were depicted as recovering their ancient rights in a
popular struggle in the narratives of the books in the 1880s, this interpretation and the possibility of reading 'the people's struggle' in socio-
political terms steadily declined over the 1890s and later as more emphasis was increasingly placed on the personalities of the major characters in the conflict. After the passing of the Third Reform and Redistribution Acts in 1884 and 1885, which granted more working-class
men with the suffrage, and with the steady rise in the popularity of
Victoria as an icon of the nation and empire, fewer texts seemed to
dwell on a potentially populist reading of the struggle for liberty. The
progressive extension of the franchise and unquestioned popularity of
the monarch as demonstrated by the response to her Golden Jubilee in
1887 seems to have pushed reader authors to return to a more royalist
and personalized history of constitutional progress. For example, the
personal attributes of Charles I were sometimes divorced from his
political situation in a manner quite unlike that of the characterizations of King John or Edward I. Charles was held to be personally
worthy, especially as a good father – a fact educationalists must have
thought would appeal to children – but he was nonetheless a bad
king. Cromwell, meanwhile, was disliked but was nevertheless a great
warrior, leader, and law-bringer. Books such as the 1901 Chambers's

'New Scheme' History Readers compared Charles's rule to that of King John, but did not suggest that Charles was personally wicked in the same way. Cromwell, in this same account, seemed to have many personal foibles, but he nonetheless 'governed wisely, keeping the peace at home, and making England feared and respected abroad as she had never been since the days of Elizabeth.'[86] John Finnemore gave Charles little sympathy, declaring with many others that his rule was like that of a despotic tyrant. Cromwell's martial successes, and even his personal governance, were contrasted as noble attributes that were the exact opposite of Charles's notion of divine right. Charles was thus seen as the problem, and the struggle over the constitution was thus the correction of his abuse of monarchical power.[87]

Indeed, while Charles was reviled as a monarch in these later books, there was much ambivalence towards his ultimate treatment at the hands of the Parliamentarians. The execution of Charles was particularly deplored, and books frequently underlined the enormity of the act with reference to the 'deep groan' that rose from the assembled crowd at his execution. Some texts noted that the event was still justified as the only possible action given the circumstances.[88] But the return of the monarchy in 1660 was then usually depicted as 'a relief' from the 'overly puritanical' period of the commonwealth, although Charles II was noted by one author as being 'quite unworthy of the rejoicing, which took place on his return.'[89] This disapproval of both the moral zealousness of the Parliamentarians and the libertine excesses of Charles II is indicative, perhaps, of the move towards moderation in late-Victorian middle-class notions of respectable behaviour and, moreover, of a changed attitude towards the place and symbolic function of the monarchy. The general shift in history readers away from the combination of dry, 'reign and battle' lists and the overt moralizing of mid-Victorian school books and towards a concentration on the role of dynamic personalities – especially in those readers intended for younger children – ultimately pushed the conflict between Parliament and the Royalists into a picturesque and romantic narrative, largely divorced from political importance, and in which a 'populist reading' lost much of its purchase.

The Constitution and the Monarchy

There was usually a careful delineation of the limited and carefully circumscribed role of the monarchy in discussions of the English constitution, but the discrete importance of the sovereign as a symbol of national loyalty was also usually stressed by the authors of school readers. Here was the core of the unresolved tension between the progressive rise of civil freedom and the political liberty inherent in the triumph of the principles of the ancient constitution – a position that was at the centre of the populist, radical-patriotic tradition of the 'freeborn Englishman'[90] – and the tremendous emphasis placed on the unifying role accorded the crown by most reader authors. Indeed, in the very same texts that provided the liberal master narrative of evolving civil and political freedoms, there can be found a 'rival' discourse to the enunciations of patriotism based on the appeal to the ancient constitution and eventual importance of Parliament. In this second discourse, the symbolic continuity of the race and the future destiny of the English nation and empire were put squarely into the crown and the individuals who wore it. Contemporary and recently deceased English sovereigns were constructed as symbols above and beyond the constitution's political settlement, in a manner that posited them as the potent cultural icons to which articulations of national loyalty ought to be addressed.

The current monarch was, unsurprisingly, more susceptible to this sort of treatment than historical ones. Some statements about the monarchy as an institution posited that the sovereign should properly hold a 'moderating influence at the head of affairs in England.' This was suggested because, being unbiased and not limited by the dictates of sectional interest, the monarch would naturally 'draw the existing government away from party [and] towards national considerations.' Such statements implicitly elevated the sovereign above, rather than merely confirmed, his or her integral place within the 'balanced constitution,' the history of which the readers had taken so much care in delineating. Indeed, with the acquisition of a vast and diverse empire, the British state was proclaimed to be never so in need of a unifying and moderating monarch. 'England' was the 'centre of an Empire,' and 'the golden link' that bound India and the colonies to the people of England was the crown. 'The existence of the Crown in England enables us to furnish our great dependencies and self-governing colonies with Viceroys and Governors, who give to them too the advantages of a moderating power lifted above the contending parties.' It was suggested that it was 'more than doubtful' that the colonies 'would submit to the supremacy of changing partisan Presidents.'[91] Some teachers, moreover, were thinking along such lines. As one aspiring teacher wrote about Victoria just after her funeral, 'in her profound veneration for all that is sacred and sublime, she was to Englishmen, both at home and beyond the seas, not only the symbol of our race, but the symbol of what is best and worthiest in our race.'[92]

Loyalty to the monarch was clearly placed on a higher order than obedience to the vicissitudes of political parties and elected government. As Malden intoned, 'we must be loyal to the Crown, for the Crown is loyal to us, and is the personification of our constitution and of our law.' This loyalty was the 'privilege of freemen, not the homage of slaves,' and was offered to the 'memory of our fathers and to the majesty of our native land.'[93] Despite the rhetoric of 'privileged freemen' this position was a significant challenge to the populist/radical discourse. The monarch in this formulation was not part of the constitutional balance worked out by the struggles of the people, but rather the embodiment, the very 'personification,' of that constitution. The implication was not that the monarch ruled by dictates of the 'popularly' arrived at constitution, but actually the reverse. Osman Newland, on the other hand, provided a more traditional and practical justification for monarchy by comparing the merits of a monarchical head of state with a republican system, and not surprisingly found the latter system singularly wanting. An elected king or president could not be trusted, Newland claimed, because corruption would necessarily accompany the election of someone with so much power. A hereditary monarch, on the other hand, limited in his or her power by Parliament, was unlikely to abuse royal privileges.[94] To a degree, this latter account might be seen as fulfilling the balancing function that Bagehot had ascribed to the crown in his prescriptive *The English Constitution* (1865).[95] Bagehot proposed that although the monarchy had ceased to be part of the focus of the constitution, it was now in a stronger position, since it was elevated above party strife. He had listed four reasons why the constitution was stronger with the monarchy in this relationship: the monarchy was the most 'intelligible' part of the political system for 'ordinary people'; it strengthened government through the force of religion; it became the centre of pageantry; and it also became the centre of the nation's morality. All these factors might be present in discussions of the monarchy in school readers, but in many the monarchy's 'true' significance and inherent value was also more generally depicted in terms of its historical and genealogical roots; in, that is, its culturally unifying potential.

As David Cannadine has observed, between the 1870s and 1914 the ritual of the monarchy changed from being 'inept, private and of limited appeal' to being 'splendid, public and popular.'[96] School readers similarly made a great deal of the ceremonial nature of the monarch. Queen Victoria, for example, was lauded both for her domestic family virtues and for her role as the 'mother to the nation.' The English people were said to owe much to this mother for both her symbolic and practical example of motherhood.[97] And unlike the somewhat problematic nature of Elizabeth I, the current queen was a paragon of womanly devotion and a worthy symbol of the majestic importance of constitutional monarchy:

The women and girls of England in particular must be always grateful for the example of what a true woman's influence on the world can be. There is not one of them whose possibilities for good have not been heightened by the reign of Her Majesty. Family life, after all, lies at the root of all society, and no political life is sound which is not founded upon the family virtues of the nation. No man can rule others well till he has ruled himself, and become a Constitutional Sovereign, and not a tyrant in his own household. Monarchy may, or may not, in remote ages, have sprung from the patriarchal rule of a father over his descendants. Certainly Constitutional Monarchy is the natural rule in the little home states, the aggregate of which make up the nation.[98]

Here again, family structure and the household was proposed as the appropriate model for children to understand the structure of the state and the role of the monarch. Such an analogy allowed for several layers of meaning about social and political identity: for the organization of the nation-state was portrayed as mirroring the 'natural' organization of the family; the father was clearly depicted as the ruler of the family, but only through 'constitutional' consent (implying some limited reciprocal duties and responsibilities among family members); and men had a 'natural' or historic role in the governance of their families, and therefore it was appropriate that they represented their entire family's interests in the politics of the nation.

Equally, significant, however, was the manner by which Victoria's genealogical heritage was moulded into English racial ancestry. The *Raleigh History Readers*, to take a typical example, noted her to be the direct 'descendant of the Saxon chiefs who settled in Wessex more than fourteen centuries ago':

She represents the growth of our people from very small beginnings to its present world wide power; and all who know of the history of our country feel a thrill of pride and joy when they think of its wonderful past and its prosperous present, with all of which our royal family has been so closely associated. When we sing 'God save the Queen,' we think not only of the queen, but of the people whose past and present life she represents. For the time we forget our parties, and we remember that, after all, we are one nation, closely related in blood and community of interest.[99]

In such pronouncements, the current queen and unquestioned loyalty to the monarch became the implied end of the story of progress laid out in the master narrative. The monarchy, by being a supposed tangible link to the past of the nation, was essentialized into being the initiator of that progress. The monarchy was no longer a constitutionally produced element in the balance of political and social interests, but the one institution that was the very representative of the nation, of the 'people.' This is also the significance of the kind of elaboration found in texts such as the 1897 *Chambers's National History* series, where obscure Saxon kings were connected to the current monarch: 'It is well to remember the name of Cerdic, because nearly all the sovereigns of England have descended from him. He was the ancestor of our Queen Victoria.'[100] Clearly, at the end of the century the moral symbolism of the monarchy was subservient to its nationalist function.

The recasting of the symbolism of the monarchy was certainly not restricted to individual monarchs such as Victoria; it applied to a variety of 'great' sovereigns that somehow fit the values of Englishness and the narrative of ascending English progress and greatness. By exploiting the easily charted genealogy of succession, the monarchy as an institution thereby became a tangible example of the genealogical basis of Englishness that is discussed in the next chapter. The fact that many monarchs in this vaunted lineage would not have identified themselves as English or of Anglo-Saxon 'stock' was simply ignored. The monarchy was depicted as an emblem of the historical continuity of Englishness and of the unifying bonds of nationality that held the empire together. The racial and ancestral links of Englishness were clearly emphasized through the repeated references to the hereditary nature of the monarch. But if this monarchical lineage was traced in an unbroken line back to the Anglo-Saxons, then the idea of continuity was inherently in tension with the notion of an elected (chosen) sovereign that was the key component of the ancient constitution.

The elevated place of the monarch in prescriptions of the appropriate contemporary situation therefore sat uncomfortably in the general

Whig/liberal master narrative because of the differing strategies for demonstrating the true nature of Englishness. Ultimately, both the Whig/liberal master narrative, as it related the struggles among 'Englishmen' and their kings between the signing of Magna Carta and 1688, and the racial-genealogical arguments for monarchical continuity consciously looked back to the Anglo-Saxons for their inspiration. Nevertheless, their explanations of the nature and symbols of Englishness were quite distinct. The line of argument developed in these readers, then, took apart the radical-patriotic notion of the 'freeborn Englishman' and melded elements of it to constitutional and state development in a way that essentially drew much of the sting of the radical position. These books sought to build national loyalty in the working classes, not just to the idea of the nation as a people, but also to the idea of the nation as justly represented by the state. Arguably, such a position may have been an uncoordinated attempt to close off to the working class the avenue of radical patriotism that Margot Finn and Patrick Joyce have revealed was so vibrant in the 1860s and 1870s. Certainly, the success of this vision of citizenship and Englishness can be traced in the dogmatic defence of the parliamentary system – and the neutrality of the monarchy – by conservatives, liberal radicals, and labour supporters alike, well into the twentieth century. One element that was clearly integral to this narrative and its vocabulary was the idea of race – of the English (or British) as being an ethnically distinct people – and it is this issue to which we turn in the next chapter.

3

Ethnicity and National Belonging

Nor ought we to overlook the necessity for so teaching as to inspire our scholars with a love and admiration for the country we live in and for the institutions by which we are governed ... And in every English school something at least should be done to make the scholars proud of this glorious heritage, and to animate them with a noble ambition to live lives and to deeds which shall be worthy of it.

J.G. Fitch, *Lectures on Teaching* (1906)

While the language of 'citizenship' and its place in the liberal master narrative was one vocabulary by which national identity was promoted, another equally pervasive vocabulary was that of 'Englishness.' Towards the end of the nineteenth century an essentialized conception of what comprised national characteristics became a key means by which the 'educated classes' sought to build a binding identity for the entire population.[1] The rubric of this 'Englishness' was seen by some as an antidote to the emergence of divisive class and other sectional sentiment, such as organized feminism, independent labour, and Irish nationalism. A distinctive interpretation of the national 'character' and culture was authorized primarily through the establishment of new national cultural institutions and a new professional elite designated to define the national culture.[2] Over time, a specific national self-identity based around ethnic claims was deployed in a manner that reconfigured the nation's self-definition and that of its 'others.' The turn-of-the-century cult of national efficiency, fed by fears of invasion and racial degeneration, and whipped up to occasionally hysterical levels by the Tory and radical nationalist leagues, was just the extreme edge of this cultural development that had permeated and transcended party-political boundaries by the end of Edward vii's reign.[3]

It is within this broad socio-political context that the use of the language of 'race' and of 'racial characteristics' in the elementary classroom needs to be situated. For the language of race in the classroom was not merely the result of the Victorian obsession with ideas of progress and categorization found in science and history writing, although this was certainly a factor. As in more elevated academic discussion, the meanings and connotations of racial discourse used in school materials and teaching were vague, inconsistent, and ambiguous. In reading books, race might be used to describe biological features, cultural attributes, linguistic commonalities, social and/or institutional traditions. The term race might be used simply as a designation of a particular group of people, as the marker of a political unit, or as an ideologically loaded signifier of an innate superior–inferior relationship. Indeed, confusion about what race really referred to is evident in the frequent connections made in some reading books among race, nationality, and language. For instance, the fifth volume in the 1895 *Avon Geographical Readers* noted:

Less than sixty years ago the continent of Europe was divided up into about sixty independent states; now there are only nineteen countries in Europe. During the last fifty years peoples who are allied in race or language have rushed together, as it were, to form powerful states.

Races, like the Germans and Italians, refused to be cut up into petty states in order to give their neighbours the pleasure of bullying them when they thought fit, and insisted on taking their places amongst the foremost nations of the world. Thus it was that the Italians, bound together by a common language, and the Germans by union of race, have moulded themselves into great nations.[4]

In this discussion of the formation of European nation-states, race and nationality were confused and conflated: a common race was distinguished from a common language, yet it remains unclear in this passage as to exactly what was meant by the term 'union of race.' In another example, it was suggested that Austria-Hungary was 'the empire of races,' with 'the Bohemians [being] a musical people' while the 'Hungarians as a race are gay and sociable; they are naturally friendly with all men.'[5] These sorts of descriptions and usage of the term race focused on its typological aspect: race marked out categories of difference, usually around perceived national characteristics. While this usage clearly did not have explicit biological and essentialist overtones, it did play on the ambiguity of the term. One reader, for instance, in comparing the German people to the English, played on the two nationalities' common racial origins, and accordingly used a positive tone of description: 'As the Germans are akin to us, it is pleasant to know that they are brave, persevering and industrious. They are also very thoughtful, fond of music, and have great love for their country, which they call their fatherland.'[6] In another, racial distinctions among European peoples carried more obvious biological overtones: 'An Italian, a Russian, or even a Swede, if we meet him in the street, at once strikes us as a foreigner. This is because the people of different parts of Europe differ considerably from each other in height, build, colour, and shape of the head, though not so strikingly as Europeans differ from the inhabitants of Eastern Asia or of Central Asia.' Moreover, a special affinity for white Americans was to be found in some readers, expressly because their racial origins were imagined to come from essentially the same Anglo-Saxon bloodlines as the English themselves.[7] As we shall see, this typological use of the term race demonstrates one facet of the vocabulary of identity.

It is evident that many authors writing for the turn-of-the-century school-book market did use the term race in a fashion that held biological overtones and essentialist connotations. Sometimes this was conscious, and in other cases it was probably unintentional. The slippage in the connotations of race, however, demonstrates another facet of language in identity construction. Reader authors used the language of race to mark out the imagined genealogical territory of English identity. As a result, when seeking to understand how English elementary schoolchildren understood their nationality, we have to question the distinction that political commentators have commonly made between English- and French-style civic nationality, with its notion of a *patria* – usually understood as a voluntary 'community of laws and institutions with a single political will' – and the 'eastern,' 'romantic,' or 'ethno-cultural' types of nationalism, which tend to stress blood ties.[8] When English commentators (and historians) have used this distinction it has usually been through a correlation between the civic model as 'good' nationalism and the ethnic model as 'bad' nationalism.[9] Yet, as Stephen Harp's study of competing French 'civic' and German 'ethnic' nationalisms in Alsace and Lorraine demonstrates, all nationalisms have a tendency to traverse these two poles.[10] The examples developed in this chapter will confirm that the positing of English national identity purely in terms of civic-political terms, as compared to the 'ethnic' bases of national identity, is clearly problematic. Such a position assumes that the English did not have a developed sense of ethnicity. Of course, many English people today may think that they have no ethnicity – that ethnicity is some kind of essential, primordial and unchanging identity found only in others – but this is a function of unquestioning acceptance of English nationalist claims, which posit the English as normative and everyone else as 'other.'

Catherine Hall has usefully examined the mid-nineteenth-century middle class in terms of their English ethnicity: that is, she has examined the 'contesting identities' and 'terrain of struggle as to what it means to be English.' The cultural identity that she suggests coalesced during the mid-Victorian decades incorporated a power dynamic and a hierarchical sense of superiority that was only peripherally related to the existence of overtly political nationalist movements and individuals. She also demonstrates that expressions of national consciousness relied on some notion of common ethnicity, and that delineation of identity, political power, and equality and inequality were all bound together.[11] Such ethnic/national consciousness, subtly implicit in a society's projected 'common culture,' can typically exercise a powerful influence on that society. By the later decades of the nineteenth century, the notion that there was something essentially 'English' about national culture was being projected onto the working masses in an attempt to forge a hegemonic bond – to create a social glue – based on the belief in common ancestry and origins. Although phrased with reference to the belief in the steady evolution of progressive liberal freedoms that was integral to the liberal-nationalist master narrative, ethnic, linguistic, and genealogical factors were projected as every bit as important as civic bonds in the configuring of English national identity.

Of course, a major difficulty for originators of this process was that not all children in England were ethnically or culturally English. Indeed, the state that governed England itself was officially organized on the basis of not one ethnic nation, but many. This factor produced contradictions in the accounts of many books, especially when it came to descriptions of the 'British' Empire. But ultimately, as we shall see, definitional problems were elided or glossed over. Significantly, however, the term 'British' was usually reserved only for descriptions involving the empire, and paradoxically (given the integral place of the empire in conceptions of the 'English inheritance') 'Britishness' was not the pre-eminently prescribed identity for children receiving their elementary schooling in England between 1880 and 1914. Instead, a hegemonic Englishness eventually came to dominate in these books, based on the language of genealogical inheritance and race. To fully understand how this discourse of race came to be deployed as part of the vocabulary of national identity in school books, we first need to briefly chart the intellectual and cultural trajectory of the ideas and images of race and racial inheritance between the 1840s and the end of the century.

Victorian Racial Typology

For the early Victorians, race was as much a synonym for type as it was a biological term marking familial ancestry or origins. Indeed, this typological usage of the term continued throughout the nineteenth and into the twentieth century, making any general judgments about the common understanding of the term extremely problematic. Even so, over the course of the 1830s, 1840s, and 1850s, under the impact of advances in social anthropology, ethnology, and other scientific strands of thought, racial discourse took on more biological and essentialist overtones, particularly in the linking of innate biological and cultural characteristics and traits to classifiable human types.[12] This 'scientific racism' postulated that humankind could be subdivided into discrete and fixed biological groups (although there was no agreement as to the exact number or division), which predetermined the capabilities and normal behaviours of the particular individuals and cultures found within each group. It followed from this that conflict between individuals and groups was the consequence of their innate biological constitution. The authority of these observations stemmed mainly from their articulation within the scientific world. However, once a readiness to denote cultural or physical differences as expressions of biological race developed, so too did the temptation to equate such classifications with social progress, and to suggest that such differences implied natural inequalities and justified racial hierarchies. The moral and cultural chauvinism of earlier periods was thus transformed into an understanding of biological race as the preconditioning factor of all behaviour for individuals and, by extension, of the past, present, and future of whole societies and cultures.[13]

Although there was little contemporary consensus as to the precise functioning or classification of racial essentialism, extrapolating from the biological connotations of race and theorizing on the superior or inferior qualities of particular races were certainly widespread practices in educated circles by the last third of the century. Too much has perhaps been claimed about the direct influence of Robert Knox's 1850 publication *The Races of Man*, but books such as this and that of the Bristol physician Dr John Beddoe certainly laid the pseudo-scientific epistemological base on which racial discourse in Britain rested until after the Great War.[14] The rise and popularity of anthropological and ethnographic societies in the mid-decades of the century, the widely publicized debates between the proponents of monogenesis and polygenesis, and later those centring on the concept of evolution itself, were all forms of testimony to the vitality of this new form of racial discourse.[15] Evidently, the ideas in these works had a wide influence not only among the scientific elite, but also among the literary set, appearing in various forms in the work of such early Victorian luminaries as Thomas Arnold, Charles Kingsley, and Thomas Carlyle.[16] Those in political circles were equally liable to draw on racial discourse: the Conservative statesman Benjamin Disraeli suggested to the House of Commons in 1849 that 'Race implies difference, difference implies superiority, and superiority leads to predominance.'[17] Earlier he had claimed, in the words of one of his novel's protagonists, that England's greatness lay primarily in its people's 'blood,' that 'all is race; there is no other truth.' Meanwhile, the prominent Liberal radical Charles Dilke, a little later in the century, confidently and triumphantly asserted that 'the gradual extinction of the inferior races is not only a law of nature, but a blessing to mankind,' and the 'love of race among the English rests upon a firmer base than either love of mankind or love of Britain, for it reposes upon a subsoil of things known: the ascertained virtues and powers of the English people.'[18]

Although the respect accorded the physical sciences was essential to the validation of racial thinking by the Victorian educated elite, for the most part the specialized debates of the various subdisciplines remained beyond the pale of the broader reading public. The dissemination of racial discourse to a wider audience, at first through formal education and then through mass-produced literary products, was taken up by popular historians and geographers, novelists, journalists, and pulp-fiction producers. Historians in particular were widely read, respected, and eminently influential throughout the Victorian era. Most of the important and popular historians in the third quarter of the century, including Kingsley, E.A. Freeman, Bishop William Stubbs, J.R. Green, J.A. Froude, and even to a certain extent John R. Seeley, espoused particular variants of racialized discourse, frequently those of racial Teutonism and/or Anglo-Saxonism.[19] The evident popularity of these historians and (later) geographers[20] meant that ideas about race and its connection to identity were integral to the nationalist histories written and consumed in the decades prior to the end of the century. The distinction between 'high' and 'popular' culture ought not be made too sharply, for some historians were certainly extremely popular and widely read, and some histories, such as J.R. Green's *Short History of the English People* (1874), had a very wide audience, selling more than 32,000 copies in its first year of publication and more than 500,000 copies in the following decades.[21] However, social attitudes were equally influenced by factors beyond those of intellectual and high cultural pursuits. Historians and other recent critics have claimed that activities in the British Empire and their reporting in the press, their representation in popular entertainment and portrayal in other popular cultural practices, had a profound effect on domestic attitudes towards the idea of race, both in confirming previously held prejudices and social chauvinism and in providing a cultural yardstick against which personal experience might be judged.[22] Widely reported events such as the Indian Mutiny (1857) and the Governor Eyre controversy (1865–6), for instance, seem to have had a role both in hardening attitudes about the deterministic nature of race and in the further dissemination of negative stereotypes within racial discourse.[23] As we shall see, these racial stereotypes were increasingly to be deployed in mainstream educational culture.

Writing Racial Discourse

Racial discourse certainly found its way into the vocabulary of elementary schoolchildren via the reading books that were published between 1880 and 1914. Paul Deslandes has convincingly demonstrated the degree to which a racialized discourse of identity infused undergraduate culture at the ancient universities.[24] Since many of the authors of readers were exposed to university culture (as were the journalist and politician authors of the civics readers) and themselves became academics, it should thus not be a surprise that this racial discourse also found its way into elementary school readers. But, as noted previously, it was not just academics who wrote these texts. Alongside the academics of specialized disciplines such as history, geography, and English literature, two other large groups of reader authors are discernible, although all three groups had important aspects in common.

After academics, the second cohort of reader authors were university trained 'educationalists.' Sir John Adams (1857–1934), for example, who was to become the first professor of education at the University of London, was simultaneously editor of several literary and general reader sets, including the widely used *Blackwood's Literature Readers* (1899). Adams and his older colleague J.M.D. Meiklejohn (1836–1902) – who held the first chair in education at the University of St Andrews and who was himself a contributor to a reading-book series, the *Chambers's English Readers* (1880–2), as well as many geography texts – began their training in Scotland and moved to England to take up posts in the newly forming schools of education. Born in Glasgow, Adams was schooled at St David's and Jordanhill Training College at the University of Glasgow. He started his educational life as headmaster at Jean Street School and then at Campbeltown Grammar School. In 1890 he was appointed principal of Free Church Training College, Aberdeen, and then, in 1898, was made rector of Free Church Training College, Glasgow. By 1902 Adams, who was a leading proponent of Herbartian, child-centred ideas, had taken the position of principal of London Day Training College, and that same year he was appointed professor of education at the University of London. Other figures of note among educationalists and teacher-training instructors were Dr S.S.F. Fletcher (1872–1916), who was master of method at the Day Training College, Cambridge, between 1897 and 1916 and the author of several Pitman's readers and texts, including sections of *The King Edward History Readers*; William Lawson, instructor at St Marks College, Chelsea, and the author of Collins's *Manual of Modern Geography* (London 1888), Oliver and Boyd's *The Geographical Primer* (1889), *Lawson's Junior Class Geography* (1891), and the senior text *The Geography of the British Colonies and Possessions Abroad* (1887); and T.J. Livesey, who lectured at Hammersmith Training College, was the author of *Primer of English History* (1877), and was a contributor to the *English History Readers* (1881) and *Granville History Readers* (1885, revised in 1902).

There was yet a third large group of reader authors. These were aspiring professionals: secondary and grammar school headmasters, principals, and senior instructors. While some may have started their actual teaching careers in elementary schools, very few of those who wrote readers seemed to have remained in the elementary system for long. Notable as exceptions to this trend were C.H. Wyatt, author of *The English Citizen: His Life and Duty* (1894), who was secretary of the Manchester School Board, and the editor of *The Jack Readers* (1904), a man named Hayward, who was the headmaster at a Birmingham Council Elementary School.[25] Although it is difficult to be certain, it does seem that the number of new reader sets written by this particular group was in decline by the turn of the century. Indeed, authors in this category often transcended the period of transition from amateur generalists to disciplinary specialists. A prime example of this was the prolific Reverend Edgar Sanderson (1838–1907), author of *Outlines of the World's History* (1885), contributor to Blackie's *Warwick History Readers* (1895), and editor of the popular *Century Readers* (1901) among others. Educated at the City of London School, he received his BA in 1860 and his MA in 1866 from Clare College, Cambridge. Sanderson was appointed assistant master at Kings Lynn Grammar School in 1861, was assistant master at Stepney Grammar School in 1862–3, and was assistant master at Weymouth Grammar School between 1863 and 1865. He was first appointed a headmaster at Stockwell Grammar School in 1870 and then served as headmaster at Macclesfield Grammar School from 1873 to 1876 and at Huntingdon Grammar School between 1877 and 1881. Thereafter he retired and devoted himself to the writing of books, of which his school texts seemed to have been the most successful.

On the whole then, by the end of the century the educational background of reading-book authors was the university or at least the teacher training college, and all aspired to professional status. There were, of course, some exceptions: J. Finnemore, for example, the author of several reader sets, was primarily a popular novelist, as was G.A. Henty, who wrote the *Sovereign Reader* in 1887; Charlotte M. Yonge wrote both history readers and edited general collections, and despite a lack of formal training her educational works remained extremely popular in Anglican National Society schools throughout the period.[26] A few authors came from the highest reaches of the social hierarchy, and a few had managed to work their way up from humble beginnings. Ultimately, however, it was the fact that almost all had university degrees or teacher training college diplomas to put forward as their professional credentials, rather than a connection to a religious denomination, that was key to their success as authors and editors of elementary school readers. This de facto professionalization of authorship in elementary readers was perhaps a reflection of the general process whereby the coalescing boundaries of the new academic disciplines of history, geography, and English literature were being justified by their practitioners at the university level.[27]

It was this professionalization of authorship, combined with the mass commercialization of the market, that led, arguably, to the remarkable degree of homogeneity found in reading books. While individual authors sometimes stamped their own personalities on their product, often this was of a stylistic nature. These variations, important though they were, were of a minor nature compared to differences found among the formal texts used in secondary and higher-grade schooling. Reviewers of education texts tended to concentrate on textbooks and provided only cursory reviews of readers, presumably because of their essential similarity and the foreknowledge that they would be vetted by local educational authorities before getting into teachers' hands – something that the *School Board Chronicle*, at least, entirely favoured.[28] On the other hand, formal textbooks sometimes received intense scrutiny. Many of the hostile reviews in the early school board period stemmed from religious and denominational disputes, but not always: Morris's *Class Book of English History* and Curtis's *A School and College History of England* both received negative reviews in the *School Board Chronicle* and sparked a running debate over the way in which the Saxon period should be described.[29] Later, texts such as Fletcher and Kipling's bloodthirsty and militantly nationalistic *School History of England* received a highly critical review in the moderate *Educational Times*. The language of race and of national culture used in elementary school readers, however, received little or no comment in the educational press.[30]

Indeed, elementary school readers relied heavily on the language of race, both in terms of setting up negative stereotypes of others, and in reinforcing the positive values of the child's own presumed ethnicity. Moreover, there was little attempt to justify, reconcile, or explain the differing interpretations and generalizations about race that circulated within these books. The boundaries between race, ethnicity, culture, and national identity were cloudy and ambiguous. Concentric circles of racial belonging and identification were present in these books,

ranging from the 'races of mankind' based simply on colour to considerations of the subracial groupings within each colour, following what
would now be called ethnic divisions. For the purpose of analysis,
these are simplified here into two levels of discourse: in the remainder
of this chapter we shall examine the treatments of 'racial' nationality
within the British Isles; in the following chapter we shall examine the
'others' to which racial self-identity was contrasted.

Nationality and Ethnicity: The Anglo-Saxon Ideal of Englishness

Overwhelmingly, it was the ideas of 'Englishness' with which English
elementary schoolchildren were expected to identify. The predominance of 'English' over 'British' as the preferred designation of the
national community in the school readers of this time might seem to
be a form of convenient shorthand or, at worst, a minor Anglo-centric
proclivity on the part of authors writing for the English market. Certainly the boundaries between the two were at all times somewhat
ambiguous. However, although it is true that English and British were
used interchangeably by the authors of a few texts, most used the
terms 'the English' and 'the Englishman' in a selective manner in their
narratives. Whereas the empire in general was almost universally referred to as being British, and the composite nature of the United
Kingdom of Great Britain and Ireland sometimes explained as a union
of races, those personal and communal traits deemed part of the national and imperial heritage, especially the virility, heroism, justice,
and glory that were represented as the very foundation of nation and
empire, tended to be phrased as attributes of Englishness.[31] Inherently,
then, there was an unresolved tension within the texts (and classroom
culture in general) between English identity and British identity. This
tension did not manifest itself as a binary opposition. As we shall see,
Englishness derived more from a constructed ethnicity, while
Britishness derived from a supposed sense of loyalty to the (multinational) state. Being English automatically made one also British, and of
course one could be Scots, Welsh, or Irish (or also be a white colonial)
and still claim a British identity.

However, by focusing on the values and culture that were distinctly
English, a claim was being asserted that Englishness was itself at the
core of the 'best' British values, and those on the 'periphery' did not
have the same 'right' to speak for the whole.[32] This was part of the
hegemonic impulse of the rubric of Englishness. The relationship be-

tween English ethnicity and those ethnicities in what was coming to be known as the Celtic Fringe was constructed through the framework of essentialized racial discourse. Thus, it was taken as axiomatic that everyone in English elementary schools should and would identify themselves with Englishness, that this was the 'true essence' of British greatness, and that the claims of Celtic nationalists – mainly Irish, but also growing among the Welsh and Scots – could simply be discounted. Of course, not every school-book author was actually English, nor consciously viewed Englishness as superior to Scottishness or even Irishness. However, from the mid-1880s on, claims about the national culture in English elementary school books became increasingly homogenized, and the distinctiveness of the Celtic component in that culture was either entirely absent or substantially qualified.

This happened through several discursive manoeuvres. Sometimes there was a simple equating of the personal and communal traits, characteristics, institutions, and activities of all the various British peoples with the term English. This is a classic position of a *staatvolk*, a group that dominates a multinational state numerically, politically, and culturally. Such a group tends to think of the overarching state as the political extension of *their* national identity, and they tend to perceive no distinction between their nationalism and loyalty to the state.[33] Thus, from the English point of view, references to the United Kingdom as England and its English-speaking inhabitants as English were clearly intended as positive designations. Yet this had the implicit effect of marginalizing the contribution made by the other nationalities of the British Isles to the achievements of the collective state, of nullifying the differences between the various cultures and societies, of passing over in silence or simply appropriating the distinctive character of the minority cultures, and in general, of discounting the influence of the so-called Celtic Fringe and other minorities on the English centre. For instance, H.E. Malden's civics reader of 1894 asserted confidently:

We are by birth English men or English women. Though we be born north of the Tweed, or among the Welsh mountains, or across St George's Channel, this is the name to the honours and responsibilities of which we have succeeded. For the name English cannot be properly confined to one tribe among the many of all who have succeeded to a share in the English constitution and to the heritage of the world-wide British Empire, which Scots, Irish, Welsh, Northumbrians, East Anglians, Cornishmen, and Kentishmen have helped to build up and defend. We talk of the English constitution because, though

Scotland had a constitution of its own, this constitution was partly founded upon that of England, and was finally merged in that of England. The English way of government was the one which finally prevailed in Great Britain and Ireland.[34]

Such a view conflated the identity of all who lived within the British Isles with that of the state, and with English governance and traditions. Because the 'English way' had prevailed in the state, all were English 'by birth.' Clearly the differences between the component peoples paled in comparison to the significance of the importance of the English heritage.

A slightly different view was that of J. St Loe Strachey's evening continuation school reader, in which the native-speaking of the English language was the marker by which Englishness might be judged for all the citizens of Greater Britain. This was phrased in terms of a hard-won privilege:

Is it fair to Scotsmen and Irishmen to talk of 'Englishmen' doing this or that, or of the rights and duties of Englishmen when we mean all the inhabitants of the United Kingdom and not merely those belonging to the various counties of England? We cannot help but think that it is fair to do so; and for this reason ... A man may be a Scotsman or an Irishman, and rightly proud of the race to which he belongs; but he is also an English speaker ... Everyone who speaks English as his mother tongue has a right to be called English; and no one to whom the language of Shakespeare and Scott is native need feel ashamed to be called English. He is English, and why not call him what he is?[35]

In Strachey's case, the Irish and Scots were judged to be different races from the English, and yet their differences were negated by the overriding importance of English culture (expressed as language and literature), one of the exemplars of which ironically happened to be a Scot. Often, however, such admiration for Englishness was accompanied by an implicit hierarchical ordering of the other identities within the British Isles. Not only did the English dominate the British Isles in terms of geographic features, population, and commerce, but in the second half of the nineteenth century they also succeeded in setting the terms of the cultural representation of the nation-state.

This dominance can be seen in a quick overview of the school materials presented to English children that purported to explain the boundaries of their nation and nationality. After the 1880s, characterizations

of the British as a mixture of peoples were quite rare for books intended for the English elementary system prior to 1914, and much
rarer than in the books intended for the secondary and elite Public
schools. English values, institutions, geography, history, literature, heroes, and monarchs took precedence over or even occluded those of
the other nationalities and minorities within the British Isles. Thus, in
books intended for the English market, the very inclusiveness of Englishness as an identity effectively marginalized the culture of the Celtic
Fringe. For example, neither the geography of Scotland or Ireland nor
the histories of any of their national heroes figured very largely. Wales,
meanwhile, was almost invariably treated as a fully integrated and
minor appendage of England, and it was almost never indicated that
any of the population living in England itself might be anything other
than of Anglo-Saxon stock. In sets of geography readers, the first volume of each graduated series to cover actual geographical locales was
usually devoted entirely to England and Wales, a fact that, given the
structure of the curriculum, inevitably meant England alone became
the centrepiece of geographical instruction. In contrast, Scotland and
Ireland tended to be put together in a different, later volume, which
could include other parts of the empire and sometimes the rest of
Europe.[36] One exception to this trend was *Arnold's Geography Readers*
(1894), which in the English edition relegated Scotland and Ireland to
another volume, but in the Scots edition of 1897 reversed this and had
Scotland form the basis of an entire volume and England, Wales, and
Ireland included in a later 'catch-all' book. Usually, however, the
amount of space devoted to Scotland and Ireland, even in many readers intended for those markets, was minimal in comparison to the
treatments of England, even when taking into account the relative
differences in population and area. And the textual grouping of these
locales with other 'bits' of the empire or Europe was analogous to
depicting them as appendages, colonies, or even extraneous foreign
countries.

This organization of content within reading books reflects the way
in which educationalists promoted their use as the basis for lessons on
geographical and historical topics. Manuals written for the purpose of
instructing teachers suggested that students be first taught details about
their immediate surroundings, then, using readers (and maps, if available), move out to consider the mother country, both physically and
politically.[37] For students in England, of course, this meant consider-
ing England first, then the other components of the British Isles, and

lastly the whole of the British Empire. The best way of explaining to children who they were and whence they were from, wrote educationalist J. Gunn in 1895, was through the use of pictures rather than maps – which were too abstract for the younger students – and/or through the use of 'the class reading-book,' which 'generally contains many stories or descriptive lessons' that were 'related to the geography lessons.' As a substitute for visual materials, 'all such lessons' in the reader 'should be made use of as illustrations of this topic.'[38] A little later, F.H. Hayward, a leading proponent of Herbartian educational ideas, seconded this use of readers with the suggestion of focusing on travel stories and narratives that indicated the matching of people with places: 'Men are interested in the earth mainly because it is the arena of their struggles, failures, and achievements.'[39] Naturally, students should start with their 'own' people and places and move on to consider those in other lands. This pedagogical strategy of moving from the immediate and local to larger and more abstract scales was one that could be readily endorsed by the new educationalists' view of 'child-centred' approaches. It was affirmed by Joseph Cowham in his *New School Method* in his assertion that the best classroom texts were arranged from 'the simplest notions of an organized community to the complex conditions under which the various forces of national life are today arranged.'[40] As we shall see, those teachers who followed this advice – given the reading books available to them – necessarily privileged a reading of England as locus of identity and Englishness as the appropriate national culture.

There is plenty of evidence to suggest that many elementary teachers did follow this method of physically placing their students in the world. Lesson plans in school logbooks indicate that this was the case. For instance, the head teacher of Christ Church National Girls School recorded the nature of geography lessons to be taught by standards in 1888: 'Std. I. Plan of the class, etc. Std. II. Size of the world, map of England; III. Physical and Political Geography of England, with special knowledge of Surrey; IV. British Isles and British N. America; V., VI., VII. Geo. of Europe.'[41] Sample logbooks from other schools, both board and voluntary, in London, Manchester, and Bristol, followed similar patterns.[42] The syllabus laid out in St Philip's National School for Boys, Bristol, in 1904–5 is particularly instructive in the way in which the relationship between England and the other component groups of the British Isles could be structured in the teaching regime: 'Std. II. Illustrations by reference to district and to maps of England and the world divisions of land and water. Std. III. England and Wales. Physical features, work of the people, means of communication, special knowledge of Gloucestershire. Std. IV. Scotland, Ireland, Canada, our colonies generally and their value. Std. V. British South Africa, Australia, India. Std. VI & VII. Trade routes, latitude and longitude.'⁴³ In this case, the immediate locality and England are the areas of primary identification, while Scotland and Ireland are grouped together with 'our colonies generally.'

If we turn to the actual content of the readers, we clearly see the primacy of English concerns. Scottish history, for instance, was all but ignored in readers detailing the history of the British Isles; the few Scottish heroes chosen for inclusion were figures such as Wallace and Bruce whose primary importance was in their relationship to the English, albeit in their resistance to English incursions. Very few history readers noted that James I of England was also simultaneously James VI of Scotland or indeed that there had ever existed a line of independent Scottish monarchs.⁴⁴ History readers with separate editions for both English and Scottish Education Codes were practically identical, there being only a small portion of the chapters or stories (typically one or two – in addition to those of Wallace and Bruce – out of forty or so) in the Scottish editions that were devoted to Scots heroes and myths, while the remainder of the text remained identical to the exclusively English history of the English editions. The only other change was the replacement of 'English' with 'British' in most references to the wider empire after 1707. Ireland fared even worse: the only references to it in history readers were usually in regard to its conquest by and submission to the English. The dominant position of England within the United Kingdom was thus given tangible significance in the amount and type of knowledge about the component groups of the British Isles provided to English children. This vision of the British Isles was often accompanied by an explicitly racialized explanation of the differences between the component nationalities.

A positive means of using the discourse of race to explain English identity under the rubric of Anglo-Saxonism/Teutonism was present in an increasing number of readers prior to the end of the century. The Celtic Fringe was as a consequence implicitly cast as linked but distinct from the English. This was particularly so in the case of Ireland and the Irish, although it was also true, if somewhat less explicitly, of representations of the Scots and Welsh as well. Unsurprisingly, even smaller groups, such as Anglo-Irish and English Catholics, Jews, the

English black population, and immigrants of other European ethnic backgrounds, were entirely ignored. The characterization of English-ness as pertaining solely to Anglo-Saxon origins reveals the primacy attached to English identity. The degree to which civilization had been attained, the very 'greatness' of the entire United Kingdom and British Empire, was not explained as deriving from the experience of all the component ethnicities/nationalities, but rather from the peculiar ori-gins, character, heritage, and transplanted institutions of a single ra-cial group to which not all the inhabitants of the British Isles belonged. The Scots, Welsh, and Irish, discussed in terms of their Celtic ancestry and of their displacement to the fringes of the land by the extraordi-nary Teutonic invaders, were not only marginalized geographically, but were often excluded from the symbolic representation of the na-tion as well.[45] This portrayal of the ethnicities within the British Isles in terms of their race or tribe was not new, but the distinctive connota-tions and implications drawn from this connection, and the increasing use of Anglo-Saxonism as an explanation of British national and impe-rial greatness, was a quite novel and highly significant development. The evolution of Anglo-Saxonism, and the somewhat broader Teutonism, and their relationship to general racial discourse deserves its own brief discussion, since both were particularly prominent in school readers.

Although the myth of the pre-eminent and primordial character of Anglo-Saxon England had its origins in the sixteenth century, there was in these early views little interest in specific biological characteris-tics – innate physical or intellectual attributes – that separated the Anglo-Saxons from other peoples. Anglo-Saxon virtues and superior-ity were defined in largely cultural and political terms rather than through genealogical 'blood ties' or biological essentialism.[46] Links were made between the Anglo-Saxons and their Germanic ancestors, but it was Anglo-Saxon institutional arrangements that were accorded at-tention and praise, and not individual or collective racial traits. This began to change with the flowering of late-eighteenth and early nine-teenth-century romanticism, and the work of such historians and writ-ers as Sharon Turner and Sir Walter Scott.[47] Scott's treatment of the Saxons in *Ivanhoe* was extremely important in transmuting ideas about the Anglo-Saxon race, from extolling institutional excellence to cel-ebrating individual and collective racial attributes; from 'dry-as-dust' accounts of Anglo-Saxon land-tenure systems and common liberties to 'a story of virtuous flaxen-haired Saxon maidens and sturdy, blue-

eyed Saxon yeomen.'[48] This romantic vision of the Anglo-Saxons remained in the ascendant until well after the end of the century. We
can see the impact of this in the work of a young pupil-teacher at a
Bristol teacher training college in 1902. She submitted an essay to the
school's quarterly magazine on the subject of Harold, the last Saxon
king:

> Remote and obscure though the Saxon Age now seems, the memory of Harold
> yet shines out unsullied, and gleams along the ages to pale the feeble light of
> his successors. A mysterious charm enshrines the name and personality of
> Harold, such that any attempt to explain or describe threatens to break the
> spell.
>
> A Saxon in form as well as in spirit was Harold; gold-brown hair, parted
> from the temples and flowing in waves to the shoulder, framed a countenance
> inexpressibly sweet and calm, yet ever tinged with a certain melancholy which
> seemed to divine the sorrowful future of him upon whom it sat; the deep blue
> eye which bespoke the purity of soul within, and often with its gentle gaze
> convicted the guilty or reassured the innocent; the form – tall, perfectly pro-
> portioned and athletic; – all, as Lytton says, 'were singularly characteristic of
> Saxon beauty in its highest and purest type.' But particularly striking was the
> quiet dignity and gentle majesty which rendered the form of Harold almost
> god-like in its bearing, and which set him apart as a leader and ruler of men ...
>
> How did our Saxon King atone for this one deviation? By a lifelong devo-
> tion and sacrifice to England! His bitterest enemy, who else knew no fear,
> confessed that he feared the great Saxon for that 'in the breast of Harold beats
> the heart of England.'[49]

The element of romantic nationalism in this future teacher's vision of
her Saxon heritage is quite striking. Most interesting is her ready acceptance of the stereotypical physical characteristics of the Saxons found
in school-book narratives and illustrations. But as was noted of racial
discourse in general, it was the development of the new scientific
disciplines in the middle decades of the century that really gave respectability to biological interpretations of racial Anglo-Saxonism.

Indeed, despite the claims of the philologists, from the 1850s scientific writers such as Knox were disputing the connections between the
Teutonic peoples and other Caucasians. In Anglo-American circles a
vogue developed for separating the Teutons and their Anglo-Saxon
sub-branch from other racial groups and hardening the imagined differences between them. This had the effect of further widening the

distinctions between related ethnic groups. Moreover, contemporary nationality and racial difference typically came to be intertwined in such a way that historians writing about the English past increasingly came to speak of the influence of the 'English race' or, more often, 'the Anglo-Saxon race' on the progress and development of English civilization. Popular historians as diverse in their outlook as Green, Freeman, and Froude were in part responsible for Anglo-Saxonist views coming into the elementary school curriculum. Passages such as the following (taken from the opening pages of Green's *Short History*) in simplified form came to feature as commonplace in history, geography, and literary readers:

For the fatherland of the English race we must look far away from England itself. In the fifth century after the birth of Christ, the one country which bore the name of England was what we now call Sleswick, a district in the heart of the peninsula which parts the Baltic from the Northern seas ... Although they were all known as Saxons by the Roman people who touched them only on their southern border where the Saxons dwelt, and who remained ignorant of the very existence of the English or the Jutes, the three tribes bore among themselves the name of the central tribe of their league, the name of Englishmen.

These were the English. We do not know whether it was the pressure of other tribes or the example of their brethren who were now moving in a general attack on the Empire from their forest homes, or simply the barrenness of their coast, which drove the hunters, farmers, fishermen, of the three English tribes to sea. But the daring spirit of their race already broke out in the secrecy and suddenness of their swoop, in the fierceness of their onset, in the careless glee with which they seized either sword or oar.[50]

History written as the evolving progress of the Anglo-Saxons thereby enveloped English national identity within a sheath of highly specified racialized discourse.

The cloaking of Englishness within the myth of Anglo-Saxon racial perfection was assisted by, and clearly had a reciprocal effect on, the treatment of the other races within the British Isles. It was affirmed that 'the ancestors of the English race, and the founders of the English language, law, and freedom were three tribes called the Angles, the Saxons, and the Jutes.' And, despite their primitive beliefs, these three groups displayed all the characteristics of the modern stalwart English. It followed that the Welsh, Highland Scots, and Irish were differentiated from the English on the basis of their Celtic racial background. Their breeding explained their particular vices and virtues and, for some authors, presupposed a somewhat subordinate status for them.[51] The relationship between the Celtic Fringe and the English centre was sometimes phrased in terms of an ancient race struggle. *The Young Student's English History* reader of 1881 concluded its account of the Anglo-Saxon conquest of Roman Britain by noting: 'The conquest of Britain was indeed partly wrought out after two centuries of bitter warfare. At its close Britain had become England, a land that is, not of Britons, but of Englishmen.' Explaining why this had to be so, the author continued, 'the Britons, abandoned to themselves, were destined to be driven out, or extinguished, or absorbed, according to that apparently inevitable law of nature by which the weaker race disappears before the stronger.' In the author's mind there was no doubt about the importance and continuity of this process, as it was then proudly asserted that 'we are that stronger race, the race of the Teutons and Scandinavian Vikings.'[52] To reinforce this point about the Anglo-Saxon struggle to drive out the Britons/Celts from the most valuable lands and into the wilds of the Cambrian mountains and Scots Highlands, many readers explained that the term Welsh was the ancient Saxon term for outsiders, and that people descended from the ancient British race 'still resided there.'[53] It was sometimes conceded that these past struggles had been superseded, largely through the amicable largesse of the English themselves, and the Celtic peoples were said to have been given the opportunity to join in the prosperity of the English.[54] One reader suggested that the actual intermixing of the English with people of Celtic extraction had produced 'the finest race in the world.'[55] Yet, in these very same texts, a hard distinction was still made, for example, between the Highland and Lowland Scots, and the largely 'pure' Celts of Ireland were contrasted with the more Anglicized and incorporated Welsh.[56] Such distinctions were exemplars of the overarching connection made between the ancient Anglo-Saxons and the nineteenth-century proclivity to impart special importance to the appellation 'English.'

For overwhelmingly it was Anglo-Saxon racial characteristics – love of liberty, courage, patience and reserve, honesty and plain dealing (characteristics that were depicted as essentially masculine) – and not Celtic influences that formed the primary basis of Englishness and, by corollary, British national greatness. Numerous readers, whether they were historical, geographical, literary, or civics-oriented, commented

on the intimate connection between the Anglo-Saxons and those qualities that were thought especially worthy in contemporary English national life and institutions. The historical study of the Anglo-Saxons
was praised over and against other ancient/classical peoples on the
grounds that 'in the hearts of these uncultured sons of the German soil
[were] noble qualities of character and disposition unknown to the

author then noted: 'Now, most of the Anglo-Saxons had light hair and
blue eyes. I expect, if you look round your school, you will see that
most of the girls and boys have got light hair and blue eyes. That is
because they too are Anglo-Saxons, like the little slaves who were
taken to Rome so many years ago. Perhaps, if you look in the glass
you will see that you too have light hair and blue eyes. If you have, I
think you too must be an Anglo-Saxon.'[59]

Genealogically transmitted cultural traits were also ascribed to the
Anglo-Saxons. Skills and attributes praised in modern England were
imagined to have had racial origins. Warning the child reader not to
dismiss the original Anglo-Saxons as heathen savages 'like some of
the black people you have read about,' one author noted, 'you must
not think that the English, at the time we are talking of, were foolish ...
[they] were good sailors and brave soldiers, hard working farmers
and skilful smiths and carpenters; and they could take care of themselves, and hold their own whether at work or play.'[60] Literature read-

ers even offered the racial origins of the English as a reason for the extent, depth, and superior nature of the country's literary output. The 1899 *Simple History of English Literature* explained that 'it was the Teutons that brought into our literature and our national character the strong love and struggle for whatever is good, and right, and God-like, that is the pride and strength of our country and its literature.'[61]

Political and civil virtues were also accorded racial significance, although here slippage between the biological, ethnic, and cultural connotations of race was particularly acute. In their discussion of the rights and freedoms that accrued to 'every Englishman,' the authors of citizenship and civics readers consciously went back to the precedents of Anglo-Saxon local government. Oscar Browning noted that 'if we wish to understand the institutions of the England of to-day, we must go back to the Anglo-Saxon forms of social organization, and to the Teutonic institutions with which they must be classed.'[62] And W. Beach Thomas explained that the liberties inherent in the largely decentralized nature of English government corresponded 'very nearly to the old meetings and councils that arranged local affairs a thousand years ago.'[63] The radical historical tradition of the 'ancient constitution' was thus infused with racialized language.

Indeed, history and tradition meshed uneasily with the racial rationale of English identity. The 'Whig' tradition of charting the historic growth of English liberties had been a prevalent, if contested, interpretation of what constituted English identity from early in the nineteenth century. But this tradition was remoulded at the end of the century to accommodate the increased importance given to racial typology. In the early 1880s the implicit theme of the rights and freedoms that 'all Englishmen' had gained through the constitutional struggles of the past was still common. As one of the writers of the *Chambers's History Reading Books* of 1882 put it: 'All Englishmen are now agreed that we greatly owe the freedom we now enjoy to our forefathers, who resolved to bleed and die on the battlefield rather than submit to the arbitrary will of misguided kings.'[64] Similarly, all the stories in the *English History Reading Books* of 1884 were chosen because they indicated points of interest from the 'middle period of English history' (from the Norman Conquest until the Glorious Revolution of 1688), since that 'was when the constitution of England was being settled.'[65] But by the 1890s these constitutional explanations were wedded to explicitly racial classifications, producing combined racial-historical narratives and genealogies of the nation. This is best demonstrated by examining discussions of an event – the Norman Conquest – that presented problems for a racial approach to history.

Writers in the early 1880s found the arrival of the Normans to be somewhat problematic, but they could pass over the difficulty by examining domestic constitutional developments and the impact of the Hundred Years War. The Normans might be acknowledged as a different race from the Anglo-Saxon English, but this was expressed in political and cultural differences rather than biological or deterministic terms. Thus, in Book III of the *Chambers's History Readers* it was posited that all the 'misery and bloodshed' of the French wars did produce a positive result, for it 'bound the English nation together as one man.' By fighting together against a common enemy, 'the races of Norman and Saxon forgot their differences, and learned to glory in the common name of Englishmen.'[66] The fighting of a common enemy was enough to bridge what amounted to surface political or cultural tensions, and thus the Normans could be unproblematically absorbed into the historic march of English progress.

Authors of school readers in the 1890s and later, however, commonly used two different approaches to account for and explain the significance of the Norman Conquest. The first of these variants pointed to the blessings that the infusion of Norman blood had conferred on the Anglo-Saxon/Teuton stock – an explanation that stressed the Normans' own Teutonic origins, and a denial that there was any fundamental racial difference at all. In *Black's Story of the English People* of 1905 the student was told that 'the Normans soon mixed with the English, and the two races became one nation. It was easy for them to mix, for English and Norman were really brothers in blood. The Norman was a Northman, just as the Saxons and Danes were. When the two races were joined, a very mighty nation was the result. The spirit and charm of the Norman together with the solid strength of the Saxon have formed the English-speaking people of today, the people who rule so much of the earth, and whose language is spreading so widely.'[67] Authors stressed the beneficial attributes the Normans brought to their 'blood' merger with the Saxons; as the Standard VI *King Edward History Reader* of 1901 observed, 'the restless energy of the early English, united with the intelligence of the Norman French, has led to the formation of a rich, powerful, and progressive nation, ever foremost in the cause of freedom and justice.'[68] In this interpretation the differences between the Normans and the Saxons were more fundamentally rooted in racial origin, yet the two were still essentially compatible – since they had a common ancestry in their Teutonness – and therefore the characteristic traits of each were seen to be harmonious and not in conflict. This was particularly stressed in English grammar books: one noted that when the Norse invaded the French coast, they 'forgot their mother tongue and became French in speech, though not in blood,' and thus, when the Normans subsequently invaded England, the language that 'they contributed' to modern English was largely 'the romantic element, which is now numerically greater than the Teutonic, though the words are in less frequent use.'[69]

The second common discursive strategy discounted Norman virtues, minimized common ancestry, and stressed the struggle for dominance between the two peoples. Ultimately, the weaker Normans faced eventual assimilation into the intrinsically stronger Anglo-Saxon English race-culture and customs.[70] G. Armitage-Smith noted in his 1895 reader for older elementary students: 'The Norman Conquest of 1066 brought in a race of sovereigns accustomed to feudalism, who strengthened central authority and kingly rule; yet they, too, learned that they could not, with safety, resist the will of the people. When disposed to encroach on the liberties of their subjects, they were coerced into confirming Saxon popular rights.'[71] In this version – basically the 'Norman Yoke' thesis lacking the earlier radical political message – the survival of the English language was taken as evidence of the Normans' eventual submission to the stronger English character. *Chambers's 'New Scheme' Readers* portrayed the language issue as symptomatic of a fierce Darwinistic struggle between the ruling Normans and the subject English. The end was never in doubt, for the language and customs of the 'sturdy' English folk, unlike the patrician Norman culture, could easily accommodate new influences without succumbing to them, and as a result the sole use of French died out.[72] The intrinsic superiority of the English language, and implicitly of the English themselves, was thereby confirmed.[73] As another *Chambers* reader stated simply: 'For some time after the Norman Conquest, the upper classes spoke only Norman-French, and it seemed probable that England would become Norman in speech, manners, and customs. But the English people as a whole kept to their old tongue and their old habits, and in the end it was not England which became Norman, but the Normans who became Englishmen.'[74] In both of these variations, the common result was an explanation of the period of Norman conquest that, while temporarily removing Anglo-Saxon governance of England, in no way diminished the qualities that made Englishness exceptional. If anything, in fact, the Conquest was cast as a positive development since it provided a test of racial character. The weaker races were assimilated and the best traits of former oppressors were incorporated into a rejuvenated English character. A stronger race imbued with the 'ancient,' 'traditional' qualities of the Anglo-Saxons and the refinements of the newer arrivals was thus the welcome result. English racial identity, expressed through its language and culture, remained favoured and superior.

Race, Citizenship, and the Empire

This equating of racial with ethnic/national characteristics, and the concomitant conviction that to be English was to be superior, dovetailed with the ideological imperatives of late-Victorian imperialism. Theories of racial hierarchy based on colour could supply justifications for European imperialism and colonialism in general, but the finer gradations of racial distinction could be used to explain England's (or more correctly, Britain's) own special role and success. School readers were full of references to the particular characteristics of the ancient Anglo-Saxons and the special proclivity, justness, and destiny that they bequeathed to the modern English so that they might 'colonize,' 'civilize,' and 'rule others.' Imperial expansion was, in fact, clearly presented as an integral part of the English racial mission, and ironically, given the narrowly constructed English ethnic chauvinism of the Anglo-Saxon narrative, 'Little Englander' views were virtually absent in school readers after the late 1880s. This accorded with textbooks produced for all levels of schooling: as one formal text from 1891 stated simply, 'The story of the growth of the British Empire is the story of the expansion of the Anglo-Saxon race,'[75] and H.O. Arnold-Forster's hugely successful *Citizen Reader* asked the child 'to remember that the great *nation* to which you belong, and of which I hope you are proud, is bigger, far bigger, than the ... little islands which make up the kingdom of Great Britain and Ireland, and that it extends everywhere the English language is spoken by men who live under English law and under the English flag.'[76]

If there was an evident contradiction between the grounding of identity in Englishness and the ideology of imperialism, it was simply papered over in most texts. Despite what might be said about the composite nature of the British Isles, it was usually the racial, cultural, and moral characteristics of the Englishmen that were represented as the *raison d'être* of the empire. One history reader from 1896 noted that 'no race could have built up this empire unless it possessed the qualities of honesty, courage, energy, and endurance,' and another (from 1902) that the Englishman's 'energy and perseverance enables him to face the difficulties of opening up a new country, and his independence of character drives him to new lands.'[77] A 1899 geography reader explained that 'wherever [in the world] the Englishman appears he carries with him law, order, and progress; and British supremacy means the reign of freedom, justice, and industry.'[78] Meanwhile, H.E. Malden's civics reader of 1894 suggested:

The kind of life, religion, law, government which spreads with the English race does not represent the highest ideals of a single Englishman, but it does represent the practical working compromise arrived at by the interaction of the ideals of all Englishmen. It is expressed by the political and social constitution which we have been endeavouring to set forth in outline. It is the work of our race – it is our work ... We do prefer then surely that the English race with its laws and customs, should spread and multiply in the earth rather than other races, and that it should absorb other settlers, not be absorbed by them, if they cannot exist separately side by side. Let us exert ourselves therefore to keep, to extend, to improve the kind of national life which we have preferred.[79]

Some geography readers pointed to the skill and industry through which the resources of the British Isles had been turned into commercial and industrial wealth. 'Englishmen are by nature both industrious and clever' and 'hence England has become rich through a wise and clever use of the wealth she naturally possesses.'[80] The special character of the English was even invoked to distinguish their worthy and just empire from those of other contemporary European powers.[81]

Regardless of the manner by which the readers dealt with the contradiction of presenting an English ethnicity as the basis of the British Empire, the implied logical extension of these racial character expositions was that imperial expansion was not only justified, it was inevitable and necessary. The Englishman was not only 'specially fitted to explore and to colonise, and to direct the efforts of nations who are less civilised than themselves,' such activity was actually necessary if the English were not to lose their characteristic vigour and virility at home. Expansion and colonization served to prevent the English at home from 'sinking into that slough of idleness and vice' and to increase self-respect and public morality.[82] The connection between Anglo-Saxonism, English citizenship, and the basis of the late-nineteenth-century empire was thus deeply embedded in the narratives in all types of elementary readers. History readers in particular focused and simplified the relationship between the innate characteristics and traits of the Anglo-Saxons, the launching of colonial expansion in the reign of Elizabeth I, and the present-day duties of each English citizen.[83] Essentialized and gendered character traits were proposed as the initiators of this English imperial growth. It was proclaimed that there was something inherent in the Englishman that had led to the English nation's lead in world-imperial affairs.

As the rising generation of English 'citizens,' schoolchildren were entrusted with the special responsibility of 'not letting down the race' at home or in its civilizing mission abroad. Such exhortations as that found at the end of the 1905 *Black's Simple Introductory Reader* were common: 'Let us remember that we, too, are English. In our hands lies the future of our great race. Let us resolve to do all we can to uphold the fame of our country, so that fresh honours may yet be added to the Story of the English people.'[84] In this view, both civic obligation and the imperial mission were implicit in the racial superiority of the English. As the highest up on the racial scale it was the duty and responsibility of the English to rule those 'lower down.' It was figured in 'citizenship' readers as a form of contract with the 'lesser races.'[85] The conflating of national civic duty with the interests of 'race' and empire was thus a transparent domestic social prescription: supporting the empire and maintaining the race entailed forgoing factional conflict on the basis of party, gender, or class. The responsibility of citizenship and empire was placed above all others, revealing a degree of defensive anxiety on the part of reading-book authors. Some readers, such as Malden's *The Life and Duties of a Citizen* (1894), portrayed the failure to live up to the social-civic ideal of imperial citizenship as being catastrophic: 'If the majority of Englishmen were to refuse to do their duty, to neglect the means by which their country has been made great and free in the past, to choose to become lazy, extravagant, tyrannical, careless of the rights of their neighbours, careless of the common interest, then the government of England would become corrupt and weak, the empire would be lost, trade would disappear, and those who might be past feeling shame and disgrace would be found out by what they must feel, universal distress beyond the experience of any bad times we have known.'[86] Others authors, through historical allusion to the Babylonians, Greeks, and Romans, pointed to the temptations of such luxury and laziness: temptations that had destroyed these previous empires.[87]

The exhortation of classroom materials to imperialism, and the building of a worthy masculinity that would sustain it, was composed in a fashion that necessarily appealed across class divisions. On the one hand, it is unlikely that the authors of readers – a new generation of 'professionals' whose self-conscious purpose was the defining of the national culture – would consciously think otherwise: they were promulgating their own view of the structure of reality, without thought of how differently that reality might be perceived by those in other social situations. National character descriptions couched in the vocabulary of race were used by these authors as a means to positively identify an imagined community. In the literary output geared towards the elementary classroom racial discourse was clearly used as a socially binding rhetoric: a language of identity inducement. The nation was shown to be comprised of one people, historically and genealogically united. Socio-economic and political divisions paled in comparison to the fact of race. The construction of Englishness as a de facto ethnicity – regardless of its inherent contradictions – thereby promoted the notion that the working masses *should* accept the existing social and political fabric of their society as part of the natural order of things.[88] This was not hypocritical propaganda, but rather in these authors' minds a 'reasonable' conclusion given their inherently nationalist world-view. Of course, as we shall see in the next chapter, for any group to be considered 'included' there must be others that are 'excluded.' Exhortations to the Englishman's 'place' in the imperial nation might have other socially specific contexts as well however, for on the other hand, the professional middle-class educationalists and authors of elementary school readers were immersed in their own social and cultural contexts, which no doubt had effects on their perceptions and unconscious prescriptions.

The late-Victorian 'social question' – what to do with the low-income masses that 'blighted' the inner cities – was one of these other important contexts for contemporary considerations of the aims and, therefore, the content of elementary schooling. For instance, in April and May of 1895, the Anglican National Society's official teachers' organ, *The School Guardian*, ran a two-part article entitled 'Emigration – England's true and only solution to the social question.' In this piece, the author asked pointedly, 'How many hundreds of thousands in our great towns and cities ... who might to-day by timely emigration have been bringing up their children honoured and honourable citizens in Australia, New Zealand, South Africa, Canada, *have been lost* by this herding together in wretched courts, lanes and alleys?' A 'terrible legacy and harvest of evil' had resulted in leaving the wretched 'to cumber and poison a land in which they never should have been born.' After citing Seeley – 'one of the truest friends of the workingman that England has ever seen' – on the benefits and encompassing identity of empire, the author continued: 'He saw no exile to the Englishman in urging him to go and replenish "Greater England" ... For Englishmen should never forget that England nowadays lies all over the world – Australia, South Africa, New Zealand, Canada, all is England nowadays, and is being brought nearer to us daily by the ever increasing facilities for reaching those greater homes of our race by the countless inventions of modern science.' In the second half of the article, the author then concluded that it was 'no exaggeration of facts to state that we are reaping to-day in the masses of shameless, evil-living, Godless socialism, defiant atheism, into which these poor herded wretches have fallen, the inevitable harvest which neglect most surely sows.' And finally, after then citing Froude, the author proposed that the only solution to the 'social problem' was to send all the surplus population to the colonies.[89]

This author, an Anglican bishop, was not alone among educationalists in proposing an emigration scheme as the means to settle the socio-economic ills of society. In the 1890s, manuals of method for elementary teachers sometimes justified a knowledge of geography among the working classes in similar terms: 'England is said to be over-populated, and fields for emigration are essential to relieve the surplus population, and to carry out the advisable and beneficent planting of the earth by English people.'[90] It would be grossly overstating the case to suggest that elementary school materials deliberately constructed the ideal of the 'Englishman' and of the imperial English nation in a fashion that promoted the emigration of the poverty stricken among the working classes. But clearly, some educators saw the idea of 'Greater England' in these terms, and suggested to teachers, who after all were 'in the front lines of the social question,' that they might as well. As examined in the following chapter on constructions of the racial 'other' that necessarily accompanied English self-identification, the vocabulary of race contained within school readers could have various interpretations and uses. And the evident anxiety among the professional middle class about the 'degraded' nature of the working classes, and indeed, that the empire might save the English from racial degeneration emanating from the 'lower orders,' can certainly be read into the lexicon of identity found within classroom materials.

4

Imagining the Racial 'Other' Within

The national pride of England is proverbial. History and geography are so taught that children cannot fail to be impressed with the greatness of the British Empire. In all the schools by means of these studies is nourished that national spirit which, though sometimes giving rise to ludicrous self-satisfaction ... is a source of genuine patriotism, ever ready to find expression in the service of the country, whether on the land or on the sea.

James C. Greenough, *The Evolution of the Elementary Schools of Great Britain* (1903)

The building of communal identity requires, of course, both an 'us' and a 'them.' The insider/outsider dichotomy is integral to the construction of a sense of community and belonging. Given the emphasis they placed on the language of an English ethnic community that was noted in the previous chapter, it should not come as a surprise that the reading books used in elementary schooling also provided racialized 'others' against which English identity could be compared. These were descriptions of, and commentaries about, people that were visibly unlike the white, Anglo-Saxon English. Sometimes such characterizations were accompanied by explicit statements about the inherent inferiority of these 'others,' and sometimes they were not. All, however, contained elements of racial stereotypes; all had significant implications for the lexicon of identity being presented to the elementary schoolchild.

Racial stereotypes have received generous attention from historians of imperialism. As Katherine Castle's *Britannia's Children* has neatly detailed for British history texts and comic books and, even more recently, John Willinsky has argued for 'Western' education in general, the construction and replication of racial stereotypes were fundamental in justifying proposed or existing imperialist practices. Racial stereotypes and the language of difference provided what Castle describes as 'the supporting cast in the story of empire, without whom the testing of self in conflict or the assumptions of [British] superiority became meaningless.' Willinsky, meanwhile, describes the creation of structured notions of fundamental difference through various educational disciplines as the integral 'educational mission' of European imperialism over the past five centuries.[1] There is much merit to both of these analyses, and this study in no way disputes their arguments about the promotion and use of 'racialized' stereotypes for the legitimization of an imperialist world-view, both within Britain and in the 'colonial curriculum' in the empire itself.[2] Rather, this chapter will move a step beyond the imperial propaganda argument and stress how an imperial identity was entirely naturalized as a part of the 'innate' inheritance of the English national community. This is because arguments that stress only the legitimating of imperialism do not adequately address the full significance of the imagery and narratives about non-white peoples as they appeared in elementary education. For something entirely missing from many imperial propaganda perspectives is the socio-economically divided context of educational practices in turn-of-the-century England.

Both Castle and Willinsky (and, indeed, many of the historians writing in the shadow of John M. MacKenzie's immensely influential *Propaganda and Empire*)[3] examine the images and narratives of race with little attention to the social conditions of their deployment. They assume the existence, in other words, of what nationalist ideology was actually trying to construct: an ideologically undifferentiated community, in which all the members shared similar interests and perceptions. Willinsky tends to concentrate on the accumulation and organization of knowledge among the educated elite and presumes simple diffusion downward through society over time. Castle reads history textbooks (the vast majority of which were the formal type used in secondary and elite schooling) and comic books (whose readership she never really defines or analytically explores) as if they were all equally available to the entire population. Castle's coherent and fairhanded analysis of the images and narratives in her sources is thus not balanced with any real attention to the conditions of their production or consumption. Her presumption that the texts and comics worked together to propagandize the needs of imperialism may indeed hold true for their reading by adolescents of the middle class and lower middle class (and undoubtedly some of the older children of the working classes as well) who were their likely audience. But what Castle is describing is at the end of the childhood process of inscribing imperial-national ideals: the symbols and narratives of imperialism would make sense because the youth exposed to them had already learned the key elements of their composition.

Moreover, it should not be forgotten that different groups within English society 'experienced' their state's imperialism, just like they 'experienced' nationalism, in entirely different contexts. The needs of empire may well have required the mobilization of the entire population, but a direct connection to the governance of that empire was still tenuous at best for much of the population: for those at the lower levels of society the context and messages of reading about other races in the empire were not necessarily the same as for those who would one day go out to rule it. Of course, one of the major arguments of this present study is that a vocabulary of national identity was deployed in elementary schooling by professional middle-class authors and that this was a means by which working-class children came to identify with 'their' nation. But, as should by now be apparent, the social context of this deployment mediated the possible meanings. Moreover, as will be made clear in this chapter, the images of the 'other' – the outsider – concerned not only the delineation of community boundaries, nor only the legitimization of imperialist practices, but were also the markers of domestic anxiety about the 'racial' state of the 'English,' and were carriers of implicit social prescriptions. For just as the 'us' in the rhetoric of national belonging was fractured along gender and socio-economic lines, so too the 'other' reinforced the double-edged nature of national belonging as it was presented to working-class schoolchildren: not only marking out the place of the English in the world, but also defining the 'place' of the working classes within the English nation itself.

In addition to marking out the imperial-national boundaries, there were alternative contexts in which the language and images of 'race' and of the 'other' were deployed in public discussions in the later nineteenth century. Most significantly, arguments about the degeneration of the English 'race' – usually referring to the 'physical deficiencies' of the urban 'lower' orders – first began to appear in the 1880s.

The result of these growing fears about 'hereditary urban degeneration' was the rise of social imperialist, national efficiency, and eugeni-
cist arguments, and the development of what G.R. Searle has called
National Darwinism – a broadly based movement that peaked in the
years following the Anglo–Boer War.[4] A connection between the rhetoric used to describe different races and that used to describe different
socio-economic classes was not new to the last decades of the century.
But it has been suggested that the biological and essentialist strands in
racial discourse hardened and became so prevalent in the second half
of the nineteenth century due, in part, to these concerns with racial
degeneration. Douglas Lorimer has argued that the 'experience of class
relations within England' was translated into racial terms, even by
those 'untouched by personal experience of the Empire.'[5] Lorimer
posits that the Victorian quest for gentility was threatened by the
advancing spectre of equality demanded by the working classes, and
as a result, individuals conscious of their middle- and upper-class
status nurtured the rhetoric of race so distinctions in status could be
maintained.

The nature and tone of the language used by middle-class commentators to describe the 'lower orders' could indeed bear a striking re-
semblance to that used to describe 'subject races,' particularly in accounts written in the last decades of the century.[6] Andrew Mearns's
Bitter Cry of Outcast London and the journalism of George Sims collectively described the urban poor in the heart of the imperial capital as
'foreigners,' 'outcasts,' 'natural curiosities,' and savages akin to the
'Aborigenes [*sic*], and the South Sea Islanders.'[7] Both Sims and Mearns
used this kind of language to shock the middle-class public into action, for as Mearns exclaimed (with capital letters for extra effect), 'the
gulf has been daily widening which separates the lowest classes of the
community from our churches and chapels, and from all decency and
civilization ... THIS TERRIBLE FLOOD OF SIN AND MISERY IS GAINING ON US.'[8] The
language of another race living in the midst of the imperial metropolis
was intended, not in a biologically determinist sense, but to spur the
state or other philanthropic activity to drag this 'other race' out of the
degradation that threatened English 'decency and civilization.' But if
easy transmutations in the languages of race and class applied mainly
to the literature intended for the middle and upper rungs of English
society, what of the material written *for* the 'lower' orders in their
schools? As the previous chapter argued, the answer to this question
is that the dictates of building 'Englishness' resulted in the supposed

racial differences between classes *not* being stressed. The differences between 'races' were instead those between the presumed normative English Anglo-Saxon and the imperial and non-white 'other.' But a reading of these images and narratives within the context of the late-Victorian fear of 'racial degeneration' indicates that domestic social prescriptions intended for the lower classes could also find their way into the value judgments ostensibly made about racialized 'others.'

Geography and Otherness in Elementary School Readers

The presentation of the racial 'other' in the late-Victorian and Edwardian elementary school was most often found in geography readers. Educationalists and government officials increasingly favoured geography as a means to help promote a sense of the national culture, much like they also favoured history – the discipline to which it was often explicitly connected.[9] Even during the 'worst days' of the payment by results period (mid-1860s to mid-1880s), geography had remained one of the most popular 'class' subjects (an extra subject to the formal curriculum that could be examined only on a 'class' or collective basis), far surpassing history. During the 1880s and 1890s professional advocates of geography, such as Archibald Geikie, explained that geography 'furnishes a just conception of the fatherland in all its aspects, and passes thence to broad and intelligent views of the world at large. By thus widening the youthful experience of men and things it helps to stimulate habits of reflection and self-reliance, and strengthens the character for the future affairs of life.' To accomplish this task, educationalists regularly suggested the use of readers, because the 'the class reading-book generally contains many stories or descriptive lessons which can also be related to geography lessons, and all such lessons should be made use of as an illustration of this subject.'[10]

When justifying the inclusion of geography in the curriculum, whether formally or informally through reader use, educationalists and teachers, especially in the 1880s and 1890s, usually made reference to its importance in stimulating interest in the empire.[11] In the years around the Anglo–Boer War a full-scale debate erupted in the pages of at least one educational periodical about the momentousness of teaching imperial geography in elementary schools.[12] However, some educationalists in the Edwardian years expressed caution in this use of the subject. Adamson in 1907 pointedly stressed, 'It is important for the future of the empire that we should all remember that the majority of British subjects do not speak English, and are not even European in race. This is one reason more for cultivating the widest possible geographical sympathies.'[13] And others, such as Welton, viewed the proper teaching of geography as a means to combat the inculcation of 'a narrowly patriotic good': that since 'Christianity teaches that all are brothers,' then to 'all – white, black or yellow – must the hand of fellowship and friendly interest be extended' and geography was a means to promote an understanding of this responsibility.[14] Moreover, while explaining that 'a clear conception of Geography is a necessary part of the training of citizens in a democratically governed country,' the authors of *The Teaching of Geography in Elementary Schools*, published in 1910, were nevertheless critical of the prevalent practice of spending a whole year of geography instruction on the British Empire, which had 'doubtless been prompted by sound motives of rousing interest in the Colonies, but [was] nevertheless bad Geography.'[15] Their argument here being that the empire did not accord exactly to geographically based divisions of the world. Significantly, however, these authors all still relied on racial characterizations in their suggestions on how to teach different geographically defined areas to children. For instance, in their description of the people of 'Mediterranean countries,' they suggest that the teacher explain how 'the people are of a happy, artistic, volatile, and sometimes rather lazy temperament.' The Teutonic people of northern Europe were, on the other hand, of an 'energetic, persevering character,' and thus it was not a surprise that they had 'created the modern industrial system.' Ultimately, although questioning the use of the empire as the basis of 'an area of instruction,' these authors summarized the moral and material progress of a civilization based on the qualities of race.[16]

The strictures of these later promoters of geography seemed to have had some effect. Geography readers continued to be produced between 1880 and 1914 in sets, moving out from the local to the national and then imperial, and lastly out to the whole world. But in the Edwardian years more and more series became increasingly literary in their descriptions. Often these later accounts took the form of a descriptive trip around the world, with various passages that expressed wonder at the strange and exotic sights to be found 'out there.' Educationalists from around the turn of the century had actively promoted the idea of teaching geography through such narratives.[17] Constructed as adventure, narrative descriptions were clearly attempts to spark the curiosity of children with glimpses into the mysterious: into a world that it was expected few of these children would ever see first-hand, but which, they were repeatedly told, was 'strange,' 'different,' 'peculiar,' 'funny.'[18] Moreover, these 'descriptive' geography readers were produced, like the historical readers, by established professional academics. An excellent example was A.J. Herbertson (1866–1915). Educated at Edinburgh University and the University of Freiberg, where he was awarded a doctorate in 1898, Herbertson's scientific background was broad, having been both a surveyor and the private teaching assistant of Patrick Geddes before his formal university training. A specialist in climatology and biogeography, he was appointed professor of geography at Manchester University (1894–6) and, in 1899, was brought to Oxford by the enormously influential imperialist geographer Halford Mackinder, whereupon Herbertson became reader at the newly founded School of Geography. Herbertson, with the help of his wife Frances, wrote and edited several elementary geography reader sets, including Black's popular seven-volume series, *Descriptive Geographies from Original Sources* (1901–6).

Although constructions of another world beyond the experience of elementary schoolchildren were sometimes highly romanticized by these authors, they also characteristically involved the explicit division of humankind into highly generalized 'race types,' accompanied by cultural, social, and moral value judgments. Such passages were anything but simple descriptions of the different types of 'strange' people within a geographically defined space. In hundreds of passages found within all sorts of geography (and also history and literary) readers, cultural, social, and moral judgments were made about people based on physical 'race' criteria. Not only colour and physical stature, but notions of beauty, personality traits, trustworthiness, and degree of civilization were all catalogued according to essentialized racial standards that reflected as much about what these writers imagined themselves to be as it did what they perceived to be the nature of their subjects. Indeed, reader sets were often structured and written entirely around skin colour categorizations.[19] In 1905, the *Collins' School Series: Over Land and Sea* readers explained: 'Mankind have been divided into many varieties differing chiefly in the colour of their skin, in their hair, their features, and the shape of their skull ... The principal divisions of the human family are the Caucasian or White race, the Mongolian or Yellow, the Malay or Tawny, the Negro or Black, and the American Indian or Red race ... It is hardly necessary to say that the people of Europe belong to the white race, which is by far the most civilised.'[20]

Beyond explaining the basic division of peoples within the world into racial groupings, the narrative descriptions that followed were devoted almost entirely to explaining the *difference* between these groups and that of the (presumed) white English schoolchild. Unfamiliar, peculiar, alien, exotic: it was in these terms that the otherness of non-European cultures and peoples was depicted. As such, the representations of non-white, non-European peoples almost always took the form of simplified racial stereotypes.[21] It was here that the convergence of racial categorization and the construction of otherness became manifest. For exotic and picturesque personal character/cultural traits were usually combined with sweeping generalizations about racial disposition. Capsule descriptions of black Africans in these readers invariably made a point of describing the physical features that differentiated them from the 'white man' (i.e., skin colour, 'woolly hair,' 'thick lips,' 'flat nose'), enjoining that 'as a rule he [the black man] is not very pretty,'[22] and frequently bracketing such descriptions with judgments on the 'savagery,' 'ignorance,' and 'idleness' of the African.[23]

In longer accounts, the picturesque story or 'narrative picture' was advocated to keep the children's attention, and to focus their learning on the distinct 'qualities of each race.'[24] George Bosworth's *Narrative Geography Readers* (1910) described African-American children as 'pickaninnies':

The boys have round, fat heads, with curly, woolly hair. Their thick lips are very red, and their teeth are as white as pearls. All the children are plump, and love to lie in the sun and do nothing.

Pickaninnies love bright clothes and favour such colours as red, green, and yellow. It is always a gay scene when the negroes in their smart clothes are seen at work in the cotton fields, or among the sugar canes.

The little black children are well cared for by their parents, who give them very fine names, such as Sambo, and Lancelot for boys, and Diana, May and Lily for girls ...

These children are never so pleased as when they are singing or playing music of some kind ... They are not bothered about work, but they have a real good time of leisure. They are never in a hurry, and their life seems to be given over to song and happiness.

They go to school it is true, but they do not make good scholars. When they leave school they do the same work that their fathers and mothers have done before them. Indeed, to look after sugar plantations and cotton fields is the best work for negroes.[25]

This passage and the illustrations that frequently accompanied such descriptions – playing as they did on long-established stereotypes of the African-American – are revealing and significant in several respects. Such stereotypical depictions of 'the happy, childlike native' ought not to be understood as fanciful or inadvertent mistakes. The 'childlike native' was an icon that acted as a 'root metaphor' and helped 'make static and manageable' the 'flux of reality.'[26] Within a schooling system based on stages of growth and chronological development, school books (arranged, as they tended to be, in graded levels) were a fundamental part of the very definition of those stages and of the human characteristics assumed to be present at each. Since children were thought to be naturally inquisitive, educators believed that 'they were attracted to, and best instructed by, simple, natural things.' It was deemed that the depiction of 'simple people in natural conditions would be appealing and quaint to children who were (temporarily) like them.'[27] In the representation of the black 'native' or African-American there was *no* development from a state of childhood to one of adult civilization. Since they were 'poor scholars' a sense that education was 'wasted' on them was indicated, reinforcing the notion that they, as a 'race,' could not advance to the civilized state that white English working-class children, through the generosity of their social 'betters,' might be expected to attain. The black adult's seemingly inevitable lot was the cotton or cane fields, yet it was suggested, in this and in many other readers, that unless compelled to work blacks and 'natives' would rather spend all their time in idleness and leisure than in hard work.[28]

The ideological results of such a representation were multifaceted. The icon of the childlike native could be cast against the projected development of the English working-class child, providing a sense of identity, security, and superiority, regardless of the facts of the actual background and prospects of the schoolchild. Even the lowliest working-class child could feel in some sense 'superior' to the forever-childlike black native. Such a view could also be advanced as the most relevant explanation of why certain peoples of the empire could not be given self-government or democratic freedoms.[29] As Mangan sug-

gests of colonial stereotypes in general, such images functioned precisely to order and make sense of the world, to facilitate a 'perceptual
blindness' that protects a society from complexities and information
'likely to produce stress.' They arise out of 'a culture's need to have
control over its world,' since no matter how this control is manifested
– political power, social status, economic domination – 'invariably it
establishes an appropriate vocabulary and set of verbal images depicting significant *difference*.' For it is this difference that threatens order,
security, social solidarity, and control.[30] The icon of the infantilized
native could also be used as a prescriptive counter-example: morality,
discipline, and a work ethic were lacking in the 'pickaninnies' because
of their racial background; they were, in a word, degenerate. If working-class children did not grow up to be moral, disciplined, and good
workers, were they not equally racially degenerate and unworthy of
English citizenship?

The depiction of the non-European 'other' could indeed be very
much an equivocal one. This is more clearly evident in another common narrative device used to keep the child's attention: the inversion
of the subject and object roles in the text. Instead of child readers
having the 'other' described to them, the 'other' explained himself or
herself to the child reader directly, or described the reader of the book
from the 'other's' perspective. In the second volume of the 1894 *Arnold's
Geography Readers*, for example, a section entitled 'Children of Other
Lands' had a 'Little Chinese' boy poke fun at the cultural habits of the
white man:

A white man, who came here to teach us about God, said that our country
was the queerest in the world. He said that we do everything the wrong way.

Of course he was wrong and we are right, only it was not polite to tell him
so. He said that our books began where they should end, and read backward;
that our workmen should stand and not sit at their work; that we should take
off our caps and keep on our shoes when we enter a room.

He must have come from a queer country, for he laughed when I shook my
own hand. He thought I should shake his.

He did not know how to drink tea. He wished to spoil it by mixing it with
milk and sugar.

This passage certainly reinforced notions of racial difference and superiority. The rhetorical 'Little Chinese' stresses the queerness of the
white man, and yet, for the child reader, it is the habits of the Chinese

that would seem exotic and strange. Indeed, the gulf between the Chinese and Europeans is highlighted by this mode of presentation, which takes things undoubtedly familiar to the child – milk and sugar in tea; the reading of books (like the one in their hands); the doffing of caps and shaking of hands; and standing when working – and inverts them. Taking familiar and common experiences and calling them strange is not likely to produce a response that would question 'our' habits and the 'queerness of us,' but would highlight the strangeness of 'them,' of 'how funny *they* must be.' Such a manoeuvre naturalized 'our' custom. This attitude was further conditioned to the point of revulsion, given prevailing English cultural mores, when the child reader found out from the same 'Little Chinese' that his food was 'mostly rice; but we eat such animals as rats, kittens, and little dogs.'[31]

There is, however, another way in which this passage perhaps ought to be read. For this passage also resonates with the long tradition of calling upon an 'other' to point out the ills of one's own society, and using an outsider to suggest a different, better example. In particular, this passage invokes the convention inherent in Addison's eighteenth-century notion of the 'polished Oriental' coming to London and re-flecting on the way in which Europeans behaved. The passage could have been used as a means of pointing out the virtues of politeness, 'proper' work ethics, and social deference. Presumptions about the proper way for working-class children to deport themselves – doffing of caps, standing at work – are highlighted with the admonishment about interference from a superior, as in the 'Little Chinese boy's' phrase 'it was not polite to tell him so.' Such a reading contrasts with viewing this 'other' strictly in terms of imperialism, and/or the missionary's overweening zeal to change Chinese customs. Of course, the belief that the Chinese (and Japanese) were better behaved than Europeans was still a stereotype, but it is one which social prescrip-tions about the deficiencies of the domestic order might be expressed without critiquing British society directly.

A marked degree of ambivalence in the depiction of the Chinese and their culture is itself evident in the extent and depth of reading-book discussions of the Chinese generally, perhaps reflecting the fact that, formally at least, China remained outside of the empire. Few other native cultures or 'races' outside of the empire were even men-tioned in school readers. The somewhat esoteric dwelling on the 'Chinaman' must surely have been because he was commonly viewed as a mysterious figure, and China as an exotic and puzzling place that had resisted English or European control.[32] For example, in one 1886 reader it was stated, 'There lives a wonderful race of men called the Chinese. Ten times as many as live in our country. And the funny thing about them is that they are all alike, so that you cannot tell one from another. They are yellow men. How would you like to be yellow? They all do their hair in the same queer way. They cut all of it off except in one place at the back of their heads.'[33] Once again, in this capsule description, the strangeness of the people (they are 'queer' and 'funny') was put in terms of their difference from the white English 'norm.' The direct questioning of the child reader ('how would you like to be yellow') stressed the physical distinction between 'them' and 'us.' White children might be able to wear their hair in the described 'queer' way, but this fashion was unavoidably linked to an 'inferior' culture and understood in the context of the stereotypical phrase 'they all look the same.' The answer to the question was clearly expected to be a negative. Yet, despite the attempt to produce a sense of their exotic disposition, this account still refers to the Chinese as a 'wonderful race,' a positive appellation that indicates a grudging respect or admiration.

The closed demeanour of the Chinese, their independence, and their collective eschewal of European customs, religion, and trade were likely responsible for the uneasy juxtapositions of cautious and admiring descriptions of Chinese culture with the traditional negative stereotypes applied to an 'inferior people.' This binary presentation of the Chinese, while sometimes hinting at the need to be vigilant with regards to them as a potential 'yellow peril,'[34] nevertheless assured the reader that the mysterious Chinaman was ultimately not a serious threat to the British Empire and its subjects.

Non-white native cultures *within* the empire, meanwhile, were depicted as 'other' in a variety of ways in school reading books. It is through the distinctive representations of different groups that we again see the necessary corollaries to the cultural construction of otherness, that of interdependence, and domestic social prescription. For although the white English child was considered the norm to which every other race or culture was compared, and to which everyone else was ultimately depicted as inferior, there was clearly an evident hierarchy of racial types and a range of attitudes towards imperial native subjects. In one sense, the maintenance of a proper sense of order was key to many of the descriptions of the non-white 'other,' precisely because they were frequently placed within the context of discussions of the British Empire. As Kiernan has suggested, 'order was from first to last the grand imperial watchword,'[35] a dictum that applied not only to the practical ruling of the empire, but also to its representation at home. As it was the indisputable destiny of the English to expand into, conquer, and rule other parts of the world, so too was it necessary to demonstrate the dependence of the native peoples of the empire on the imperial centre. The various peoples of the empire were simultaneously 'other' – and clearly inferior – to the English, and yet also part of 'the most glorious Empire the world had ever seen.' English imperial-nationalism *required* an acknowledgment of these people as both 'others' and dependants. The visual illustration found in the opening pages of the third volume of the 1896 *Britannia Geography Readers* graphically depicts this necessary interdependence. In this pictorial representation of the empire, four images of the aboriginal peoples found within India, Africa, Canada, and Australia surround a picture of the Houses of Parliament. Britain, the 'mother country' and centre of the empire, is represented by a building symbolic of its institutions and government. The various areas of the empire are symbolized not by buildings or landmarks of their own, but by 'lesser races,' wearing their 'native' dress. The symbolic implications of this arrangement are twofold: first, the whole tradition of English/British national politics and culture and its evolution over many centuries is contrasted with the barbaric simplicity of the subject peoples of the empire; second, the interdependent nature of the relationship between the subject races on the margins and the civilizing centre is depicted through the image of the 'Mother of all Parliaments' and the diverse peoples under its benevolent sway.

A better sense of how imperial classification and its significance for how the middle-class authors viewed English society can be fleshed out if we examine how three non-white 'native' groups from within the boundaries of the late-Victorian empire – subcontinental Indians, Australian Aborigines, and New Zealand Maori – were depicted in the common reading material of elementary schooling. The newly ascendant language of evolutionary and social Darwinistic theory allowed peoples to be ranked according to their state of 'civilization' and 'evolutionary development.' This procedure was somewhat complex and not without its contradictions. In general, distinctions of colour and attainment of civilization largely seemed to correspond: the In-

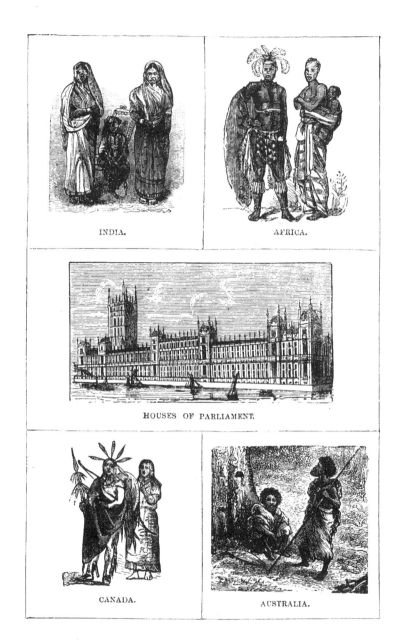

'The Empire,' from *Britannia Geography Readers* III (Edward Arnold 1896), 4.
Reprint permission granted by the British Library.

dian was judged to have achieved the highest level of civilization, the Maori was viewed as somewhat less advanced, and the Australian Aborigine was given by far the lowest status.

A variety of reasons can be detected in the differing treatment given various 'subject' races in school books. For example, received knowledge about ancient Indian civilization, the affinities between European languages and Sanskrit, the extended length of contact between the Indian subcontinent and Europe, and the importance of India to the substance and image of the empire all predisposed the British to view the Indian peoples in a different light from the other 'savage' and 'barbarous' races of the southern hemisphere. However, as we shall see, the relationships among the three groups of people and the British were not nearly as unequivocal as they might appear on the surface. For instance, while it was conceded that Indians had attained a state of civilization, they were depicted as a 'docile,' 'passive,' and 'dependent' race, and hence were essentially feminized as well as infantilized. The Maori, meanwhile, though still 'barbarous,' were depicted overwhelmingly as a vigorous, 'manly' race, and were in some ways much more *admired* by the British than were the Indians. The Aborigine, having failed to develop anything even approaching civilization, was denied either a masculine, feminine, or even infantile character, but rather was represented as a degraded savage, so low on the evolutionary scale as to be barely human at all. The implicit purposes and significance of these variations provide some clues as to the various domestic prescriptions that informed these views of the world beyond the everyday experience of the working-class child, and so we shall explore the significance of each of these depictions in turn.

Imperial India and Infantilized Indians

The relationship between the peoples of India and the English was complicated by earlier prevailing views about common linguistic origins. Because of the research of the mid-nineteenth-century philologists, and their work on Sanskrit, some texts suggested that subcontinent Indians were a race distantly related to white Europeans. In such instances, however, 'corrupting' influences – usually framed within what Edward Said has traced as the discourse of 'Orientalism'[36] – and ideas about wholesale racial degeneration were proposed as factors that had led to the lower racial status of the Indian. In this mass of claim and counter-claim, the blurring of the contemporary definition of race becomes apparent. Discussions of common origin in some texts invoked race as a marker of only linguistic similarity. They pointed to the fact of tremendous racial diversity within the Indian subcontinent itself. Other books resorted to climatic theories of race, or made biological distinctions between the peoples of the south and those of the north. The degradation of the Indian races and the decline of their civilization were sometimes explained as the result of millennia of invasions and 'cross breeding.'[37] As one text noted, 'The mass of the population is of a dark aboriginal stock, and the proportion of Hindus to Muhammadans varies in a perplexing way ... In Bengal even more than in other parts of India it would be a gross error to imagine that Hindus must be the original Aryans, and Musalmans the descendants of foreign invaders.'[38] The classroom reading books of the end of the nineteenth century were exactly like their formal textbook counterparts in their disdain for the riot of competing linguistic and religious groupings that was the result of the Indian 'racial' medley. Racial diversity and a degree of historical racial intermixing were sometimes blamed for the *reversal* of evolutionary progress. The threat of the racial and/or moral degeneration of a race – in the case of the Indian, a once proud and powerful people – was therefore presented.

Within the confines of racial discourse, considerations of the peoples of the subcontinent frequently began with an account of their former 'greatness,' followed by some generalizations on their 'decline.' Initially, Indians were thought to have been a 'manful' race who 'wrote thoughtful books' and made 'wise laws.' Over time, however, the 'Hindoos degenerated, grew cowardly and superstitious,' and developed effete and effeminate characteristics that prevented them from defending their homeland from marauding invaders. This decline was occasionally explained in terms of the effect of a particular climate on the composite character of the race. In the volume on India in *Macmillan's Geographical Series*, Henry Blanford explained that the primary cause of the degeneration in the racial character of the Indian was the hot and humid climate of the Indian peninsula, which sapped the population's vigour. In a similar vein, *The Raleigh Geography Readers* noted that 'to live in warm, damp air softens both body and mind. So rich people in India are not ashamed to grow fat and lazy, while the poor, who have to work as well as they can, lose their spirit, and would like to be idle if they could.' Such views harkened back to Enlightenment notions of climatic determinism, and suggested that race was historically mutable and not biologically essential. And yet such views often sat side by side with clear assertions of the immutability of race, as when India was referred to as a 'curious jumble of races' that did not mix because it would be like mixing 'oil and vinegar.'[39]

Regardless of these contradictions about the mutability of race, such explanations implicitly feminized and/or infantilized native Indians and contained implicit social prescriptions. While certain groups had retained something of their 'manliness' (the Sikhs and northern Muslims, for instance), the vast majority were 'timid,' 'superstitious,' 'weak,' and 'dependent' when compared to the governing British.[40] Even the distinction between the light-skinned northern 'Aryan' races and the darker-skinned people of southern India was commonly marked in terms of gendered language: 'The people of India are not all of one race, nor do they all speak one language ... In the north the people are tall, fair, manly, strong, and warlike; in the south, slight, dark and timid.'[41] No doubt such distinctions were made in accordance with the theory that Europeans were distantly related to the 'Aryans' of the northwestern parts of India (particularly, Punjab, Sind, and Rajputana),[42] but also probably because these northern peoples demonstrated more resistance to British rule than any other group within the boundaries of the Indian Empire. Exactly who was considered worthy of the designation 'manly, strong, and warlike' was never consistent, however, since, as another reader put it, 'the fact is that the Bengalees, with whom we had first to do were so slavish and timid that any bold soldier among them would be like a dog driving a flock of sheep.' If the majority of Indians were not 'manly,' equally they were not yet adults, and perhaps never would be. Compared to the mature English, all the Indian peoples were considered to be at an early stage of their 'schooling' in development: they were 'stuck at the ABC of civilization.'[43]

Of course, in another sense, elementary schoolchildren were also learning the 'ABC' of their 'own' civilization. Positing the Indian at an early stage of the civilization alphabet simultaneously suggested dependence on their English 'masters' for further instruction – indicating a use of a discourse of race that allowed for future development – and the necessity of English working-class schoolchildren to learn their own 'place' in the order of things. Moreover, the fact that India had once had a worthy civilization, and that racial degeneration was caused by a combination of climate and 'innate' factors or proclivities, could also be read as a cautionary prescription: 'When the peoples of Europe were still ignorant barbarians' Indians 'made wise laws, and could defend themselves manfully as well as obey their rulers, qualities without which there cannot be a great nation.' But 'by and by the Hindoos degenerated' and 'could no longer keep to themselves the rich country that tempted invaders.'[44] Racial degeneration and effeminacy were somehow related. The ability to defend 'manfully' one's nation was posited as the characteristic of a vigorous race. Needless to say, the English did not suffer from the debilitating effects of a tropical climate, as geographical accounts of the British Isles were sure to stress – sometimes in direct contrast to areas such as India.[45] Such a direct comparison was also frequently encouraged by teachers' manuals of method: 'We can depict the qualities of each race; we can clearly show the dependence of its new advance on its geographical conditions; but we must also keep in mind the necessity of a previous state of culture in order to allow the geographical conditions to become operative.'[46] As another manual remarked, it was vital that children be made to see that 'nations are influenced very largely by the physical conditions of the areas they occupy.' Since England had 'a temperate climate' it had become a powerful nation. Indeed, '[n]o nationality has ever developed first-rate rank under either tropical or arctic conditions.'[47]

Keeping such exhortations in mind, then, it became clear that elementary schoolchildren were doubly privileged: they were of English heritage and they lived in a locale and climate that allowed them to succeed as a race. And should the implications of the socio-economic context of such a message be missed, one teachers' instruction manual spelt it out:

It is quite possible, too, that by the time boys now finishing their schooling are middle-aged men, the Eastern nations, with their great supply of cheap labour, may be our great manufacturing rivals. Is it well that the ordinary Englishman should, as he too often does, interpret the motives of all other nations, even Oriental nations, as if they were Englishmen? Cannot he learn about these nations to know at least the need of caution in forming his opinions as to their probable actions and feelings?[48]

It was clearly incumbent on schoolchildren not to squander their advantages, but to strive to live worthily, to accept their position in society, and if possible better themselves. And it was also incumbent on teachers to make sure that children understood the stakes involved. If the working classes slipped into racial degeneration, if they allowed themselves to become slothful, lazy, and vicious and not learn the 'ABCS' of civilization – as had the Oriental nations – then they risked passing the economic advantage over to those people, who might 'catch up.' Economic prosperity in the future thus meant learning the lessons of failure of past civilizations. And unlike the elite schools and universities, wherein the model societies of the Greeks and Romans were still the main examples, the lessons for working-class children were to be drawn from the now subordinated peoples of the empire.

The treatment of Indians in these texts was usually more comprehensive than that accorded other subject races within the empire, no doubt because of the more than two hundred years of British imperial activity in the subcontinent prior to the time that these books were written. Indeed, the empire loomed large in accounts of India and of Indians as a people. In a very real sense, representations of 'The Indian' were constructs entirely dependent on the interrelationship of the British and the natives of the subcontinent, abstracted from the historical context of their interactions. The Indian was consequently depicted as a curious mixture of docility, timidity, and passivity on the surface, with a latent 'treacherous,' 'untrustworthy,' 'fanatical,' 'ferocious,' 'cunning,' and 'cruel' persona lurking just below this surface.[49] This latent 'treachery' in the idealized Indian's character became manifest in the two events of the Indian past most widely reported and described in the school history, literary, and geography readers of the turn of the century: the Black Hole of Calcutta and the 1857 Mutiny.

Katherine Castle has demonstrated how events such as the Black Hole and 1857 Mutiny were totally decontextualized in history textbooks, since they provided no account of why figures such as Suraj-u-Doulah or the Sepoys in 1857 were in conflict with the British.[50] The same is true of all the various types of reading books of this period. Imprisonment in the Black Hole was depicted as being unjust entirely because English individuals were subjected to an Indian despot, and not because of the situation or any actions on the part of any historical figures, whether English or Indian. The event was depicted in entirely ahistorical terms: it was mythologized as an evil wrong perpetrated by 'them' against 'us.' The important symbolism of this parable was reinforced by the mysterious manner of the injustice. For not only were the English imprisoned, they were subjected to treatment beyond the boundaries of any English experience. An extremely common refrain was that the suffering of the victims of the pernicious

Suraj-u-Doulah was too appalling to describe, they were so changed by their 'one night's suffering, that not even their best friends would have known them.'[51] Significantly, this 'unspeakable' anguish stands in marked contrast to the extremely graphic descriptions of other historical tortures and punishments, carried out by other natives and by the British themselves, that are gleefully provided elsewhere in these texts.

The sparking of youthful imaginations with images of tortures 'that no pen could describe' was, in fact, an effective way of demonizing the abstract 'Indian.' Castle has usefully pointed to the depiction of the Black Hole in history textbooks as focusing on the 'evil' character of Suraj-u-Doulah. In the majority of readers this particular Indian prince became the very archetype of the 'treacherous Indian.' As Castle herself concludes, the icon of the treacherous Indian prince became a composite figure demonstrating the Indian native's inherent cruelty, emotional and moral licence, lack of manliness, and disregard for human life. His failings were thus 'indicative of the shortcomings of Indian leadership.'[52] It is within the mould of this figure that the subsequent actions of *all* Indian individuals in conflict with colonial rule could be placed. Descriptions of 'trouble in India' immediately brought about the complete inversion of the image of the docile and dependent Indians who remained subservient to their imperial rulers. Whatever their grievance, any conflict with the English brought to the surface the dangerous latent potential for treachery that lurked beneath the apparent calm of the Indian Empire.

Consequently, we find in accounts of the other great conflict story of British imperialism in India, the 1857 Mutiny, the same language of 'latent treacherousness' and 'unimaginable horrors' employed to depict the Sepoy mutineers and their actions, which being both fanatical and ferocious, were 'too horrible to be described.'[53] The 'horrors' of that 'awful' and 'dreadful' time, although never explicitly detailed, were ones that the protagonists would apparently never forget. The immediacy of the danger was further emphasized by the reminder that 'there are men and women alive today who were children in Lucknow. They remember the awful time of the Mutiny as if it was yesterday.'[54] The device of relating the events in terms of childhood experience could be a powerful one. In this case it was of the order of 'look how lucky we are' compared to our forebears, since it was they who had to endure and subdue the great treachery that was manifested in the Mutiny. It implied, in fact, that the events had a direct impact on the lives of ordinary men and women in England, as well as having repercussions in India. The consequences of the Mutiny were the normalization of British rule over India and the convergence of imperial affairs with considerations of what it was to be English. While the Mutiny was depicted as an aberration, and not part of the normal relationship between the British and Indians, it was nevertheless a lesson in the nature of the Indian's essential character and an apprehensive warning to future generations. This illustrates what Homi Bhabha has suggested for colonial stereotypes in general, that iconographic images like that of 'The Indian' were inherently unstable – as anxious as they were assertive.[55]

The 'Manly' Maori

In contrast to the basically Orientalist depiction of the Indian, the representation of the Maori peoples of New Zealand in school books was very much in the 'noble savage' vein of eighteenth-century travel descriptions. There seems little doubt that they were one of the 'lesser races' most admired by the British in the late-Victorian period. The adjectives used to describe the Maori in readers included 'noble,' 'brave,' 'skilled,' 'fine,' 'strong,' 'active,' 'well-shaped,' 'handsome,' 'intelligent,' and 'superior to the majority of barbarous races.'[56] The *Avon Geographical Readers* provided a typical description of the Maori people in 1895:

Of all the people whom we call savages, they were, perhaps, as we found them, the most civilized. They lived in houses; had stone weapons and tools of their own; cooked their food with fire; stored up food so that want and famine were uncommon; had a system of laws; and treated their wives well; but they ate their foes when they could kill or catch them.

They are an active people; the men average 5'6" in height, and are almost equal in strength and weight to Englishmen. In their former condition they wore matting; now they wear European clothes; formerly they pulled out their beards and were tattooed; now they wear beards and the young are not tattooed.

They have never learnt our language; on the contrary, they have compelled many people in New Zealand to learn theirs; but now they are melting away. A remnant of them still dwells around the lakes of the North Island.[57]

Almost all descriptions, like the one above, noted the physical appearance of the Maori in positive terms, and many commented on the skills of Maori carvers and craftsmen and on their seafaring and military prowess. But the attributes that seemed most to have impressed reader writers were the well-developed systems of Maori law and private property, their 'civilized' treatment of women, and their adoption of certain western ways (including Christianity), while managing to retain a stubborn independence, symbolized by the careful guarding of their language and their tradition of martial excellence. Of course, this view of the Maori, while containing a touch of admiration, held none of the earlier view of the 'noble savage' as being a guide to virtue. In effect, the Maori were still 'savages' and were always designated as being of a lower order than Europeans. The mild admiration for them held by English school writers stemmed from a belief that the Maori had independently come to demonstrate many of the character traits, and even proto-developed some of the institutions, that the English cherished or *should* cherish of themselves. Domestic social prescription is again evident here: the Maori were thought to be diligent, thrifty, decorous in their interpersonal relations, obedient of laws, and held private property as sacred.

Reader authors made exceptions for, and even justified, those Maori vices that in the representation of other cultures were routinely used for the purpose of demonization and condemnation. In particular, the supposed proclivity of some Maori tribes to practise cannibalism was downplayed and glossed over, or even accorded somewhat sympathetic justifications of 'having been tempted to become [cannibals] by the great scarcity of animal food' and that they 'believed that the character of a brave warrior passed to the person who ate the flesh.'[58] Other accounts stressed that the Maori had given up 'other savage customs': that with the taking up of Christianity they were even closer to becoming truly civilized.[59] Given time, the Maori might progress beyond their savagery and further develop a civic society, although within this ideology there was no chance of their ever becoming the true equals of the white Europeans. Nevertheless, the respect given the Maori was significant, and it accents another of the functions of the differential construction of otherness. The somewhat favourable depiction of the Maori helped to put into context for the child the trouble that the British experienced in subduing them – troubles that they would no doubt come across in their history reading. The Maori, although clearly 'other,' were sufficiently imbued with the positive attributes of English civilization to be a tough opponent. As with the treatments accorded the Afghans and Zulus, there was a subtext of grudging admiration in many of the readers for any people who successfully resisted (if only temporarily) British imperial expansion.[60] These were people who demonstrated 'manly' independence and resourcefulness, something that should be cultivated among the lower · orders of England, lest dependency and effeteness drag them, and the rest of the society, backwards down the evolutionary scale. Moreover, it heightened the sense of British achievement in bringing New Zealand into the imperial orbit, and emphasized the value and worthiness of having made the effort in the first place. The majesty and wealth that had accrued from the largely peaceful British domination of India demonstrated one side of the English imperial character: the perceived English proclivity for trade and good government; the conquering of worthy adversaries, such as the advanced warrior race of the Maori, pointed to another, namely the myth of British martial excellence, and chivalrous conduct to a defeated but worthy opponent. In both cases, examples could be made of positive and negative characteristics found in other races.

The 'Lowly' Aborigine

No such sympathy or admiration was bestowed on those at the bottom of the racial hierarchy, the 'lowly' Australian Aborigines. In most accounts the Aborigine rated among the 'lowest races' of the entire world, and descriptions of Aborigines typically commented on their physical 'ugliness,' 'wild savagery,' 'unintelligence,' resistance to western civilization and the male Aborigines' 'abominable' treatment of their own wives and children.[61] The contrast between the Maori and Aborigine in these readers is quite striking. One telling example of the different treatment accorded the two cultures was the complete dismissal of the Australian native's craft, martial and survival skills, characteristics of the Maori that had been highly praised. The use of the boomerang, for instance, was not an indication that the Aborigines were an intelligent people. Instead, the failure or lack of desire to 'learn the arts of civilization' was heartily condemned.[62] Indeed, far from praising the skill with which the Aborigine crafted uniquely skilled hunting weapons, it was noted that although 'the weapons of the Australian natives are much better than their other implements,' this was not impressive, because 'killing is the science to which a savage gives most attention.'[63] Thus, whereas the male Maori was praised for his warrior prowess and finely made weapons, the Aborigine was derided for his ingenuity in the 'science' of killing.

Another clear difference between the representations of the Maori and the Aborigine was in the matter-of-fact way in which the population decline of the Australian Aboriginal peoples after contact with Europeans was noted. The precipitous decline in the numbers of the Maori was, to a degree, accorded some sympathy. *The Warwick History Readers* noted the 'sad sentences' of a Maori proverb: 'As the white man's rat has killed our rat, so the European fly is driving our fly away. As foreign clover is killing our ferns, so the Maori himself will disappear before the white man.'[64] Similarly, the *Royal Osborne Geography Readers* lamented the 'doomed' future of the Maori peoples. The extinction of the Maori people was viewed as more or less inevitable, but none the less regrettable. Such simple statements about extinction carried very different connotations in discussions of the Australian Aborigine. A geography reader from 1900 provided a conventional comment on the subject of native population decline: 'The Black Fellow is fast disappearing before the onward march of the white man, and in a few years will probably be extinct.'[65] In this case, the simple 'facts of life' of racial extinction were mediated by the extremely low opinion held by the British of the Australian Aboriginal peoples. Whereas the Maori, for all their savagery, were resourceful and independent, had adapted to some of the white man's ways, and had resisted others in a noble and manly manner, the Aborigines were 'degraded and debased,' neither resisting nor learning from their new British masters. Their relationship to the white settlers was, to many authors, one of irrelevance, and as such, their demise ought not to be considered by the schoolchildren reading about them as a great loss to humanity. One reader from 1899 explained:

We found this vast country inhabited by a peculiar race of savages, who, in many respects are among the lowest of the human race. The 'Blackfellows,' as they were nicknamed by the settlers, are rather dark brown, with thick hair, and a coating of grease and dirt that hides the natural colour of the skin. Herded together in wandering tribes, they have no fields or villages, and only faint ideas of religion, government, or comfort. They go naked as willingly as not, unless they can get blankets or cast-off clothes from the white people ...

The men, too, are often seen to be strangely marked, in accordance with their savage practices and notions of ornament. The common punishment among them is to run spears through the fleshy part of the offender's arms and legs, so that one given to thieving bears all his life signs of this bad character.[66]

In this text the Australian native was considered akin to livestock 'herded' together, and of so primitive a state as to be 'still' indulging in such 'barbarous' practices as body piercing (a common, yet largely ignored practice of the Maori as well). It was consistently doubted whether the Aborigines could ever join the ranks of 'civilized man' – whether, indeed, they should be considered as cannibals at best. But even this account was more sympathetic than most, for it at least did not depict the native Australians as being a positive threat to the white settlers. Their demise was a simple fact of the 'natural law' according to which the less worthy race died out before the advances of the more worthy one.[67]

Some authors were much more strident in their views about Aboriginal population decline. John Finnemore's *Black's Literary Readers* (1906) was a typical example of the more uncompromising view, suggesting that it was a 'good thing' that the Aboriginal peoples were in decline. Such an outlook was justifiable, suggested Finnemore, because of the very savage and barbaric nature of the Australian native race. Finnemore indulged in extremely hostile negative stereotyping of the Aborigines:

'Blackfellows' hunt in the bush, and fish in the rivers, and some of them are very dangerous. They will kill any white people who fall into their hands.

The first white men who landed on the shores of Australia found that the blacks were not to be trusted. Sometimes the blacks would attack the boats ... The blackfellow is a very low form of savage. He cannot learn so well as blacks in other lands. He only counts up to five. After that he uses a term which means many.

The blackfellows are very cruel to their women, the gins. The women have to do all the hard work, and carry all the loads. Even then they do not escape the cruel blows from the waddy, a big heavy stick. At times of great hunger, the blackfellow has been known to kill and eat his own children.[68]

In Finnemore's view the Australian native peoples were a positive menace to white civilization, demonstrated not only by their antipathy to the white settlers, but also in their treatment of each other. He touched on just about all the areas in which condemnation could be marshalled against another race: cannibalism (of one's own children, no less, a horror that probably redoubled on itself when it is considered that this text was intended for children); horrendous and 'unmanly' treatment of women; undisciplined violence; antipathy to the benefits of white civilization; no outward signs of 'intelligence'; and an absence of any morals or decent values such as honesty. With seemingly no chance of redemption – the Australian being less able to advance than even other black natives – the sooner they died out the better it was for all concerned. It was beyond the bounds of Edwardian morality to advocate the active aiding in the extinction of such a race. But the best that could be done for them, another text indicated, was to protect them from outright oppression and let nature take its course, since 'the country which they inhabit must eventually become a white man's land.'[69]

Allotted no sympathy, no admiration, nor even a sense that they were either once or ever could be a worthy race, the Aboriginal peoples of Australia were thus represented as merely a hindrance to progress and the spread of English-led civilization. This particular construction of otherness fed back on the self-characterization of the imagined English themselves: as just, noble, and forthright in their relationships with imperial native groups. It was also a domestic social lesson. The Aborigine was depicted as less than fully human, but the common refrain in these descriptions was that the Aborigine would not learn or adapt to civilized society. The fate of any people who would not learn or adapt was dictated by social Darwinian precepts. They were weak, and unwilling or unable to change. Far better, it was suggested, to allow the British settlers in Australia to sweep them aside and to build a society worthy of their original English homeland. The Aborigine was thus the least *necessary* of the imperial native groups discussed here. Yet their representation confirmed the general construction of race types present throughout school books. The lowest physical type was correlated to the lowest moral type and thus had the least human 'worth.' Students in the elementary school, reading about the debased life of the Aborigine, would no doubt see themselves as further up the evolutionary ladder. But without 'civilization,' without respect for the laws, without developing the proper attitudes towards their peers and social superiors, might not they too slip back down into the 'ABCS' of civilization and be pushed aside in the onward march of racial destiny?

5

'The Home of the Race': The Familial Imaginings of National Identity in Elementary Schooling

The need of elevating domestic duties and of dignifying home life is considered urgent, and many teachers regret that only a small number of girls enjoy the advantages of lessons in practical cookery and other housewifery operations.

Alice Ravenhill, 'Moral Instruction and the Training of Girls in Elementary Schools in England,' in M.E. Sadler, ed., *Moral Instruction and Training in Schools* 1 (1908)

The language of 'family' and of 'home' seems to have been seen by turn-of-the-century educationalists as especially appropriate for children. Images of family, of home, and of mothers were frequently used as signifiers of belonging by elementary educationalists especially when demonstrating ideas of national continuity. They were used to help explain abstract concepts such as the 'nation,' and to demonstrate the hard-to-describe sentiment of national loyalty, by imparting a 'natural' or Promethean sense of the social order and of collective identity. In the vocabulary of family and home in the elementary classroom we consequently witness the intersection of social, gender, and pedagogical ideologies within a consciously national discourse.

A simple example of the deployment of these types of metaphors and narratives can be found in a volume of Nelson's 1909 *Royal School Series*, wherein the historical nature of English place names was prefaced with the assertions that 'the dearest word in the English language is the word "home"' and that 'no other language has a word which means exactly the same thing' as 'home.' When thinking of 'home' the English cannot but have 'tender thoughts' because the '"home" carries with it the idea of a family bond.' It is this bond, the reader continues, that has united the English for centuries, and thus exploring the English sense of home had much to 'teach us about our forefathers.'[1] Given a privileged status and explicitly connected to a sense of Englishness in reading books, the English idea of home implied both a sense of natural order and a genealogical and historical rootedness. In this particular case, this passage on the 'dearest word in the English language' preceded discussion of old English place names. Associating the word home with Anglo-Saxon rural settlements posited the Anglo-Saxons and the rural environment as the quintessential roots of the modern English.

The opening lines of *The Waterloo Citizen Reader* demonstrate the sometimes prescriptive connection made between a highly structured ideal of home and its correlative, family, and a stable overarching social order. Despite the 'constant growth of individual obligation' the resilience of the family over the course of history had proved that most societies were evolved through 'the patriarchal model.' And the 'life of a typical home of to-day gives us an image of the State and its functions true enough to serve as a starting point.' For it was the father who 'regulates the family life, he it is who reconciles the clashing of interests of the members of the household, he it is who preserves peace, sees that all have their rights, and sees that all do their several duties.' According to the author the result of this arrangement was the greatest happiness possible for each member of the family. This sort of analogy was not new. However, by the end of the century the social concern that was operative in such accounts tended to be phrased in terms of the overall national well-being. For, just as the rhetoric of 'good citizenship' tended to be used to cloak prescriptions of social deference, so too the ideal of the familial home as a place where the collective good came before that of the individual was used as a metaphor that telescoped familial duty up to the larger community of the nation itself. Thus, just as 'cheerfully obeying' the rules of the family household promoted the happiness of the family as a whole, taking care to do 'work in the best possible way' and remembering to do all the duties required by the state ensured the happiness of all the nation.[2]

Arnold-Forster pointed to this same social context when he explained that 'at home it is sometimes your duty to deny yourself some amusement or advantage for the sake of your mother or sisters; or again, as you may possibly have to suffer some pain or inconvenience for their good; so it often becomes the duty of men and women, when they grow up, to deny themselves advantages, to suffer loss or pain, not that their own friends and relations among whom they live may be the better, but that all the people of this country may gain, that England may do what is just and right.'[3] When the nation was symbolized as a home, everyone had his or her own special place, roles, responsibilities, and duties. It was both hierarchical and interdependent and functioned for the benefit of all so long as everyone knew and kept their station, and was willing to accept the necessary sacrifices that such (extended) familial ties required.

Pointing to the nation as an extended family and explaining the role of the individual in terms of his or her responsibilities to 'siblings,' 'motherland,' and 'forefathers' were clearly not narrative devices new to this period. Like the organistic and anatomic metaphors of society also sometimes used in school books, antecedents of this kind of rhetoric can be found in texts from the medieval and early modern periods.[4] Nonetheless, the type of familial metaphors and narratives used in the promotion of an inclusive national community between 1880 and 1914 are striking, and as they interacted with other messages invoking ideas about race and citizenship, an analysis of their construction can shed more light on the ways in which social and gender ideologies were incorporated into and helped shape the nationalist narratives presented to elementary schoolchildren.

Such an analysis effectively puts into doubt the claim that English/British 'civic-legal' style nationalism was always of a qualitatively different order than East European 'ethnic' style nationalism. The basis of English nationality was conceived not only as racial/ancestral, but also through reference to the primordial and unbreakable bonds of familial attachment. Thus, although at the level of political theory a distinction between eastern- and western-style nationalisms may be ascertainable, and even though there was certainly a degree of the civic conception of nationality in the prevailing notions of citizenship, in the education given the children of the English masses such a hard distinction was not sustained. Educationalists and the professional school-book authors suggested that the national community should be bound together by an amalgam of ethnic and family ties to which the civil-legal traditions were merely an accompaniment. Along with myths about common racial ancestry, the implied sense of 'blood' relationships among the English was symbolically represented to children through a host of metaphors and narrative devices playing on familial themes. Indeed, familial metaphor and racial discourse often intersected in constructions such as 'racial motherhood' – which was a particularly potent attempt to draw women into a sense of national duty and responsibility. Civic-legal definitions of the nation, while clearly advanced, were more abstract than notions of blood ties and family duties, particularly for those sections of the population (half the male labouring population and all women) who were still deprived of many of the political-legal trappings of nationality and citizenship.

Given that late-nineteenth-century notions of the family and the family home were structured around notions of the proper ordering of gender difference, a second important reason for dissecting the familial metaphors of national belonging is that it illuminates the other half of the story regarding how gender ideology was incorporated into and cross-cut the meanings of national identity promoted to working-class and lower-middle-class children. In particular, we can see how in these books women were incorporated into the overall nationalist narrative, and also explore how the construction of a domestic femininity was suggested as the appropriate correlative of civic masculinity. This last aim is particularly important, as there is a danger of focusing on the role of masculinity alone as the ideal by which English/British national identity was transmitted to children – a tendency that has surfaced in much recent writing on the domestic impact of late-Victorian and Edwardian imperialism.[5] This has been the result of concentrating only on the masculinist nature of the contemporary imperial-nationalist discourse. It has become fashionable to argue that a 'British imperial identity' was, in the decades straddling Victoria's death, increasingly constructed around a race and class-specific image of predatory masculinity, or 'imperial manhood.' There is, indeed, something to this idea of an imperial masculinity, which, defined as a political category as well as a personal and social identity, offered 'privileged access to social resources and the concomitant capacity and duty to exercise control over the self and an array of inferior Others, such as women, children, colonized people, foreigners, or even animals and the natural world.'[6] But as Laura Tabili has stressed, explanations of this process of masculine identity construction, 'with its recourse to a Manichean Other that embodied those characteristics excluded from the masculine ideal,' must also include an acknowledgment of the symbiotic connections joining such binary oppositions as masculine and feminine, Occidental and Oriental, 'man' and 'nature.' The elementary school was not an elite all-male preserve, after all, and the proper school training of the working-class girl was thought to be every bit as indispensable for the future good of the nation as was that of the children of the upper and middle classes and the working-class boy.

The conceptions of professional middle-class educationalists and authors regarding appropriate masculine and feminine roles within society both helped constitute and had a reflexive effect on the expression of their nationalist imaginings in this period.[7] Incorporated into the general purposes of elementary schooling, these imaginings were universalized: what these educationalists and authors believed was naturally 'right' and 'proper' came to be prescribed by them as appropriate for all elements of society. This is not to say that actual working-class gender/social roles developed solely out of the prescriptions of middle-class educationalists, scientists, and authors.[8] It is also certainly not the case that contemporary gender ideology, consciousness of social status, and nationalist ideology fit together as a seamless or uncontradictory whole. Rather, it is suggested here that the cultural construction of national identity within the classroom relied upon, and helped reinforce, wider social perceptions of gender difference and the belief that there was an obligation to subordinate gender, social, and political equality to the dictates of 'national duty.' Thus, the professional middle-class construction and projection of an idealized femininity and its association with 'traditional' domesticity and motherhood should be considered as a correlative to the fabrication of the active, worldly, and virile imperial-nationalist masculinity evident in the understanding of 'good citizenship' that was detailed in a previous chapter.

'Home' as a Gendered Metaphor for the Nation

Comments such as 'England is the home of the race,' patriotism is 'founded on the love of home,' and 'we love England because it is our home,' littered the pages of the books used in elementary schools, as well as the rhetoric that teachers and commentators used when explaining the role and purposes of elementary education.[9] These assertions were, to use Raymond Williams's term, a 'structure of feeling': an attempt to convey those special qualities of England as a place and as a nation that could not normally be easily explained or described by using a metaphor pregnant with known and knowable meanings. The image of 'home' for many reader authors seemed to capture the essence of the unique sense of belonging that they wanted to convey. It was 'right and natural' to love one's home and family, and hence in the same way it was 'right and natural that we should love our country.'[10] The imaginative force behind the patriotic and nationalistic imagery of home relied on the meanings that it conjured in terms of family relationships, relationships that in turn depended on the gender perceptions of the late-Victorian professional middle class.

Robert MacDonald has aptly described the overarching historical narrative about England/Britain presented to schoolchildren throughout this period as the 'Island Story.'[11] In this narrative the island home of the English developed from its deep Anglo-Saxon roots through the period of Norman despotism, bursting forth into full flower under Elizabeth I, and since then, had progressed through the spreading of its civilization and justice all over the world. Since the readers tended on the whole to stress the importance of the empire rather than take a 'little Englander' line, the home metaphor was frequently invoked in descriptions of the relationship of the metropolitan centre to the periphery of the empire. In commonplace rhetorical flourishes, England was the 'forever home' to its overseas sons and daughters: the colonies and dominions were the children (in various stages of maturity) of the 'mother country.' The island-story narrative was based fundamentally on the assertion that historic Englishmen had set out to conquer, subjugate, and rule others, and they had been successful because this was their destiny. This narrative was bolstered by overt declamations of imperialist nationalism on the part of educators who warned teachers to be wary of the 'vague, feeble, emasculated philanthropy or altruism' of the 'little Englanders,' and that instead, only the 'genuine and manly love of country' of imperial patriots ought to be taught in the classroom.[12]

England in this narrative came to be represented as the little island home of a worthy race of people who were now spread out across the globe. The first lines of *Macmillan's New History Readers* capture something of the most muted variants of this narrative, commending the rise of a modest homeland and its place at the centre of a vast empire: 'In this book we shall read about some men and women who have helped make this great Empire; and we shall also learn how the change has come about that these small islands have become the home of Englishmen.'[13] Other texts were far more bellicose, sometimes pointing to the smallness of the English homeland compared to its imperial possessions. The *Highroads of Geography* series noted under the heading 'The Motherland' that 'size was not everything,' for although small, the island home of the English had produced 'the foremost people in the world,' who had won for themselves 'vast lands beyond the seas.' This proved that the 'best goods are often packed in the smallest parcels.'[14] Meanwhile, the *Britannia Geography Readers* proclaimed of the empire: 'We know that it is the greatest empire the world has ever seen, and the British flag floats over wide regions in every part of the globe, but even then we are unable to comprehend the vastness of our Empire.'[15] The poetry contained in literary readers also made much of the apparent contrast between the modest home and the immense hinterland, with the seemingly larger than life accomplishments of 'the Englishman' straddling both:

There's a land that bears a world-known name,
Though it is but a little spot;
I say 'tis first on the scroll of Fame,
And who shall say it is not?
Of the deathless ones who shine and live
In arms, in arts, or song;
The brightest the whole wide world can give,
To that little land belong.
'Tis the star of earth, deny it who can;
The island home of an Englishman.[16]

As the true and original island home of all those who had ventured forth to found the empire, and despite its imperial acclaim and power, England itself was basically 'small,' 'cosy,' 'modest,' 'quaint,' 'pleasant,' and frequently, 'rustic' and rural – although the bustle of the cities and the power of industry did also receive some mention. The power and strength of the nation in this rhetoric thus did not derive from the territory of England itself, although there was nevertheless something about English soil that was special and sacred, but rather from the English people, who had left their home in order to search out adventure and spread the welcome trappings of English civilization.

If the power and strength of the British Empire were depicted as laying in the unique characteristics of the people who had conquered and now ruled it, England itself was thus figured as a home in both the sense of a familial abode and as a hallowed geographical space that, despite its physical failings and small extent, nevertheless compelled powerful bonds of attachment. Volume III of *Arnold's Geography Readers* explained directly to schoolchildren that many English men and women had left England, but that a powerful reciprocal relationship still existed between 'them' and 'us':

Go where they may, no matter how grand and how beautiful other lands may be, no matter how rich they may become, no matter how long they stay away, they never forget their native land.

Other lands may have fairer skies, higher mountains, broader rivers, wider plains, or more extensive forests, yet there is something wanting that the wanderer finds only at home. As it is with them, so will it be with every true man, woman and child. They will always love the land of their birth.

We are English people, and whether we stay at home, or sail away to other lands across the ocean, we shall love Old England as long as we live, and be proud to say, 'I am an Englishman.'[17]

The Britannia Geography Readers echoed these sentiments, suggesting that 'we love England because it is our native land, and the home of our friends, we are proud to know that our country is worthy of our love.' It was this love that made England 'first among the countries of the world,' and although other countries had 'warmer climates and fairer skies, higher mountains and longer rivers, wider plains and vaster forests and gayer flowers and richer fruits,' no other country 'on the face of the globe' equalled the English homeland.[18] Unsurprisingly, this powerful love of home that was imagined to exist within the breasts of all English men and women was frequently presented as having a specific racial origin. The Anglo-Saxons were considered to be of a special quality precisely because of their formidable love of home: it was they, 'a very strong race of men, tall and fair, and very handsome' with their 'blue eyes and yellow hair,' who brought into being this love of home.[19] Since the Anglo-Saxons were the forefathers of the English who had spread around the globe, then England, the 'first' true home of the Anglo-Saxons, was thus the true home of all the English wherever they might currently reside. A view of England as the 'home of the race' – of all Anglo-Saxons worldwide – was also indicated in the rhetoric about England being the 'mother country.' The very first chapter of the 1903 *King Edward History Readers*, entitled 'The Mother Country and Her Children,' noted after a few inspiring lines from Scott that there were thousands of descendants of the Anglo-Saxons who had never seen 'the land of their forefathers' and yet 'speak of the old country as Home, for they have learnt its story from their parents and their friends, or from books.' Despite the fact that many 'are natives of countries many times larger than England, countries that are thousands of miles away,' they nevertheless 'always think lovingly of the little island home of their forefathers who left it, in the years gone by to make a new home for themselves.'[20] It is significant that typically it was 'our forefathers' or the 'loyal sons' of the 'mother country' who left to found new colonies and engage in adventure and commerce and/or civilizing missions. 'From the Mother Country, her brave sons have gone forth, and by patient industry and enduring courage, have created great, strong, healthy children of the Empire.'[21] In such passages, the mother country, England – 'our home' – was rendered as the figurative maternal source and supporter of the prosperous and virile sons who had spread the English race around the world. The mother country remained the eternal guardian of English values: the sheltering, caring home to which imperial/world travellers could return to escape from the pressures of their overseas mission and the challenges of spreading English civilization against the obstacles of 'savage' lands and peoples.[22] This symbolism and imagery suffused these readers in a wide variety of forms, playing on the images of mother and father/son, family and home, as a means to explain the bonds of affection it was thought elementary schoolchildren should develop towards both their nation and their countrymen overseas. Racial and familial metaphors were thereby conjoined in their presentation of the ancient roots, historical continuity, and future destiny of the English nation.

One revealing example from this pervasive familial discourse can be found in a general reading book from 1885. This text noted how some English emigrants in Australia – the text does not make it clear as to whether these 'recent' emigrants were freemen or convicts – had taken a skylark with them to remind them of their English roots:

The lark's song brought their English homes to their hearts, if not to their longing eyes, and many a memory of a happy childhood came back to them. They gathered round as the bird sang his wonderful song; and there, in that land of exile, many of those sons of toil remembered the prayers learned at their mothers' knees, and the innocence and hopes of their childhood and youth.

The hills and the valleys of their far-off English homes rose before them, and their hearts softened. Truly, the skylark preached a sermon to them – a sermon in song. And who can doubt that it did 'do them good.'[23]

In this passage, the emigrants' home was equated with an idyllic England typified by the image of an idealized mother and childhood. The skylark's song brought to these men – for the passage speaks only of them as being 'sons' of toil – a sense of both their spatial and emotional relationship to home. Their hard work in a distant and unforgiving place far removed from the land of their 'true' homes was here made more tolerable for them by the bird's evocation of things cherished. And clearly those things cherished were intended to be readily identifiable for the children reading the text, which indicates, perhaps, that these educational writers believed that elementary school students would identify with this sort of rhetoric precisely because they were in a very real sense highly dependent on their parents, particularly their mothers. Yet the bird's song also suggested that what they missed was somehow distinctly English, namely, the connected images of the English countryside and a mother.

In a similar vein, Arnold-Forster related in one of his 1893 readers a story about the events at the Albert Hall to mark the 1887 Queen's Jubilee. He noted that a great crowd of dignitaries and officials from all over the empire had assembled and, during Victoria's entrance, stood and heard a 'great singer' sing 'Home Sweet Home':

As the sweet, clear voice rang through the hall it seemed as if the same thought had come to all who were there. All the men [from the colonies] had their own happy homes in the land from which they came, but they felt that there was one other land, which to an Englishman must always be like home too, and that is the dear 'Old Country' from which they, or their fathers before them, all came, and which they still love.

I need not tell you that that 'Old Country' is our own dear England. There were many who, as they heard the beautiful notes of 'Home Sweet Home,' could not prevent tears coming to their eyes, and we may be sure that Queen Victoria who for fifty years had reigned over her people, and who had loved them so much felt the words of the beautiful song go to her heart.[24]

These sorts of passages were playing on the emotional connotations of home and family life. They were suggesting to children that the feelings they should have for their place of birth, and for their fellow countrymen, regardless of whether they knew them or not, should approximate that of their feelings towards their actual home and the members of their own family. The emotional attachment due to the imagined community of the wider nation and empire was here made comprehensible by using terms that conjured more limited relationships and communities.

Some readers took the emotional connotations of the home icon even further and presented the love of home as an almost uniquely English attribute, and that this love of home defined one of the most important of all English national characteristics. One author claimed that the chief characteristic of English men and women is their love of "home."' Englishmen separated 'from the home and native soil' frequently succumb to 'home-sickness, a real disease, known to the science of medicine.' This 'worthy feeling of attachment and duty to the country in which we live and to the nation at large' was explained as the essence of patriotism.[25] The Reverend C.S. Dawe suggested that the English were 'an eminently home loving race,' and G.F. Boswell explained that the English had a peculiar 'thrill of pleasure at hearing the song "Home Sweet Home,"' because 'English life has always centred in the home, the *Ham* of the early inhabitants of this country.'[26] John Landon's teaching manual concurred with this assessment, encouraging teachers to have all their classes sing 'Home Sweet Home' in an effort to aid in the 'implanting of patriotic feeling' in their students, and much of the poetry collected in many readers seems to have been chosen for this same purpose. Indeed, of the seventeen poems contained within Book IV of *Arnold's English Readers*, seven reflect directly on the English home and/or garden – the most obvious being 'The Merry Homes of England' – out of a total of nine that explicitly celebrate/eulogize England and Englishmen.[27]

As we can see from the above examples, within the confines of the overarching 'Island Story' the iconography of the home metaphor was often interconnected with another narrative of Englishness in this period – English ruralism. The contours of this narrative united the idea of the English home with the image of the distinctly southern English countryside and village life.[28] John Ahier has identified a tendency among twentieth-century textbook writers to represent rural life as 'undivided from nature' and to mask other divisions; in effect, to naturalize and romanticize 'both agricultural labour and patriarchal family forms.'[29] This tendency, however, was already being substantially developed in the materials of classroom culture in the period 1880 to

1914, where the national ethos imprinted into characterizations of the English landscape were linked to its supposed insularity, tamed and crafted form, stability and order.[30]

Both in their descriptions of rural conditions and in their accounts and general disdain for the process of urbanization, text- and reading-book authors presented to their child readers a mythic view of English village life that incorporated domestic and social harmony in their narrative of national origins and progress. The English village was represented by many authors as both something typically English and as something that was fundamentally better than the urban conglomerations that had developed over the course of the eighteenth and nineteenth centuries. Inhabitants of the village were depicted as having a 'charm and innocence rarely found in towns.'[31] Moreover, the association between the countryside and the 'home of the English' was commonly made. Central to this idealization of historical and contemporary rural conditions within school readers was the supposed social harmony and idyllic family life that were bound together by the close proximity of the family and home to nature.

The two most consistently idealized and romanticized historical periods in regards to the evocation of rural Englishness were that of the Anglo-Saxons and 'Merrie England' of the sixteenth to eighteenth centuries. This is perhaps to be expected given the key place of these periods in the historical narrative of the island story. The naturalization of home and family life within the rural locality, however, also demonstrates the degree to which the patriotic rhetoric and the projection of a national identity relied on the gendered meanings implicit in the icon of the home.

In their accounts of both the Anglo-Saxon era and the period of 'Merrie England,' school readers suggested that rural/village life was simple, innocent, and governed by nature: by the seasons and the fundamental order and purity of the English countryside. Not only were the Anglo-Saxons thus depicted as the true and original ancestors of the modern English, but their perceived organization of society and way of life was also seen as being both quintessentially English and one of natural social concord. One reader noted that nearly all of the Anglo-Saxons lived in the country and that 'most free Englishmen possessed a plot of land. The English were therefore a nation of farmers and herdsmen delighting in a simple out-of-door life.'[32] This particular vision of the idyll of English rural existence was renewed, after descriptions of the manorial bondage of the 'Norman Yoke,' in the representations of 'Merrie England.' The exact dates of this epoch, of course, varied quite considerably, but most reader authors seemed to have viewed the sixteenth to mid-eighteenth centuries as fulfilling the dictates of this 'golden age.' During Elizabeth's reign it was suggested that 'the different classes of society were much together, and there were few dividing barriers. Life was spent then more in common and more in the open air.'[33] And another reader noted of the early seventeenth century that the English delighted in their rural existence, that 'village life was a happy life' because 'folks were friendly with each other.' Women would spend their summer evenings 'spinning at the cottage doors' while 'the men sat on the long benches outside the alehouse and talked about the crops.' Meanwhile, 'young men and boys wrestled and leaped, and played many quaint old games; or boys and girls sang the old country songs and danced the old country dances together on the green.'[34]

Such mythic images of contented rural life embraced a view that the 'traditional' was best and sagacious; that the 'natural' and proper order of things included women – 'spinning at their cottage doors' – blissful in their own sphere of home, and of men conversing on worldly matters in the highly public space of the local tavern. Social harmony and national progress, it was intimated, had been assured for centuries as long as there were such 'yeomen' industriously tilling their fields (but, of course, willing to take up arms for their country when called upon, and adept at such activities as use of the longbow),[35] with their wives aiding and supporting them from the steps of their thatched cottages. In these books, then, social and gender divisions in no way threatened the attainment of national concord, because a hierarchical social and gender order was entirely naturalized.

This circumscribed idyllic vision was further strengthened by those authors who ventured to suggest that the great urbanization and industrialization of the late-eighteenth and nineteenth centuries had wrought a partial unravelling of the national social fabric. In particular, it was held that the wrenching of women out of the rural domestic economy had had disastrous consequences for the moral health of the nation. As one author commented on the great changes of the nineteenth century: 'Thousands of women, also, were employed in the factories and mines where it was well-nigh impossible for them to keep clean-hearted and womanly.'[36] The passing of 'Merrie England' was thus here rendered as the ruination of 'ordinary women's' femininity, through the destruction of her domestic life.[37] This theme was often highlighted by passages on the evils of female and child labour in the early part of the century. Immediately following such observations, however, came triumphalist accounts of how such excesses had been curbed by the social legislation (particularly the various Factory, and also later Education, Acts) of the mid-nineteenth century.[38] The general trajectory of many of these texts, at least in their detailing of urbanization and related questions, was thus to chart a path from a point of original virtue, through a period of jeopardy and discord, to that of the contemporary period in which, due to the efforts of great statesmen, reformers, and educators, the proper values of 'manly' masculinity and domestic femininity could again be aspired to.

In overtly patriotic rhetoric the symbolism of the home clearly depended on the meanings associated with the family order and perceived gender roles. Whether describing England in terms of the relationship of the mother country to her children, as 'home to the race,' or, as in 'Merrie England,' as a romanticized and idealized homeland where stable familial relationships bound together the nation's social fabric, the signifiers of home and mother country relied on a particular domestic ideal: on the icon of a caring, supportive, nurturing mother in the safe, harmonious, cosy and orderly confines of the familial domicile. But to explore this association properly we need to further delineate the evolving nature of the gender ideology of this period, and how it intersected with both the structure of the curriculum and the meanings encoded into the content of elementary schooling.

Gender Ideology and the Ideal of Home

The elevation of motherhood during the Victorian period has received considerable attention from historians.[39] The religious and moral arguments characteristic of the early to mid-nineteenth century concerning the role of women – and of men as providers for, but also as the heads of, households – were reformulated towards the end of Victoria's reign. In the mid-decades of the nineteenth century this domestic ideal was presented as desirable in that it provided stability for the individual in the family, and ensured the proper standards of bourgeois morality in society. Davidoff and Hall have demonstrated that ultimately the domestic sphere included men just as much as it did women: that the mid-Victorian middle-class man's success in business or the professions often depended on his proper ordering of family commitments; that masculine self-respect required an exacting code of public behaviour and indulgence in family life. Women, largely denied access to the public sphere (although never entirely), were rhetorically given sway over the domestic sphere through their supposedly superior claim to moral and spiritual values. Of course, male authority still headed the domestic sphere: the belief that the household was itself a microcosm of the political order – with the husband listening to and taking into consideration the interests of the other family members, but nevertheless having final say – was vigorously stated by the Evangelicals early in the century.[40] But by the end of the century, the shared nature of the middle-class domestic ideal was changing. The harmony that was seen as created by men and women working together in their roles at home was giving way to one in which femininity – the social construction of women as wives, helpmeets, but especially as mothers – came to represent the domestic sphere itself, while masculinity was increasingly divorced from the dictates of domesticity altogether and came to be represented as residing solely in the public sphere.[41] This conception was increasingly evident in school readers where discussions of domesticity in both the contemporary and favoured historical periods were clearly associated with the status and role of women. Nelson's *Royal Star Readers*, for instance, noted in 1887 that 'boys should learn those things which will best fit them for the common business of men whereas girls should seek that knowledge which will best qualify them to discharge their duties as women,' which was 'as housekeepers,' and, curiously enough, as 'heads of families.'[42] The changing identification of the home with women alone came to colour subsequent pronouncements of English racial history. The National Society reflected this association by indicating that despite the savagery of the Anglo-Saxons, they placed tremendous 'sanctity' in the idea of home: 'Children revered their parents, were ever ready to serve them, and even to die for them if occasion so required.' Indeed, the home was special because 'they held that there was something sacred in a woman.'[43]

The reasons for this shift to a further separation of the 'separate spheres' concept occurred for a number of reasons. Biological, medical, and anthropological scholarship – grounded in the observable and inescapable differences between men and women – both bolstered and legitimized the older cultural myths and religious traditions that had enforced earlier gender hierarchies, and helped transform the domestic ideal. After mid-century the differences between the sexes came to be predicated increasingly on the evidence, knowledge, and assertions of professional experts – doctors, academics, researchers – and the construction of gender difference became similar in general structure to that of racial typography. The differences between men and women were thought by many to be essential, 'natural,' and immutable. Using the powerful language of science, basic biological traits – reproductive functions, physical attributes, genetic heritage, perceptions of intelligence – were increasingly made central to definitions of both gender and ethnic identity.[44] The physical and cultural differences between women and men were placed along a spectrum of value that frequently invoked the metaphor of master/servant, and the interdependence between the superior and subaltern sex was acknowledged as operating in this relationship.[45] Thus, just as colonial rule was justified on the grounds that colonial subjects were saved from their own violence, corruption, savagery, and barbarity by their European masters, a critical precept of the perceived inequality between sexes was that the weaker sex ought to willingly accept the public authority of the stronger. Men argued that women's 'nurturing, domestic and spiritual talents' made them suited to the domestic setting, while their 'mental and physical frailty,' and their 'inability to act successfully in the public spheres of economic life, politics and high culture,' should be protected by male legal, political, and social authority.[46] Men increasingly came to be identified with their occupations and public duties rather than with their households, and women with their moral and maternal function in the domicile.

Women's demands for influence in 'a space apart,' and what John Tosh and others have convincingly argued was a flight from the mid-century middle-class conception of domesticity, were also critical in the reshaping of the ideal of separate spheres. The rise of the 'New Woman' and arguments about curbing the moral corruption of men through reference to the idea of separate spheres had something to do with this,[47] as did the fact that professional middle-class men were distancing themselves from the home by preferring to remain bachelors or marrying late, by sojourning to homosocial institutions and activities, and by going overseas to work in the empire.[48] Ultimately, however, it was the tremendous emphasis placed on domestic motherhood in the second half of the century that defined the ambiguous and doubtful position of domestic fatherhood.[49] This is not to suggest that either the idea or the actuality of the middle-class family home dissolved. Rather, middle-class men at the end of the century no longer saw themselves quite as tied to the family environment as their fathers and grandfathers had been, and masculine values increasingly ceased to be those that combined adherence to both public and domestic spheres.

The significance of this shift on elementary education lies in the fact that in this essentially middle-class vision a great deal of symbolic importance was put into the idea of the home as a feminine space. This was a place girls ought to identify with as peculiarly theirs, and the ideal that boys ought to identify with as the most important thing to uphold and defend. Within the nation a binary connection between genders was therefore presented alongside the constructed binary opposition of gender. As one contemporary teachers' manual explained, the aim of history lessons, such as one on the Armada, was to show how the love of country united brave men, not for themselves, but for the 'defence of hearth and home.'[50] The abstraction of loyalty to nation, when couched in terms of home and family, was thereby constituted in terms of different but complementary roles for each sex. Both the structure and the content of elementary schooling came to reflect these ideals of gender division and connection as they were reproduced in the writings of professional middle-class educators. Equally important, however, was that this discourse manifested itself not only in the form of textual pronouncements, but also in the very organization of the curriculum and the physical structuring of the elementary school itself.

The Professional Imagining of the Home and the Structure of the Curriculum

Ellen H. Richards, the pioneering American domestic science educator, indicated at the end of the century how social and national values had come to coincide in the importance accorded the icon of home:

The Englishman's house is not only his castle ... it is conceded by so able an observer as Edmond Demolin that [it] is the secret of Anglo-Saxon superiority.

If we accept the conclusion of thoughtful students of human evolution and assume that what is represented in the term 'home' is the germ of Anglo-Saxon civilization, the unit of the social progress; that no community rises above the average of its individual houses in intelligence, courage, honesty, industry, thrift, patriotism, or any other individual or civic virtue; that nothing which church, school or state can do will quite make up for the lack in the home, then we must acknowledge that no subject can be of greater importance than a discussion of the standards involved in home life.[51]

Here the home was held to be not merely an oasis from the pressures of the public realm, but also an important symbol for the nurturing of national values and for any understanding of the duties and rights of national citizenship. The social realm, simultaneously universal and intensely personal in the mid-nineteenth-century vision, was broadened to a self-consciously national and racial scope at the turn of the century. Richards's own understanding incorporated a mid-century view of the shared nature of the domestic environment. She noted the growing national importance of the domestic sphere, but did not perceive this sphere as an exclusively female one. However, in her prescriptions for domestic education, it was only women who were to be instructed in the vital importance of the home. Women were to be entrusted with the necessary domestic values and allotted the task of renewing the purpose and values of home life. Their example, particularly as mothers, would lead to the proper development of other civic virtues. It was suggested that 'the home has survived the shock of losing most of the intellectual and religious education of the children,' but will 'it bear the amputation of the material industries represented by the kitchen?' Richards answered her own question with a resounding yes, so long 'as the home is that place of *moral* education where the *mother* is, the mother to world-children, if not those of her own flesh and blood. The home still means the perfection of the child life for which it exists. It is the ideal which will preserve the Anglo-Saxon superiority if anything is able to do it.'[52]

Women were thus given the role to make the home both a symbol and a reality worthy of being revered and defended by men. Many English educators also explained that only through the combined efforts of male public activity and female private sway could a 'true English home' worthy of its hallowed representation result.[53] The Englishwoman's identity was confirmed in her realization of this ideal: 'The attainment of this ideal should add immensely to the permanent stability of the country, for no nation can rest on surer foundations than that in which the most capable women, those most highly trained, are the housekeepers and the mothers.'[54] Sara Burstall, headmistress of Manchester High School for Girls, suggested in 1907 that the role of schooling (in this case for middle-class girls) was to form deserving

Englishwomen who would strive, through their 'normal work ... to be the maker of a home, to be a wife, and above all a mother.'[55] Boys, on the other hand, required an education that fitted them for the difficulties of an active public life, endeavouring to support and defend family and the home ideal.[56]

For some, the supreme factor in the 'stability of the national character' was the coordination of the parents in creating a proper home. Schooling for middle-class girls was thus meant to give them a sense of the wider importance for their future life responsibilities and their duties as integral participants in English society and the nation. Alice Ravenhill, who, from the turn of the century on, was one of the most active in the movement to extend formal domestic education to girls of all classes, prioritized her aims for domestic/hygienic instruction in 1909.[57] Most important was the need to associate 'the practical training given to girls in domestic subjects with a sense of the enormous national importance of their work and the substantial contribution to the State made by every intelligent, conscientious home-maker – however exalted or however lowly her position.' Second, it was important to 'show girls that they, even more than the teaching profession, have a responsible educational, as well as national, duty to perform in the right care of the physical and moral welfare of the home life of the community; for which purpose, some training in the domestic arts and hygiene is indispensable.'[58] While middle-class parents, with some help from private schooling, could be relied upon to furnish the appropriate atmosphere and resources for the proper training of their children, the capabilities and outlook of the working classes were viewed with more pessimism. State intervention was assessed as needed, and indeed was increasingly used at the turn of the century in an attempt to reform what was seen by many in the middle classes as the undisciplined and excessively independent working-class youth culture.[59]

In part this stemmed from some commentators perceiving a collapse of the home as a functioning model of national citizenship. Bernard Bosanquet, for example, explained the relationship of the citizen to his family in prescriptive terms that suggest he believed there to be a decay in the familial fabric of society: 'The home is after all, an element in the common good of the community; the wife and the children are not playthings, nor animals to be fed, nor instruments of social or industrial advancement, but are members of a great nation, that has a past and a future, and relations of duty and participation in a common good, binding together all its citizens.'[60] This was echoed by W.F. Trotter, who, after his assertion that 'the home is the nursery of citizenship' where 'one learns obedience, sympathy, self-sacrifice, and acquires the idea of common interests,' lamented that since 'the discipline of the home is invaluable,' it was 'a national calamity that there are so many people who have never experienced it.'[61] These observers were remarking on a supposed absence: for Bosanquet in society as a whole, in Trotter's case perhaps only of certain classes. The symbolic purpose of the home ideal as a national value was being assigned great importance at the very same time that the actual existence of this ideal among much of the population was being questioned. Several moral panics arose over the 'immorality' and irreligiosity of the urban working class and the problem of 'juvenile delinquency' at this time, spurred, in large part, by the apparent findings of the large numbers of middle-class social investigators.[62]

In 1896 William Morrison explained that the problem of criminal juveniles, for instance, was explicitly connected to these individuals' lack of a sense of familial attachment and responsibility, because in 'most cases they find themselves in a large city without friends, without family ties, and belonging to no social circle in which their conduct is either scrutinized or observed.'[63] Similarly, Mary Barnett's *Young Delinquents: A Study of Reformatory and Industrial Schools* (1913) suggested that although the Education Act of 1870 had revolutionized the life of working-class children, it had 'not restore[d] to them the normal home-life of which they had been deprived.'[64] This 'normal' home life was presumably one based on a middle-class model. John Gillis has suggested that such concern over the licentiousness of youth lay behind late-nineteenth-century middle-class social reformers' attempts to impose on juveniles of all classes – via the 'discovery' of adolescence – a period of dependency on adults through the educational, welfare, and leisure organizations that they controlled.[65] Middle-class bias towards viewing their own values as universal meant that their values were thought applicable to the working classes as well, and feelings of class superiority meant that any constraints about expressing anxiety over the glorification of the family ideal in the middle-class context did not apply when discussing that of the 'lower' classes. Consequently, imposing on poor families the mores and values of the middle-class domestic ideal was regarded as a potential cure-all for the perceived ills of society.[66] If the working-class wife, for example, were to provide the 'cosy home' of the domestic ideal and was ready for her husband's return from work with nutritious meals and a clean and tidy, if humble, abode, then home would provide a refuge for the working man from the hardships of the outside world, 'would prove an antidote to the lure of the pubs or streets,'[67] and would ultimately allow for the development of a sense of national belonging, responsibilities, and duties. This, in turn, would create the proper role models for the children of the family, who would endeavour to obey their parents, not wander into immoral or indulgent habits, and would thus also develop the proper attitudes of respect for domesticity and respectability. Moreover, as Jane Lewis has also argued, despite the evident middle-class bias in social reform measures that presumed the desirability of the male-breadwinner model of family life, 'working-class wives accepted in large measure the primacy of their responsibilities to home and children and the secondary nature of any wage earning they might engage in.'[68]

The perception of a disintegrating social order fuelled by the failure to live up to the domestic ideal resulted in encouragement of the games ethic, muscular Christianity, and manly 'character building' for boys of all classes, and the rise of compulsory domestic instruction and training in racial 'motherhood' for girls. This sort of reformatory sentiment, and the concomitant desire to renew a sense of the national importance of the home, was reflected in many of the reading books given elementary schoolchildren. H.E. Malden suggested this obliquely when he noted that being 'proud of our country and our Constitution does not mean sitting down to admire it, nor shouting out praises of it, nor marching in procession to its honour and glory and our own.' Rather it meant hard work: 'We are proud of our work when we turn out a job well done ... You girls are proud of your handiwork when the room is neat and clean, when the hearth is cheerful, and a good tea of your preparing is ready for your father on his return from his labour.'[69] Other school reading books intended for use in largely working-class elementary schools frequently emphasized this vision of the perfect ordering of English domestic and public life: 'Fathers and brothers often work hard to earn enough money to keep the house – pay the rent, buy food and clothing, and other things. But no matter how much or how little money is earned, the mothers and daughters are after all the keepers of the house. They can make the humblest dwelling into a comfortable English home.'[70] However, if home was to have realistic and socially appropriate resonance for the working classes, then the educational experience of boys and girls in elementary schools would have to differ from that provided to the children of the middle classes. For although couched in terms of national necessity, fairness, and the duty of all, the inculcation of the moral values and standards of domesticity was class-specific. It was thought that all young girls, for instance, should be taught the importance of domestic tasks and how to run the household efficiently, but for the middle-class girl this meant classroom learning about the 'science of cleansing,' supplemented with readings on how 'home life' was 'the basis of our civilization'; for the working-class girl, learning the importance of the domestic arts actually required getting her hands wet through practical instruction in 'laundry work.'[71] Alice Ravenhill was a particularly prominent proponent of this view. In 1909 she suggested that it was the national duty and responsibility of all young women to become proficient in the domestic arts, and to provide the 'right care of the physical and moral welfare of the home life of the community.' Significantly, however, most of her efforts were directed at the promotion of this duty in girls' elementary schools.[72]

The reasoning provided by educators for this divergence of educational practice and provision for girls and boys of different classes often had a nationalist gloss that papered over potential social divisions and tensions. Social harmony and the promotion of middle-class perceptions of respectability often underlay the dictates of 'national efficiency,' for example. It was recognized that the working-class girl would not have the resources to engage any help for her domestic chores save that of her children. She would have to do the work herself, and it was important that she know the most 'efficient and sanitary methods.' Middle-class educationalists patronizingly believed that left to themselves, working-class girls would fall into the same 'inefficient' practices as their mothers; practices that kept the working poor in poverty, vice, and degradation. With suitable training it was unrealistically believed that girls might create model middle-class household environments on their husbands' working-class incomes.[73] Similarly, boys were given vocational instruction thought suitable to their station in society and, by and large, were not encouraged to think of social advancement, but rather to revel in the vital role of efficient labour in the national community. Some provision for particularly gifted working-class boys and girls, it is true, was made in the form of scholarships to secondary schools. However, numerous studies have indicated these mainly benefited individuals in families whose economic circumstances were such that they could afford to lose the earnings of the adolescent in question, and that they were thus among the higher end of the artisanal social segment (further education thereby permitting crossover into a lower-middle-class position), or alternatively were already in a basically lower-middle-class social situation and were willing to make financial sacrifices for the sake of the appearance of middle-class gentility.[74]

Moreover, it was also well understood at this time that regardless of the dictates of the women-in-the-home domestic ideal, many working women would, for a time at least, become servants for the middle and upper classes, and some vocational domestic training in schools ensured that there would be a constant supply of cheap, pre-trained domestic servants. Many working-class parents realized and resented the social aims of mandatory domestic training in schools – particularly when in the process of learning 'laundry,' for instance, it was not infrequent that the teacher's clothes were those that were laundered.[75] This is an indication of the contradictions inherent in the promotion of middle-class gender ideology through working-class schooling, because in order to retain their status, members of the middle classes actually required that many working-class women be excluded from the middle-class ideal of femininity. For many working-class women, true womanhood through family life had to be sacrificed to the very class that promulgated the ideology of feminine domesticity, since the middle classes could 'only aspire to [their] ideals through the exploitation of working-class women as factory workers, as agricultural workers, as homeworkers, as domestic servants and as prostitutes.'[76] Educational practice was therefore an uneasy mediation between an ideal and a social-status necessity. Schooling operated to both promote professional middle-class 'national' standards among the working classes and also to ensure the continuance of existing social divisions.

Assuredly, this vision of the importance of the domestic ideal was dependent, for all classes, on the distinct and special place given to the mother in the family. Towards the end of the nineteenth century the significance of motherhood increased through the largely accepted assumptions of professionals and experts in the fields of public health and education. This occurred mainly because medical discourse at this time was in the process of reconstructing female identity around women's biological cycles and reproductive functions.[77] The dichotomies of these perceptions and practices helped exaggerate the notion of physical and psychological differences between the sexes, and reinforce opinions about the different ways in which boys and girls of all classes ought to be educated and socialized. Most significantly, this also paved the way for arguments about the importance of 'racial motherhood' in the years after 1890.[78]

Racial motherhood, as several studies have demonstrated, placed the health of the race, and hence also that of the nation, into the special domain of women. Protecting the quality and ensuring the continuance of the English race, nation, and empire by being a good mother was increasingly posited as the foremost duty of the true Englishwoman.[79] A.H.D. Acland had noted in the mid-1880s that education, intended to promote good citizenship, had to include the instruction of women in the specific role that they held in the furtherance of the nation, 'for we all know that with our women, with the mothers of the Englishmen of the future, lies the greatest possible responsibility; and the more they can in their busy lives – even more occupied and hardly worked very often than ours – become reasonably and rationally educated, the better the English people of the future will be.'[80]

Motherhood became an important public issue in the years after 1890 mainly because of the widespread fears that British national and imperial power (judged variously in terms of commercial, industrial, diplomatic, military, and/or racial) was slipping into decline.[81] In this context, concerns arose about the low birth rate of the British Isles and the quality of the human stock being propagated. Children, it was said, belonged 'not merely to the parents but to the community as a whole'; they were a 'national asset,' 'the capital of the country'; on them depended 'the future of the country and the Empire'; they were the 'citizens of tomorrow.' Good maternal practices were believed essential for the rearing of the soldiers and workers (as almost all the rhetoric around racial motherhood assumed that the infants to be cared for were male) of the future generations of the imperial race; child-rearing became a national duty rather than just a moral one, and if it was poorly done then the state was increasingly willing to intervene.[82] This meant that elementary schooling would also become the nursery of good future mothers in an attempt to preserve the well-being of the nation as a whole. Under the weight of the arguments about racial degeneration, the responsibility of mothers to the nation, and the pre-existing standard of the domestic ideal, racial motherhood became a potent symbol in this period that fused nationalist imaginings and prescriptions with professional middle-class discourses of race, class, and gender.

The Domestic Ideal and Racial Motherhood in the Curriculum

The chronology and course of development of the elementary curriculum was highly sensitive to these professional middle-class discourses about female identity and roles in the nation. The first issue to consider in this regard is that of sex segregation in the classroom. The urge to segregate by sex in the classroom had been firmly ingrained in the voluntary schools from before the inception of rate-aided schooling in 1870, but the new board schools did not seek to reverse this; rather, they took up this impulse wholeheartedly as well. Between 1880 and 1914 both systems increased their efforts to fund separate sex-segregated classrooms above the infant level (roughly age seven).[83] And although lack of funds often retarded these efforts, particularly in rural areas, it remained a priority for both systems, with the newer and more wealthy board schools eventually achieving a higher rate and more comprehensive scale of segregation. Board schools tended to be situated in urban areas and were often quite large (their average attendance being about 380, compared to the voluntary school average of about 170),[84] so although there remained many more voluntary schools than board schools, the limited number of segregated voluntary schools obscures the degree to which sex segregation was pursued and achieved in this period. More than half of the board schools in England were completely sex-segregated; many had entirely different rooms, playgrounds, and entrances for boys and girls. A large number of board and voluntary schools were partially segregated. Moreover, even in those schools that had nothing but mixed classrooms, at various points during the school week these classes were divided by sex so that different subjects could be taken separately by boys and girls. The desirability of women teaching girls and men teaching boys was found to be increasingly difficult to fulfil due to the lack of qualified male teachers and the savings for the educational authorities that female instructors provided (as female teachers commanded earnings of only about 67 per cent of the salaries of male teachers). Indeed, by 1900, there were almost three times as many women elementary teachers as there were men.[85]

The relative failure to achieve complete sex segregation and same-sex teaching was mitigated by the substantial segregation in the substance of teaching that was achieved prior to the end of the century. Elements of both the form and the content of the curriculum became increasingly gender specific. From 1870 until 1886 there were only three subjects that all students, male and female, were required to take – reading, writing, and arithmetic – although there were a number of popular optional subjects such as singing, sciences, geography, and grammar that either sex might also be instructed in. With the passage of the 1870 Education Act, however, girls were obliged to take some amount of needlework instruction in addition to the three Rs; indeed, needlework had been a widely offered option for girls in those schools that had existed prior to the 1870 act. By making gendered subjects optional and then compulsory grant-earning subjects – that is, allowing schools to receive education grants from the government for teaching these subjects – the Education Codes of this period encouraged, and later ensured, that a gender-differentiated curriculum would become the norm in elementary schooling. Theoretical domestic economy became a grant-earning option for girls after 1874, and became a compulsory subject in 1878; drawing was a similar option for boys from 1874, until it was made compulsory in 1890. Cookery was added to the Education Code as an optional grant-earning subject for girls in 1882, and instruction in laundry was similarly added in 1889. By 1900 general housewifery was also a grant-earning subject.[86]

Although permitted to take these subjects by the changes to the Education Code, the actual provision of this segregated curriculum varied from place to place. Schools in the large urban centres were actually often in advance of the national code in offering these 'practical' domestic subjects, while the poorer rural boards and many voluntary schools lagged behind. The London School Board made domestic economy (including practical cookery and laundry) a required specific subject in all its schools from 1883. All girls in Standards v and vi had to attend a course of twenty lessons at one of the designated School Board for London Cookery Centres, or in one of the specially fitted kitchens in certain London schools. The demand for new cookery centres was so great that the board had to authorize additional monies to be made available in the form of loans for all the schools wanting to build and equip them.[87] By 1900 the London School Board had set up 168 Cookery Centres, servicing the needs of 470 contributing London-area schools.[88] As a direct result of the 1888 Cross Commission report and the example set by the London Board, domestic economy, cookery, and housewifery were all specifically encouraged by the Education Department and its inspectors as suitable subjects for all girls in

England and Wales.[89] This is especially significant because although manual and vocational training was also advocated for boys, far fewer resources, and hence less instruction, was devoted to practical and vocational training for boys than it was to girls. Thus, even though the growth in the interest and supply of domestic subjects, especially after 1886, corresponds with the growth of the elementary curriculum itself, an imbalance between the amount of practical as opposed to general academic instruction offered to the two sexes increased over the course of this period.[90] The time allotted to needlework and practical domestic subjects for girls was used for academic subjects (most commonly commerce or geography, but also English, basic science, or history) and/or physical education/games for boys. Indeed, although the period 1888 to 1895 was marked by a great increase in the amount of attention given to the promotion of science, mathematics, and commercial subjects as well as domestic and manual subjects,[91] the actual provision of these new subjects was itself quite gender specific. While boys might be instructed in commerce and the physical sciences, girls tended to be given instruction in the 'theoretical' domestic sciences (hygiene, basic nutrition, household/garden chemistry and biology); girls were thought less capable in mathematics than boys, and as a result, beyond basic arithmetic the only mathematics offered girls tended to be practical 'household finance' (measurement of weights and volumes and other 'practical' knowledge needed in shopping and cooking), while boys might receive 'financial arithmetic,' mensuration, and geometry.[92] These basic patterns continued even after the demise of the block-grant payment arrangement in 1896.

During the first two decades of the twentieth century, the increasing concern over national efficiency and the rise of ideas about racial motherhood added further to the sex segregation of the curriculum, and the focus on the utilitarian schooling of girls and the importance of household and maternal care in education in particular.[93] In 1904 the Interdepartmental Committee on Physical Deterioration recommended more concentration on physical exercises and games for all children, and infant care, cookery, and household management for girls in schools were given priority especially in the eighteen months or so prior to school leaving (at age fourteen).[94] This report was extremely influential, and within a year the Board of Education required that all syllabuses in laundry, cookery, and household management be submitted to the board for approval rather than to the local inspectors. The aim of this measure was to ensure the utility and practicality of the domestic economy provisions in each area, and to encourage the further development of comprehensive education of girls in these subjects.[95] The minor backlash against the increasing emphasis on domestic subjects for girls by feminists and social and educational reformers in this period was dismissed by members of the Board of Education in 1906 and 1907 on the basis of racial motherhood arguments. They further suggested that since it was desirable that only a small minority of girls work beyond the confines of home once they were adults, the elementary school system should cater to the needs of the majority.[96] Scientific views were increasingly used to bolster the gender division of the curriculum. Eugenicists such as Karl Pearson were somewhat influential both in the drafting of the 1904 Physical Deterioration Report and among the public health officials charged with inspecting elementary schools.[97] In light of the paranoia that had developed regarding the falling birth rate and perceived racial degeneration trends, some eugenicists proposed that an academic education for girls was actually detrimental, as it would stand in the way of marriage and maternity.[98] Moreover, some medical experts had been arguing against the intellectual education of girls since the 1880s on the grounds that the strains and rigours of intellectual learning, particularly as girls approached adolescence, hindered the proper development of their reproductive systems.[99] This view held that if the blight of only the 'worst stocks' of the working-class population procreating was to be reversed, 'well bred' and 'respectable' women of all classes ought to do nothing that would hinder their chances of successful marriage and maternity. Education, in this view, ought to be directed primarily towards the goal of producing better mothers, more desirable wives, and hence more and better children.

One result of the fears about racial degeneration whipped up by the 1904 report, and the campaigns of eugenicists and the various established medical associations between 1904 and 1909,[100] was the 1910 Board of Education 'Memo on the Teaching of Infant Care and Management in the Public Elementary Schools.'[101] This document spelled out that the curriculum for girls in the two years prior to their leaving school ought to revolve primarily around lessons in personal hygiene, temperance, home nursing, housewifery, and infant care. Cleanliness and hygiene were stressed, as was the need to keep instruction simple and practical, and the emphasis on mother craft and the appeal to the 'motherly instincts of girls' was consistently framed within a need to appeal to the girls' sense of duty to both family and nation.[102] The arrangement of the gendered curriculum thus followed the strictures of the domestic ideal and later concerns about racial motherhood. While manual and technical education was promoted for boys as a means by which Britain's national commercial and industrial strength might be bolstered, the almost overriding promotion of domesticity in the elementary education of girls was justified in the first years of the twentieth century by the scientific and educational value that was accorded to it by the professional medical and public health associations, and educationalists, that influenced the Board of Education.[103] School instruction for girls in household management, cookery, and economy and instruction for boys in drawing and commercial and manual training were consistently advocated as means to help elevate poorer working-class families out of abject poverty and into 'respectability,' to help diminish the anxieties of the working family – thereby lessening social and political tensions while simultaneously maintaining the social hierarchy – and to help further inculcate among the mass of the labouring classes those values that were seen as the core of Englishness in the middle-class imagination.

Domestic Englishness and the Content of Elementary Education

While the intended recipients of specific lessons on the 'public' duties of citizenship were primarily the boys in the elementary school, girls also were subjected to nationalist proselytizing in the specific and separate subjects that they were instructed in. Through their schooling, working-class girls were told to think of their domestic training and their preparation for motherhood as having quite a lot to do with their nationality and civic membership. Educationalist Catherine Dodd suggested in 1903 that England lagged far behind Europe and America in recognizing the importance of the proper (and different) educational ideals necessary for boys and girls in the determination of national purpose. In her view, girls ought to be separated from boys 'after a certain age,' such that the distinct but equally essential duties of each sex could be concentrated and focused on.[104] The influential Alice Ravenhill, in her capacity as inspector of hygiene and domestic economy for the Yorkshire County Council, provided the following justification for the teaching of domestic economy to girls in 1903:

The home constitutes the centre of interest in any study of present social and economic progress, for it is no exaggeration to say that on the happy, healthy maintenance of family life hinges the political, commercial, and industrial welfare of the Empire. The manifest decadence of true home life in this country, though attributable to numerous and complex factors, affords certain evidence that the home is not fulfilling its function. Friction, fretful discontent, contempt for duties, which rightly performed afford scope for the employment of the highest intellectual gifts; this tale of disappointment to parents and demoralization among young people is painfully familiar in every grade of society ...

Good homes are the basis of the highest and most fruitful civilization; to secure them for the British Empire depends on her women, her schools, and her educational zeal.[105]

Such rationalizations based on imperialist rhetoric for the teaching of the domestic sciences were matched by the exhortations to teachers contained within manuals of teaching method. On the one hand, such manuals implored teachers to instruct domestic subjects in order to preserve the social status quo. Thus, an 1894 manual suggested that 'teachers should, when possible, advise mothers to encourage their daughters to become good domestic servants in preference to entering upon indifferent callings which frequently entail late hours, injury to health and exposure to temptation.'[106] On the other hand, these manuals were also quick to point out to the teacher the national and imperial importance of the domestic sciences and the teaching of hygiene and, indeed, tried to impress upon teachers the need to explain this to the girls in their classes. Volume two of the 1911 *Teacher's Encyclopedia* explained: 'Amongst the many educational developments of the last century, that of the training of girls in the Domestic Sciences may be reckoned as one having the greatest imperial importance. Woman's outlook and position in industrial, professional and social affairs, have undergone much change and advancement, but no matter in what sphere of life she moves there is no branch of education more urgently needed than that which gives her the knowledge of how to govern her own particular corner of the world wisely, healthfully, and with a true economy.'[107]

Occasionally these appeals were made directly to the students. One text aimed at working-class mothers, but also used in the domestic science classes of some London Education Authority Schools, noted: 'If every woman who takes upon herself the sacred relationship of motherhood could be led to realize how she is responsible for the future of the baby-life, and how the true greatness of the individual constitutes the true grandeur of nations, we should have healthier babies and happier homes, and the disintegration of family life would be a menace no more.'[108] Another text used in Manchester-area elementary schools from the 1890s explained in detail how national duties and motherhood and femininity were all conjoined, since 'Motherhood is the ideal of womanhood, and that a woman who has trained herself physically, mentally and morally, for the fulfilling this high ideal, will have prepared herself, incidentally, for any womanly work which may fall to her lot.'[109] Arguably, however, it was the tasks that the child was made to do, and the examples used and role models followed, rather than the didactic justifications provided in a textbook's preface and introduction, that really shaped the significance of this aspect of elementary schooling.

Schoolgirls' practical subjects such as needlework, cookery, laundry, and household cleaning, just like boys' instruction in drawing and manual handicrafts, in fact, depended more on oral and visual as opposed to textual instruction. Textbooks for these subjects, where available, were laden with pictures and diagrams and were thus expensive and infrequently distributed. Mostly the diagrams in these texts were of patterns or simple shapes and images to be copied (animals, household objects, etc.), or on the correct use of tools, or explanations of various stitches, or the rules of perspective.[110] Consequently, while the advocates of national efficiency and certain prominent imperialists frequently extolled the virtues of vocational domestic and manual training, their arguments were seldom relayed to the children directly in these particular teaching materials. For the children, the message of this instruction was only evident in the learning-by-example tasks that they were told were appropriate for them: in such activities as working in school kitchen centres and woodworking shops, and in sewing and drawing classes.

Despite the claims of educationalists and teachers that such tasks were important for the good of the nation, there was little about these tasks that could be construed by children as having much to do with their sense of national identity. Witnesses at the Cross Commission in 1887 had ruefully encouraged the instruction of domestic chores – the laying of tables and making of beds – 'accompanied by music' as early as age three in order to impress upon the young girls' minds that such activity was actually pleasurable and not 'drudgery.'[111] The impracticality of the needlework training provided to most schoolgirls was commented on by many observers, even though a greater number of interested educationalists still justified its inclusion in the curriculum, albeit in often contradictory ways that changed with the passage of time.[112] Ultimately, as Carol Dyhouse has suggested, this indicates that the practical value of needlework was entirely subservient to its symbolic importance as a marker of domesticity/femininity.[113] As late as 1909 the Board of Education was still encouraging its instruction on the basis that the subject 'appealed to the natural instincts of the girls.'[114]

It should thus not be supposed that these forms of instruction were necessarily successful in promoting the ideals they were intended to convey. The sometimes absurd nature of the practical subjects taught likely increased these girls' scepticism about the actual value of their education, and reinforced, perhaps, the resentment of many working-class parents towards the intrusive nature of compulsory schooling. However, this resentment and scepticism towards elementary schooling, as Dyhouse has demonstrated, was itself *learned* through the regiment of the family economy and the pervasive social disapproval of married women working beyond the confines of home.[115] Instruction in practical subjects during this period did nothing to undermine, and probably reinforced, this potential stigma, despite the increasing number of women entering the workforce. Thus, despite possible resentment and occasional resistance, such training likely did much to further strengthen the dictates of domestic gender ideology among the manual classes, for the lesson carried home from the vocational and practical subjects of elementary schooling for both boys and girls was that the general gender roles of their parents were correct and immutable, even if the particularities of each family rarely matched exactly the ideal suggested in the classroom. Schooling in vocational subjects confirmed that their lot, whether they be boy or girl, was decreed by structures and forces largely beyond their own agency.

The general teaching of theoretical domestic economy had more recourse to reader sets and cheap texts as the primary instrument of instruction, particularly as they became more readily available in the 1890s.[116] Generally, these books also mainly contained basic practical instructions and aphorisms, and offered mostly moral, as opposed to national, strictures and exhortations. One general text, *Good Things, Made, Said and Done for Every Home and Household*, sprinkled its recipe pages with well-worn sayings such as 'better to go to bed supperless than rise in debt.'[117] Another text detailed the importance of locating the 'home' in a 'good' neighbourhood, suggesting that a dwelling was only a 'home' when it was 'in a respectable neighbourhood' and that 'it is not poverty, but sin, that makes a neighbourhood not respectable.'[118] *Arnold's Domestic Economy Readers* contained many passages and offhand comments on the innate nature of little girls and boys – 'Did you ever know a girl who was not fond of dolls? I never knew one' – combined with a step-by-step introduction to the dictates of domesticity:

The doll's house is the best game in the world for little girls, who treat their dolls as if they were their children or their visitors. They make tea, and give parties, and talk, just as they have seen their mothers do. The next step, after playing at housekeeping, is to help mother to do the work of the house. A girl soon learns how to dust tables and chairs.

A boy who will not dirty his hands to do a piece of work is not wanted in any workshop in the land. And a girl who will not dirty her hands to make the house clean is a burden where she ought to be a help. Dirty hands may be a mark of honour, and clean hands when your mother's are dirty may be a mark of shame.[119]

In fact, these books contained an odd mixture of passages, which, as in the above quotation, frequently conflated middle-class ideals about family life (in only a minority of working-class households at this time could there have been a doll's house of the type envisaged in this quotation) with prescriptions clearly intended for working-class and lower-middle-class consumption (as in the comments about workshop and domestic labour). All in all, then, classroom vocational materials for girls concentrated on practical advice on 'home-making'; for boys, they similarly concentrated on the skills that the boy might need to earn a living in the manual labour force. The underlying messages of these texts were thus quite simple in their reinforcement of basic gender and social ideology. Domestic work, maintenance of the home, and serving others was suggested as the proper focus of women's lives; the development of manual skill and the importance of worldly toil, discipline, and duty to family, community, and society was offered as right and proper for boys.

In the reading books and texts used by both sexes to teach non-vocational subjects, particularly history, 'civics,' geography, and literature, women appeared generally only in domestic and nurturing roles, usually as the wives of figures of import, or occasionally as the home-bound symbols of the nation-empire and its principles. Anna Davin has found, in a short survey of general reading books used in London board schools, that the stories and tales presented in general readers invariably prescribed differentiated gender roles and behaviour. For example, boys were described as adventurous, daring, and rough; the girls as tidy and diligent at home.[120] The boys were 'more likely to be naughty' in these books than were the girls, and their naughtiness sprang from 'exuberance or adventurousness,' whereas girls' naughtiness was portrayed as 'tamer and less positive,' in that they were too 'self-willed' or thought too much of 'showy clothes.'[121] Davin shows that the urge to promote a social ideology of industry and morality was certainly gendered in the period immediately following the passing of the 1870 Education Act. Both boys and girls were exhorted to industry and thrift: the girls' work was always in unpaid service to their family, or as a domestic servant, the boys in industry and paid labour. Davin quotes the following verses from the 1871 Jarrold *New Code Reading Books*:

> We who have to earn our bread,
> We must all endeavour
> Strive against our laziness
> Try to grow more clever.
>
> Elder Sisters, you may work
> Work and help your mothers
> Darn the stockings, mend the shirts
> Father's things, and brothers'.
>
> Younger boys, and you may work
> If you are but willing
> Thro' the week in many ways
> You may earn your shilling.[122]

Certainly, the sort of messages about gender roles that Davin has identified in books of the early 1870s continued to be written into reading books throughout the period under consideration here. Women continued to be depicted as presiding over home, and their maternal duty was consistently elevated, while their 'public' role in the national community was minimized or ignored entirely.

Masculinity and femininity, like notions of specific races and classes, are fundamentally social constructs dependent on opposition to, and interconnection with, one another. While the nation itself was inevitably depicted as being a unified whole, the place, role, and importance of the Englishman and Englishwoman within the nation were identified in separate terms in elementary school culture between 1880 and 1914. One of the most powerful metaphors used to depict a sense of national unity and belonging was that of the home, but this icon was also formulated within the changing confines of gender ideology. Anxiety and ambivalence about the proper roles of men and women in the middle-class ideal of the home helped lead to the progressive rigidity of gender roles prescribed through schooling for working-class children. Gender, class, and nationalist ideologies converged and interrelated with one another in an attempt to provide a symbolic role and identity within the national narrative for both sexes of the still largely disenfranchised working classes. The ideal of home as both a key patriotic reference point and as a metaphor for the varying but complementary roles of the sexes within it thereby became integral to the national narrative. To simplify somewhat, the working woman's relationship to the nation tended to be conceived more in terms of her biological and maternal importance to the English 'race' – the production and rearing of healthy children, the support of men, and the guardianship of the spiritual and moral values of the English nation – whereas the working man's importance and role was that of public toil and civic duty: of respectable manly activity at all levels, whether it be in the protection and perpetuation of the nation and its institutions in politics, civil administration, the armed services, or most commonly, in manual labour.[123] To the social and moral imperatives of gender division were thus added a national, imperial, and racial duty of such great importance that it could not be left to parents alone to develop. Such a view justified increasing state intervention in educational, social, health, and welfare policies. This chapter has examined the type of domestic identity that was prescribed as appropriate for working-class girls and the means by which educationalists hoped it would be produced. While it seems apparent that in the deployment of metaphors and symbolism of national identity, home and family roles were seen as appropriate for the explanation of the emotions of belonging and loyalty, the justifications of the gender and other social divisions of labour could not so easily be explained through practical instruction.

6

Narratives and Rituals of National Belonging

There is nothing more difficult to convey than reality in all its ordinariness. Flaubert was fond of saying that it takes a lot of hard work to portray mediocrity. Sociologists run into this problem all the time: How can we make the ordinary extraordinary and evoke ordinariness in such a way that people will see just how extraordinary it is?

Pierre Bourdieu, in Priscilla Parkhurst Ferguson, *On Television* (1998)

In his comparative discussion of European nationalism, Eric Hobsbawm gave the label 'national patriotism' to the powerful new ideological currents of the second half of the nineteenth century, which viewed the state as itself embodying the goals, aspirations, and sovereign legitimacy of the nation. In this discourse, the rhetoric of national loyalty was predicated on the belief that state and nation were intimately interconnected in both figurative and material ways.[1] Loyalty to the state was articulated as loyalty to the nation and vice versa. The nature of the icons, symbols, and 'invented traditions' found in both elementary school readers and in the practices of the elementary classroom demonstrate that this process of national patriotism was also well underway in England in the late-Victorian and Edwardian eras. As has already been stressed, symbols and narratives in classroom reading were, in combination, the vocabulary of the reconfigured nationalism of the end of the century. These narratives and symbols in elementary school books, moreover, connected the building of an appropriate national identity with the social concerns of their authors.

Ultimately, this process of building national literacy – or, using Hobsbawm's term, forging 'national patriotism' – became hegemonic from the sheer interconnectedness of the many symbols and narratives of identity found in both the literature and practices/rituals of the turn-of-the-century elementary school. The various emblematic recitals of Englishness all seemed to reinforce each other, and because of their ubiquitous 'ordinariness' seemed to be simple 'common sense.' Accordingly, the rationale for this chapter stems from an acknowledgment that the division into individual discussion of motifs and narratives in this study has so far been made purely for analytical purposes. Consequently, this chapter will attempt to connect and further contextualize much of what has already been discussed in this study through three different kinds of case studies. First, we shall explore one of the most influential and integrative of national narratives found within the classroom, that of the navy and English seafaring. This narrative – that there was something special and unique in the English/British connection to the sea, and that the nation-state's navy was a foundational and heroic national institution – was a fundamental element of working-class children's school experience, both in terms of their reading and in the form of other classroom practices such as singing. This will be followed by a discussion of how the language of identity suffused classroom discussions of one of the most obvious, visible, and yet also complex and contradictory of national symbols – the flag. Deconstructing the instruction provided in the meaning of the flag, and the common, ritualized 'flag worship,' provides us with some understanding of how emblems and symbols with nationalist meanings operated together in both literary and ritual performance in the elementary school. Lastly, this chapter concludes with a brief discussion of the changing uses and meaning of organized physical exercises in the classroom – the often-dreaded drill – indicating how a physical, rather than purely imaginative, process worked to reinforce the meanings learned in the classroom.

The Navy

W.H. Davenport Adams in his popular history of England's decisive naval battles and great maritime commanders asked, 'What is more characteristically English than the Navy?'[2] For children receiving their education in English elementary schools between 1880 and 1914 such a question would have had particular resonance. Indeed, although many of the youth attending elementary schools might never actually observe a naval vessel during their childhood years, the images and metaphors of the navy and of English seafaring suffused the culture of the classroom in a manner that, like the other symbols and narratives explored here, helped invoke a sense of what it was to be English. The navy in question was, of course, the British Royal Navy, but it was a peculiarly English representation of it that found its way into the classroom. In some ways English and British were synonymous in the story of the navy's role in protecting the British Isles, but as with many of the images and symbols used in the English elementary classroom, the readers generally referred to an English view of naval tradition and heritage. Indeed, the 'story' of the navy provides an excellent example of how many of the elements of narrative Englishness operated together as a whole.

The prominent place in the English classroom accorded to images of and stories about the navy at the turn of the century has first to be contextualized within the increasing attention given to the navy by British society as a whole. Considerable attention was paid to the navy in public debate in the period after 1880, a distinct change compared to earlier in the century. In fact, during most of the nineteenth century, the unchallenged role of the British Navy in policing the world's oceans was taken largely for granted by the domestic population, and there was little public concern evinced about the state or importance of naval affairs except around specific, minor crises. This attitude changed, however, with the advent of concerns about Britain's commercial and military position vis-à-vis other European powers, concerns which were similar to those that sparked public interest in the content of formal education, and also with the added duties that were expected with the acquisition of vast tracts of formal empire. The issue of naval defence burst into the realm of public debate in the mid-1880s, and increasingly thereafter public concern over naval affairs and naval expenditures was a feature of British public opinion right up to the First World War.[3] By the mid-1890s several societies and leagues had emerged to promote the cause of the navy and its integral role in the maintenance of the nation. One example of these was the Navy Records Society, which, starting in 1893, published volumes of documents regarding naval matters (beginning with *State Papers Relating to the Defeat of the Spanish Armada*), a project that was basically designed to foster and popularize the study of naval history. The primary impetus for this society came from John Knox Laughton, whose mission was to bring to the forefront public awareness and understanding of the pivotal role the navy had historically held, and continued to hold, in the life and defence of the nation. Another example was the Navy League, founded in 1894, which was a nationalist organization dedicated to educating the public about the role of the navy in the defence of the realm.

In tune with this increased emphasis on the navy and its role in the defence of the nation, many elementary schools took up the cause of the navy. These traditions and myths were, of course, not absent from schooling prior to the 1880s. But as the century drew to a close, elementary schoolchildren were even more likely to be reminded that they lived on an island (or more correctly, a group of islands) and that the navy was the physical bridge to the wider empire, the linchpin in British trading security, and the nation's primary protection against both invaders and those who sought to deprive the English of their birthright. Support for the navy was portrayed in everyday classroom reading as simply essential to even the lowliest working man and woman: 'The fleet is England's right arm. But for her fleet England would be a cipher in the councils of Europe, might be stripped of her colonies, and could not hold her Indian Empire a year. But for the fleet, the English workingman might, any day, find his daily work gone, and the price of his children's bread half-a-crown a loaf.'[4] Indeed, using the same 'defence of the realm' rhetoric, and what essentially amounted to economic scare-mongering, the distinctly partisan case for an even larger navy found its way into some readers:

To defend our shores from invasion and to protect our ships scattered all over the face of the earth, we must have powerful fleets of men of war; for

> 'Her dauntless army scatter'd and so small
> Her island myriads fed from alien lands –
> The fleet of England is her all in all.'

The teeming millions of our people would be starved to submit to any foe who could so block our ports as to prevent stores of food coming to us from other lands; hence the navy of England should be strong enough, not only to defend our coasts, but to protect our merchant ships against all comers.

The British navy is the largest and most powerful in the world; but some of those who ought to know doubt if it is as strong as it should be.[5]

The navy thus had its supporters among school-book authors – as demonstrated by the above quotation – who used the seemingly non-partisan language of the 'nation' to explain the practical, but vital, importance of safeguarding the English food supply. And yet clearly the last line also demonstrates that a highly subjective contemporary political gloss could also be applied to historical treatments of the navy.

Nor was the navy's economic importance in protecting the living standard of the working classes the only way in which the image and role of the navy was utilized in elementary classroom culture. The navy and its historic successes and traditions were significant cultural markers of Englishness as well. English children were told that they were members of a nation-race of seafarers, and that the past, present, and future welfare of all the people of the island had depended, and would continue to depend, on English sailors and the British Navy.[6]

Alfred the Great was commonly depicted within the classroom as symbolizing the historic continuity between the contemporary English seafarers and their 'hardy' Anglo-Saxon origins. Portrayed as 'the noblest king that ever ruled over England,'[7] Alfred was a popular hero in children's didactic texts throughout the nineteenth century, primarily for his perceived selfless and scholarly character as typified in the oft-retold folk tale of the burnt cakes.[8] In the last decades of the century, however, he was also increasingly heralded for his martial accomplishments and for what was described as his key role in the founding of the English naval tradition. One text from 1890 noted that it was to Alfred that 'the English owe the idea of a navy to protect the country from invasion.' Another noted that 'he raised forts in suitable places. He built a royal navy and taught the English, who had forgotten their old seafaring habits, how to fight on the ocean. He was the first English King who gained a victory at sea over the Danes.' And numerous other history and geography reading books exalted Alfred primarily because he was 'the Founder of the British Navy.'[9] Typically these texts posited continuity from the ships of Alfred's time to the contemporary navy. The *Tower History Readers*, for example, noted that 'perhaps the wisest thing that Alfred did was to build warships, and teach his people once again to fight upon the sea. He saw, what our king and his ministers see today, that England's bulwark is her navy. We have the most powerful navy in the world, and for centuries no foreign foe has set foot on English soil.'[10] But this historical connection did not apply merely to the institution of the navy. Alfred's seaborne campaign against the invading Danes was often used to symbolize the innate, 'seafaring spirit' of the English. This sort of rhetoric invoked ambiguous racial characterizations, for once Alfred had reacquainted the Anglo-Saxon English with the lost secrets of successful naval warfare, the English forever took 'possession' of the sea as they were 'destined' to do.[11]

Books and readers from a variety of disciplines and perspectives echoed these themes. C.H. Wyatt's general civics reader, *The English Citizen*, noted that 'the love of the sea' was 'inherent in the breasts of a people sprung from a race whose greatest exploits of conquest and adventure have been intimately associated with seamanship,' while a geography reader from 1901 proclaimed that 'we are rightly proud of our forefathers, and it is for us to follow in their footsteps, to keep the place they have gained for us and to show that we are worthy of the great race which, with all its faults, has set so good an example to the world.'[12] Similarly, Herbert Hayens's popular historical-adventure text noted: 'The love of the restless ocean implanted in the hearts of our fierce piratical ancestors has never left the British boy ... the blue waters [are] his especial birthright.'[13] Numerous other geography, general, and literature readers detailed the racialized traits of superior virtue, adventurousness, pluck, and raw ability that had, since Alfred's time, characterized English seafaring.[14]

In history reading books, the 'raw ability' of the English sailor was a constant in every succeeding historical period from Alfred onwards. The *Patriotic History Readers* noted that, since Alfred's death, England's 'splendid sailors' had kept the island nation safe from any fear of invasion (discounting the notable exception of the Norman Conquest, which, as was noted in a previous chapter, was invariably treated as a special case). This was a rather generous assessment of the navy's performance, since attempted invasions of the British Isles had, in fact, not been prevented by naval action in 1215, 1399, 1470, 1485, 1688, 1715, 1745, or 1797. Nevertheless, the image of the sailor had become so sanitized and glorified in this period that even the most benign elements of the earlier 'Jolly Jack Tar' stereotype were not applied to his description. Instead, the entire English population was said to have a special relationship to the sea: the English 'have always kept up their love of the sea, and many of [our] most famous victories have been won by our navy.'[15]

The notion that the English had had a 'natural' and unbroken chain of naval successes, and that these were integral to the survival and strength of their nation, is widely evident in these readers. This pro-

jected historical continuity, linking naval and national success origi-
nating with Alfred, is clearly indicated in John Finnemore's 1901 collection of thumbnail biographies for classroom reading, *Famous Englishmen*. Finnemore described it as 'fitting' that Alfred should open
'our record of Famous Englishmen' since 'he showed to the full every
quality which has marked the greatness of our race.' Most significantly, it was Alfred who first 'built a fleet, which was the beginning
of the British Navy, the navy which now has ships on every sea, and
flies the Union Jack in every corner of the world.' And although Alfred
had been dead a thousand years, 'he is not forgotten. To this day the
English people are fond and proud of his name.'[16] That this sort of
didactic projection informed much of the elementary school's cover-
age of naval history and current geography was also revealed by the
visual materials found within the elementary schools. Decorative prints
contrasting vessels from the 'olden times' (often Alfred's longships or
Nelson's *Victory*) to contemporary naval warships hung on classroom
walls.[17] The pictorial covers of the reading books, and the special and
coveted 'picture books' in the small school libraries, were adorned
with portraits of great naval heroes, ships, and signal flags. And special events such as the commemoration celebrations of 25 October
1901 marking the King Alfred Millenary were held in many schools.[18]

   Another area in which naval imagery was particularly prominent in
the elementary classroom was in the poetry and songs that were recited aloud in class. Alfred Tennyson's 1885 poem 'The Fleet,' which
included the lines 'You, you, if you shall fail to understand / What
England is, and what her all-in-all / On what you will come the curse
of all the land / Should this old England fall / Which Nelson left so
great,' was frequently found in literature readers.[19] Sea shanties and
patriotic naval songs by the likes of Henry Newbolt, Charles Kingsley,
and the great poets of the eighteenth and early nineteenth centuries
commonly adorned the pages of readers and songbooks. School logbooks attest to the frequency and popularity of these kinds of songs
and their boisterous singing, both regularly in class and on special
occasions.[20] Thomas Campbell's 'Ye Mariners of England' was a particular favourite, included in numerous school readers and in most
songbooks prepared for schools. Its lyrics – celebrating English mariners as the 'bulwarks of Britannia' – give a fair indication of the general tone and content of most of these poems and songs.[21] In the first
three stanzas of this song we encounter many of the elements of the
navy myth as it was presented to schoolchildren: the evocation of a
sense of continuity with the ancient past; the elevation of naval he-

roes; and the sense that the English were destined to rule the waves. Another classroom favourite, expressing the same veneration of the English maritime heritage, was Newbolt's 'Admirals All,' which listed the names and exploits of the great 'sea dogs' by name, followed by the admirals Benbow, Collingwood, Blake, and of course, Nelson.[22] These songs and poems – other favourites that appeared with great frequency were Campbell's 'Battle of the Baltic,' Dobson's 'Ballard of the Armada,' Garrick's 'Hearts of Oak,' Macaulay's 'The Spanish Armada,' Newbolt's 'Drake's Drum,' Palgrave's 'Trafalgar,' and Thomson's 'Rule Britannia' – and the many more to be found in literature readers and songbooks were, in combination with the visual reminders on the walls of the classroom, interactive reinforcements of the navy narrative present in the school readers.

The didactic use of naval heroes and the seafaring myth was closely associated with the empire and with notions of racial destiny in this period, and thus echoed the general trajectories of the other major narratives of 'Englishness' already discussed. The navy was, of course, the material as well as symbolic link between the mother country and colonies – the very 'lifeline of the Empire.' Ideas about the inherent superiority of the English sailor, supposedly derived from his Anglo-Saxon descent, meshed perfectly with race discourse and the language of 'imperial responsibility.'[23] Even the 'divine providence' narrative of English freedoms and the Whig historical tradition could find expression in representations of the navy and its heroes, since the self-imposed obligation to maintain the freedom of the seas was presented as an extension of basic English freedoms. Writers could, in this regard, also point to the navy's 'unending perseverance' in ridding the seas of pirates and the slave trade. The navy's role in protecting slavers prior to abolition was, of course, never mentioned. Indeed, in most readers the slave trade only ever appeared in comments on its abolition. The navy, then, as symbolized by the men who had brought it into existence and led it to pre-eminence, protected the island home of the luminary English and their overseas dominions, and was thus the very guardian of the cherished 'English virtues' of liberty, peace, and law.

The Flag

One of the physical symbols of national belonging most commented on in school readers during this period was that of the British flag, the

Union Jack. Pamela Horn has rightly noted that an 'almost mystical reverence for the flag' developed among elementary educators at this time.[24] In both their private meetings and in their official organs, local education authorities (state supported and voluntary) debated the value of having a flagpole and a Union Jack flying in the school yard, and whether or not to have the 'national flag' in the actual classroom.[25] Imperialist propagandists were particularly keen on having the flag present in elementary schools so that the values they claimed it represented might be venerated. From the 1890s on, imperialists repeatedly claimed that children did not understand the meaning of their flag, and that they needed more direct teaching in its importance. One commentator in 1896 noted in *The School Guardian*:

We copy America in many things; would that we might copy her in educating the young to know the glories of their country's past and to reverence its flag! Our people, as everyone knows, do not care for their flag. They know nothing about it. They do not know the meaning of the Union Jack, nor how its three crosses signify the indissoluble union of Great Britain and Ireland. To them, one flag is as good as another ... the fact is, we have become so cosmopolitan that the very idea of patriotism is distasteful. We have outgrown such narrow feelings, and even in the desire that our country should keep her old place among the nations is ridiculed as 'jingo.'[26]

Despite an immediate (and accurate) counter-response from Arnold-Forster in the same journal that such claims were highly exaggerated – that elementary schoolchildren were in fact already receiving such instruction and that his own book, *The Citizen Reader* (which he claimed had sold more than 400,000 copies), was fulfilling this purpose – such claims nevertheless sparked a variety of donations and flag-buying drives. And, notwithstanding the occasional objections of trade unionists and other groups opposed to what they considered the 'jingoistic bent' of flag worship, it would seem that by the outbreak of war in 1914 a very substantial number of elementary schools could boast a school flagpole and Union Jack, and perhaps also classroom flags as well.[27]

Indeed, logbooks from elementary schools of all denominations and affiliations from all over the country indicate that, by the end of the first decade of the twentieth century, it was customary practice to have the schoolchildren march past and salute the flag on annual events such as Empire Day – the Empire Day Movement was started in 1902 by the Earl of Meath, the first official school celebration held in 1904, and by 1905 Meath could claim empire-wide observance of the event (although it was not observed in every school in the land prior to the First World War)[28] – and also on special occasions such as coronations and other 'national anniversaries.'[29] On Empire Day schoolchildren were given specific instruction on the meaning of the flag they saluted.[30] In accordance with the Empire Day Movement's provisional program, the London Education Committee explicitly directed that an address on the symbolism of the flag become part of the 1908 Empire Day celebrations. As one London teacher's entry in the school's logbook noted: 'Empire day. According to council instructions children assembled in the hall and head mistress addressed them on Empire Day and the Union Jack; at 11.30 marched into playground, sang national songs and saluted the "flag." Girls made tableau of the nation.'[31] If their frequent letters to education and teachers' periodicals are any indication, imperial propagandists seemed to have devoted a good deal of their efforts towards further increasing overt teaching about the flag.[32] Such overt proselytizing on the flag and its importance to Empire Day led to letters of protest being sent to local education authorities from labour, socialist, and pacifist groups. Often, however, as with the June 1907 protest about Empire Day and flag 'worship' by the Operative Bricklayers' Society of Battersea, such objections were politely listened to and quietly shelved or dismissed.[33] Notwithstanding the shrill demands of the imperial propagandists about the paucity of flag worship and the disapproval of labour and the left about including more, elementary schoolchildren were *already* being exposed to the 'edifying meaning of the flag' – it was one of the most frequently occurring symbols in the students' everyday reading materials.

Beyond its common physical presence on covers and/or frontispieces, depictions of the flag and discussions of its significance and meaning took many forms in reading books. Few geography, 'civics,' or contemporary history readers were without some didactic references to the Union Jack. Descriptions of its material and symbolic composition, explanations of its use as an emblem of nationality, and narratives describing deeds of valour accomplished in order to honour it all found their way into readers. The most common use of the flag was in recitals of the value of national pride. 'Who has not seen the Union Jack proudly floating from the masthead of a war-ship or the flag-staff of a public building?' asked one set of readers from 1903. 'It is merely a strip of blue silk or stuff with one white and two red crosses upon it. Yet thousands of our brave sailors and soldiers have shed their blood, and given up their lives to save it from falling into the hands of the enemy. This simple flag stands for our great country and nation. When we cease to love it, or can no longer defend it, then the great and glorious British Empire will totter and fall to pieces, like a building with weak foundations.'[34] Most accounts described the physical nature of the flag, contrasting its modest nature with the exalted emotions that this 'piece of bunting' was thought to evoke. It was explained that flags meant a great deal: that they represented all that was great and good about the nation. Moreover, the importance of the flag was vehemently asserted as a means to understanding the nature of nationality. 'The Union Jack should be honoured and loved by all of us, as it is the flag of our country, and reminds us of all we hold most dear.' Authors poured scorn on the notion that the flag was merely a 'piece of bunting' and on those that loved it solely as decoration. 'We do not, of course, revere and love the piece of bunting or the stripes, but what they represent – that is our country.'[35] Such descriptions attempted to infuse abstract meaning into an everyday object. The flag itself was but a marker of the national greatness that was suggested as its legacy. As one author stated matter-of-factly, 'We call our flag the Union Jack. It was the flag of our fathers, and it will be the flag of our children. We ought, therefore, to know what is on it, and what it means.'[36] Knowing what it meant required the use of explanatory narratives, detailing the deeds that had been accomplished to honour the nation, and extolling the distinctive values that had made these accomplishments possible. Reader authors attempted to explain the symbolism of the flag itself through reference to historical and mythical tales, and also to provide fables of the 'symbolic power' of the flag. We shall deal with each genre in turn.

Due to the composite nature of the Union Jack, most readers used the designation 'British' when describing it: 'Every nation has a flag by which it is known, and which stands for the country to which it belongs. The British flag is the famous Union Jack, "the red, white and blue," as it is sometimes called, because it is made up of these three colours.'[37] But in acclaiming the unified and unifying nature of the Union Jack as an emblem, reading books tended to stress both the core English values and the wider imperial connection, rather than simply the multinational composition of the United Kingdom: '[The] flag is used to show that some uninhabited or uncivilized country had been taken in the name of the Queen for the people of England, and that from that time it is to become part of the British Empire.'[38] Tremendous symbolic importance was invested in the flag in this regard: 'The flag of any country stands for the country itself, and those who insult the flag, insult the people ... When we speak of our soldiers and sailors defending our flag, or fighting under our flag, we mean that they are defending or fighting for their native land. When we say that any person or country is under the protection of the British Flag, we mean that the person or country so protected will be defended with all the power of the British Empire.'[39] Not only did the flag stand for the power of the British Empire, which all Englishmen and women were encouraged to defend, but the mere existence of a common flag flying over the empire was projected as being a source of untold strength.

Circular reasoning was also offered to show why it was important both to honour the unity of the empire under the flag and to endeavour to extend its sway: 'United under one flag, the world-empire will then be irresistible, and its power to do good will be great and far reaching. In order that the Empire may be held together under one flag it is necessary that its various parts should be drawn closer to one another by ever-tightening cords of interest and affection.'[40] Indeed, although some authors stressed the symbolism of the different component flags in the Union Jack, many of these same authors still referred to it as the emblem of the Englishman, and of English values. A telling example of this was the oft-reprinted poem by Mullen, 'The Flag of England,' which described the Union Jack as England's symbol of liberty.[41] Moreover, the first page of H.E. Malden's 'civics' reader explained that 'the Union Jack is the flag of Great Britain, and it is made up of three flags combined.' However, by page two the flag has become a symbol of English values and virtues and the familiar representation of the dutiful Englishman: for wherever this flag flew 'there is the home of Englishmen, and there the duties of Englishmen must be done.'[42] Arnold-Forster similarly commented that when it was properly used in any place, the flag proclaimed that beneath it was something that belongs to England, and 'which the people of England have undertaken to protect.' Whatever that something was – whether a fortress, ship, or ambassadorial residence – it was protected by the English government and people who would make sure to 'see that right and justice' were done there.[43] Another author noted simply: 'The Union Jack is a symbol of the union, which binds Englishmen all the world over.'[44]

Certain distinct values were clearly identified as existing only where the Union Jack flew. These values, a distillation in symbolic form of many of the traits considered to be characteristic of England and of Englishmen, included love of liberty, freeborn rights, indomitable courage, respect for one's self and others that have 'earned it,' and a well-developed sense of duty. A widespread device was to refer to the freedom enjoyed under the protection of the flag, and that all under it would be treated with fairness and justice. Comments regarding freedom and liberty 'under the flag' were sometimes connected overtly to the highly touted, self-imposed task of clearing the seas of pirates and slave traders.[45] At other times the significance of the flag was presented as a more general, abstract claim about British customs and law: 'Under that flag there is no slavery; no man can be arbitrarily put to death or deprived of liberty. Where it flies, it is a mark or symbol of the rule of law, order and liberty, and of the presence of Christian civilization.'[46]

Stories of the 'power' of the flag played on the themes of respect for the emblem of a mighty nation and on the flag as a symbol of justice, liberty, and 'fair play.' George Bosworth's *Narrative Geography Readers* included a story of a foreign king stepping in mud rather than on the British flag,[47] but a more common type of approach was exemplified by a Collins geography reader from 1901, which retold how 'an American poet'

has described how when there was a rising of Indians in North America, and a number of white settlers were killed, an English fur trader with his wife made a journey through the district in which the Indians were, and suffered no harm. The trader was told both he and his wife would lose their lives. But he was not afraid. He nailed a Union Jack on the top of his waggon [*sic*], and started on his journey.

'The indians knew quite well
That where those colours flew,
Then men that lived beneath them
Were mostly straight and true.'[48]

In this anecdote, as in accounts of the British suppression of the slave trade, the flag was depicted as a symbol of English righteousness, fairness, and justice. For, as the text went on to explain, if the English settlers who had gone to 'trade in the country around Hudson's Bay had been cruel and dishonest, and had treated the natives badly, the Indians would not have respected the flag of their country.'⁴⁹ A later, revised version of these readers recited a different yarn with a similar message. This time it was of how an Englishman abroad had been saved from injustice by his accusers' recognition of the 'power' of the flag:

> Some years ago, an Englishman in a foreign land was about to be shot as a punishment. The consul said that the people in that land had no right to put the prisoner to death, but they would not listen to him. When the soldiers were marched out, and were ready to shoot, the consul went up to the Englishman, and, covering him with the Union Jack, exclaimed, 'Fire if you dare!' But the officer in charge did not give the order. He was afraid to fire on the British flag. Had he done so, his country would have had to answer for the insult to the British nation. So the man was saved.⁵⁰

But lest the child reading this text came to think of the authority of the flag as being unconditional, the same reader narrated another tale about the deployment of a Union Jack that explicitly connected esteemed but restricted English values with the symbolism of the flag. This was the story of Sir Samuel Baker, 'a great Englishman' travelling in Africa who, while with a 'savage tribe,' was attacked by some slave traders:

> The king of the tribe was in great fear, and he said to his white visitor, 'let us pack and run.'
> But Sir Samuel was not afraid. He hoisted the British flag over the village, and then sent word to the enemy that he would defend it to the last.
> Knowing that if they attacked the British flag they would be severely punished, the slave traders went away without firing a single shot.
> Then the king asked Sir Samuel to make him a present of the flag which could work such wonders, but this he refused to do. He said that the British flag was respected, because those who carried it were always ready to defend it with their lives. The flag would be of no use to men who ran away in the face of danger.⁵¹

The message of this little tale, contrasting as it did the 'cowardice' of the savage natives with the English/British pluck and resolve implicit in the symbol of the Union Jack, was one that was clearly intended to convey a sense that the flag represented certain national values: particularly bravery, honour, and justice. The flag was not merely a magic totem: the flag of a nation would only be honoured and respected if 'the people or the nation is worthy of honour and respect.'[52]

The stated aim of all such narratives and descriptions was the generation of respect for the flag, not as an object, but as a symbol of national character and community. In their attempts to evoke a sense of pride about their nationality, reader authors encouraged elementary schoolchildren to consider the heroic deeds done for and under the banner of the flag. Using the romantic ideas associated with military heroes, the readers clearly associated military glory with the Union Jack. In an account of the relief of Lucknow, it is the sight of the flag that inspired both the defenders and those attempting to relieve them to press on with their struggle: 'The flag told them from afar off that they were not too late; that their work was not in vain, and that ere another day was passed they might press to their hearts the loved ones who so long had stood upon the brink of death.'[53] The glory of martial sacrifice was depicted in terms of a Union Jack–draped coffin, and offered as a reminder of the 'majesty' of the English nation, empire, and 'race' with which the children were encouraged to identify: 'When men die fighting for their country they are buried wrapt in the English flag – the Union Jack; and this honour is extended to those who have served their country well in other ways ... The Union Jack represents to men's minds the might, majesty, and honour, of England and of the English-speaking race within the Empire.'[54]

The pregnant meaning of the flag was hammered home to schoolchildren in a variety of ways, but the focus was always squarely on having the children associate the flag with a sense of belonging and loyalty to their nation and the empire, and with the values that had made them 'great.'[55] Arnold-Forster was particularly keen on inculcating a sense of the 'majestic' symbolism of the nation's flag, a goal to which he devoted several highly didactic passages in his influential *Citizen Reader*. The role of the flag in the classroom is thus best summed up by his own reader's discussion of it: 'The flag is nothing in itself; but because it stands before other people as the mark of our country, it means a great deal. It is right and useful that men should honour and love the flag, and be prepared to lose their lives in defending it, as many of our countrymen have done before now; but we must bear in mind that it is not really the piece of coloured silk that is worth fighting for or dying for, but only the honour and reputation of the country which has chosen it for its own.'[56]

The Changing Justification of Education Practice: Drill and Physical Exercises

The vocabulary of identity found within reading materials, reflected in the classroom's maps and pictures, and actualized in the rituals of flag worship and the singing of patriotic songs and sea shanties, found another corollary in the physical activities of the elementary school curriculum. The stated purposes and implied aims of physical education were varied, and as with all of the ideology explored in this study, it would be erroneous to suggest that physical education was incorporated into the school curriculum solely as a means to indoctrinate students in their national identity. However, it is also clear that, just like the in-class subjects, the form of physical education promoted in the elementary school was a product of social, political, and cultural imperatives closely connected to concerns about national identity, as much as it was based on notions of educational pedagogical advancement and psychology. A brief survey of the evolution of organized physical education through the later nineteenth century should round out our picture of how the meta-narrative and vocabulary of identity construction suffused the entire process of elementary schooling.

According to J.S. Hurt, the inclusion of physical drill in the curriculum of first workhouse and then the voluntary schools prior to the later 1850s was largely due to its perceived dual role in securing classroom order and as a means to help rejuvenate pauper men's productivity in physical labour, either alone or in teams. By demanding that all manner of classroom tasks be done in step-by-step unison, by enforcing the forming of lines before and after instruction, by the performance of stylized physical movements in the playground, and by requiring correct posture and regimented movements in the classroom, organized drill activities were thought to help teach the good habits of obedience and discipline. It was thought that these individual virtues were conducive to the instilling of a sense of law and order, and also in helping to eradicate pauperism. This would happen since, as drill taught patience, obedience, and industry, the activity would help to eradicate the 'taint of hereditary pauperism' that was the result of inbred and inherited moral shortcomings.[57] Drill was the means by which to 'secure a punctual observance of the hours allotted to rising and going to bed ... [and] to preserve uninterrupted decorum in attitude, expression, and manner during the meals and religious services.'[58] All these aims were clearly based on the possibility of reforming the individual trapped in his or her own improvidence. Drill was thought to diminish the desire of the poorer child to commit crime, to create an aversion to personal sloth and idleness, and to reduce impatience and individual disobedience. In its early formulations drill had very little to do with physical fitness or well-being.

By the 1870s drill was enshrined in the educational codes for more overtly social, as opposed to individual, moral-regenerative purposes. In 1875, to remove any possible doubt about the intentions of drill, the word 'military' was inserted into its description in the Education Code.[59] Drill was now a practical extension of the very ethos of elementary education. It was part of the process whereby children were socialized into those values necessary for the working-class individual to function in society in a properly regulated and military-like fashion.[60] In contrast, drill was not advocated for the elite Public Schools at this time, and in fact, at the Clarendon Commission on the Public Schools it was suggested by E. Warre, an assistant master at Eton, that the cricket and football fields were more appropriate than the barrack square for the sons of the upper classes. Organized drill in elementary schools now increasingly took the form of calisthenics and regularized periods of marching and parade-ground activities. A manual used in the early 1870s suggested that 'a moderate amount of drill brightens up and polishes the children of the working classes wonderfully. It teaches habits of order, regularity, silence, obedience, neatness, attention, steadiness and method.'[61] Edwin Chadwick summed up the purpose of drill as useful because it gave 'an early initiation to all that is implied in the term discipline,' namely, 'Duty, Order, Obedience to Command, Punctuality, Patience.'[62] This use of drill became popular as specialized competitions for school drill teams developed in the 1880s. At the drill competition in London in 1886, thirteen companies of forty boys each 'wheeled' and 'doubled' and 'prepared to receive cavalry.' After the drill, General Hamley addressed the boys and spoke of the excellence of this kind of physical training and of its advantage in 'cultivation of habits of obedience.'[63]

In the 1880s and 1890s social reformers tried repeatedly to have drill replaced with other, less routinized forms of physical exercise, including organized games and swimming. Innovative physical education was advocated by reformers as desirable in the 'full healthy development' of each child and as the means by which the lives of the working classes might be improved.[64] Yet despite the growing interest in the large and progressive school boards for fitness systems such as

Ling's Swedish Gymnastics, drill remained the national Board of Education's favoured and heavily promoted form of physical education until 1909.[65] Significantly, the arguments used to support the continued use of drill, and also its replacement by systematic gymnastics, also changed subtly between the mid-1890s and the first decade of the twentieth century. During the Anglo–Boer War and for some years thereafter, there was a nationwide resurgence of overtly military-style drill, including the use of dummy rifles,[66] which some argued was necessary 'to lay the foundations of a military spirit in the nation.' Indeed, a full-scale debate on the place of drill within elementary schools erupted in the House of Commons in March 1900. Numerous members of Parliament expressed their opinions that education in general and physical education in particular were not serving the 'best interests of the nation.'[67] Of course, this debate must be viewed in terms of the crisis caused by the poor start (from the British point of view) of the Anglo–Boer War.

However, significantly, much of this discussion occurred before the poor physical condition of British army recruits was widely known, and well before the committee to study the problem was established.[68] In 1902 the War Office, in consultation with the Board of Education, issued instructions to all General Officers Commanding Districts that they should assist schools in the promotion and teaching of drill whenever possible.[69] Even those progressive educationalists and social reformers who opposed the military aspects of drill, and who argued instead for organized games and the Ling gymnastics system, found that they made the most converts to their position when they contextualized their arguments with references to national and imperial priorities, national efficiency, and later, fears of racial degeneracy.[70] Thus, physical training was typically urged as a 'national concern, involving issues that permanently affected the character of the race,'[71] with commentators ominously pointing out that the 'neglect of physical training has caused empire after empire to dwindle, crumble and finally fall to pieces.'[72]

The London School Board was the largest authority to come out against compulsory, overtly military-style drill, and London schools were encouraged to use the Ling gymnastics system instead. As Hugh Philpott, the official chronicler of the London School Board, explained, at first 'the great aim of teachers generally seemed to be to get the boys to march and turn and wheel with clockwork precision and to hold themselves stiff as pokers. The Drill sergeant rather than the gymnastic teacher was their model.'[73] This was changed to a more developmental approach that stressed physical health, flexibility, and growth. However, even in 1903 it was clear that drill still had a place: 'No school entertainment nowadays is complete without an exhibition of drill. Once a year at the Albert Hall a great demonstration is given of the physical exercises taught in the London Board Schools. The programme at the 1903 display included, besides extension exercises without apparatus, displays with dumb-bells and Indian clubs, flag drill, ball drill, and fencing and quarter staff exercises.'[74] While finding adequate numbers of trained instructors for gymnastics was a major problem for the London school authorities, there was also still an abiding interest in drill and its social/national possibilities. Indeed, ultimately the arguments used to justify the Ling gymnastics system merely echoed the responses to concerns about the need for military drill. In his 1906 address on 'Physical Training in Elementary Schools,' Colonel Fox, the London County Council inspector of physical training, suggested there was a direct connection between gymnastics, physical culture, and national prowess. Fox argued that the Ling system of gymnastics was as admirably suited to retaining this physical culture as any other form of drill, and had the benefits of being less overtly militaristic and tediously rigid in form than barrack-square-style drilling. Moreover, 'the revival of gymnastics in a country' he noted, 'has been invariably brought in on a wave of patriotism ... the increase of gymnastic societies in France after the events of 1870; the great movement in Denmark after 1864; and in our own country as a result of the unsatisfactory returns during the late Boer War.'[75]

Regardless of whether it was military drill or organized gymnastics that was being promoted, the arguments used to justify routinized physical education were often very similar and usually touched on the necessities of imperial-national citizenship. A good summary of these views was provided at the 1906 Northern Educational Conference by Captain H. Worsley-Gough, who explained to the assembled teachers and educators:

Today, education is recognized as essential to fit the future citizen to take his place in the world, but the best education you can give a child is of little use unless the body be rendered fit to receive it and turn it to good account.

The supremacy of a nation in commerce or in war depends mainly on the physical qualities of the people, and an eminent spokesman, speaking not long ago on this subject, said, 'The future of the country rests with the future of the race, and the race rests with the future of the children.' It is with the children that physical training must begin, that they may grow into healthy men and women fit to be the fathers and mothers of another generation ...

There is one aspect of the question of Physical Training, which appears to me to be of the utmost importance, and that is its relation to the great problem of Imperial Defence ...

It is to be hoped that English boys and girls will always play games, but games are recreation, while physical training is education and part of the business of life. The cultivation of physical health and the development of the body is one of the highest duties of man – a duty which he owes at once to his country and to himself, for the strength of her children is the strength of the nation.

To train a boy to know how to help in the defence of his country is not necessarily to implant in his bosom the seed of aggressive militarism, while the very training which renders him capable of performing the highest duty of citizenship develops his body and muscles to meet the demands of his everyday life.[76]

Such a justification of the need for physical education – stressing its role as education, and as necessary for promoting healthy notions of duty and citizenship, even while dismissing any militaristic intent – could aptly be applied to many in-class subjects being promoted in the elementary schoolroom.

Over the course of about fifty years, then, the support of drill in the elementary school curriculum moved from a concern with individual moral regeneration to arguments about group socialization to demands for actual physical health as a prerequisite of 'national health' and military success. Significantly, 'progressive' educationalists were often at the forefront of the move towards reinvigorating interest in physical education, aiming to improve the health of the young population at the end of this period – not at an individual level, but at a social one. As Carolyn Steedman has pointed out, even the most committed progressive social activists, such as Margaret McMillan, published their depictions of working-class childhood and arguments for reform at a time when their audiences 'understood labouring children to constitute a form of social danger.' The reception of the work of social activists who sought to bring to the public's attention the 'physical deficiencies' of working-class children ought thus to be contextualized within the contemporary concern about how the ill-health and low physical standards of urban labouring youth threatened Britain's imperial prowess.[77] Despite their pushing for fundamental social (and even socialistic) reform, the arguments of such progressives thus tended to underscore rather than challenge the calls for drill or organized gymnastics made by conservatives, imperialists, and national efficiency advocates. The changing arguments regarding the need for physical education were not sudden or total shifts, but rather the gradual emergence of dominant discourses. Some elements of the older views could still be found in a few arguments about drill and national health in the Edwardian period, and arguments about the military purposes of drill were first advanced in the 1860s. This general pattern does, however, indicate a correspondence of the changing content of the curriculum to the progressive changes in ideas about the role of educational practice with regard to the reformation of the individual and his or her place in the social whole.

Nationalism, in all its guises, produces powerful narratives. In general, the construction of a national story is facilitated by the evocation of myths about the nation's own ancient origins and tales about national 'growth' and developing unity. These narratives have no closure, as the nation is always growing, developing, and reaching forward to claim its 'destiny.' Thus, national narratives, even when they are the products of a cultural nationalism that is unconnected to specific political aims, are certainly not apolitical. National narratives are constructed out of romantic ideas about the past and desires, both conscious and unconscious, about what the present and the future should look like. Consequently, national narratives are fundamentally social prescriptions. It is within the context of social prescription, therefore, that the meaning of the national narratives presented to each new generation should be situated. The heroes who had attained glory for England through their devotion to the flag, or through their deeds and activities at sea, were all extolled in a manner thought to nurture a sense of national belonging and pride. At the same time these symbols and institutions were a source of motivation to future duty. In being invited to locate themselves within this interconnected historical and symbolic inheritance, elementary schoolchildren were encouraged to identify with an essentialized English identity. Conspicuously, the object of this identity was the actual intersection of nation and state. The flag represented the past glory and the present characteristics of the people within the nation, but it was also an icon of the state and its potential power. The navy too was both the embodiment of supposed English national traditions and values that stretched all the way back to the Anglo-Saxons, but also the most powerful force in the state's protective armoury. The use of military-style drill or ritualized gymnastics in schools added a tangible, physical dimension to the unfinished national narrative: children needed to be fit and disciplined for whatever task their nation might need of them in the future.

Ultimately, national characteristics and the building of feelings of nationality through the imaginative and physical subjects of schooling were symbolically connected to state prerogatives and power. With English identity thus came various expectations, obligations, and responsibilities, each of which moved the child subject from the realm of mere identification with the English people to the realm of concrete action on behalf of the state. For as the author of the *English History Reading Books* aptly explained:

Every new step in a nation's progress brings with it increasing duties ... We boast of our freedom in England, and we do well ... Each little child, as he or she grows up, can do something.

Thousands of small right acts done come to a great deal when they are taken together. As we read what men of old have done for us, let us think of their deeds as the poet Browning thought when sailing off the Spanish coast. His mind dwelt on Nelson and the old warriors who had fought and died there for their country. Trafalgar was in front and St Vincent behind. Then he turned to think of himself, and the words that rose to his lips were

'Here and here did England help me; how can I help England? Say!'[78]

Conclusion:

'For Home, Country, and Race'

It is an illusion that youth is happy, and an illusion of those who have lost it; but the young know they are wretched, for they are full of the truthless ideals which have been instilled in them ... It looks as if they were victims of a conspiracy; for the books they read, ideal by necessity of selection, and the conversation of their elders, who look back upon the past through the rosy haze of forgetfulness, prepare them for an unreal life.

W. Somerset Maugham, *Of Human Bondage* (1915)

In December 1897 a company of the Royal Artillery stationed at Gibraltar performed 'The Babes in the Woods and Robin Hood,' a Christmas pantomime for the local British population on 'the Rock.' In a scene in the first act the children of a 'typical board school' explained to the disguised Robin Hood what they were taught daily in their classrooms:

> ALL: A model school-day you see
> 'Castle Road' chicks are we
> We learn just what we ought
> And this is what we are taught:

> BOYS: We're taught to work and play,
> A little of both each day,
> So that when we're grown up, then –
> We'll be good Englishmen.

GIRLS: We learn to sew, and clothes to make,
We learn to cook and bake
In fact you see our School contrives,
To make us English wives.[1]

We might speculate that the sight of numerous burly gunners in po-
nytails and short trousers ensured the success of this production. While
admittedly somewhat irreverent, this passage does provide us with an
apt summation of the perceived aim and methods of English elementary schooling as contemporaries understood it between 1880 and 1914.
Both the content and the context of this passage encapsulate the close
relationships among class, gender roles, Englishness, and the processes
of late-Victorian elementary education. The school's purpose was abun-
dantly obvious: its intention was not just to teach children 'their letters'; it sought a much more important and abstract goal, to produce
'good Englishmen' and 'good English wives.'

Between 1880 and 1914, elementary school-book authors wrote into
their collective product their own imaginings of what being English
was all about. And the visions of Englishness that these authors increasingly presented were of a different character than that which
was implicit in the school books produced at mid-century. Traditional
liberalism was not discarded entirely in the English national identity
promoted through schooling towards the end of the century, but it
was certainly modified. The civic idealism that had marked the lib-
eral-nationalism of mid-century gave way all over Europe to more
biological conceptions of nationality – due, in part, to the widely dis-
seminated and increasingly accepted views of Lamarck and Darwin.
Professional educators were merely responding to other academic
trends when they exploited the newly fashionable conceptions of race
and nationality to promote their own vision of Englishness that wedded racial and national identity. It was an uncomfortable marriage, to
be sure. 'Race' was as slippery a concept in nineteenth-century usage
as it is today, and the term could denote not only biological but also
social and cultural difference. Nevertheless, the authors of books for
the elementary school system frequently invoked the language of race
in their discussions of English ethnicity and national origins in a manner that easily traversed the term's biological connotations and its
possible social-cultural meanings.

The tenets of Anglo-Saxonism consequently became favoured in these
authors' discussions of English history and geography. The Anglo-

Saxon English race was contrasted with other less 'fortunate' races, both among Caucasian peoples and the 'coloured' peoples that populated and bordered on the British Empire. Patterns of superiority and interdependence were highlighted, demonstrating to working-class children their 'natural' affinity with the rest of their own race-nation and their essential difference from other races. The Anglo-Saxon English were also said to be racially suited to expansion and colonization. The ancient Anglo-Saxons were portrayed as hardy sea-rovers; they were natural adventurers, hard-working, had a virile masculinity, and were led by honest and courageous leaders. The modern English eventually mobilized these same traits in the imperial expansion that began during the Elizabethan period. Thus, the modern empire was linked to the English Anglo-Saxon racial heritage, and consciousness of the empire was thereby made integral to English national consciousness.

With the empire portrayed as a 'natural' and vital element of the English nation, the differing coloured races of the colonies were located within a symbiotic relationship with the English. Ultimately, the English needed subject races that they could help develop towards 'civilization' so as to legitimize their own benevolent self-image. The subject races were consequently portrayed in a manner that showed they clearly 'needed' this English help. This entirely self-confirming ideological legitimization of the empire not only justified the imperial enterprise (rationalizing the apparent contradiction between liberal democracy at home and benevolent despotism abroad); it also proffered a noble responsibility that was entrusted to all elements of English society. The imperial responsibility – the 'white man's burden' – was not merely directed at those children who would one day go out to administer the empire. It was also thrust onto to the working class as a means of including them in the national mission; of socializing them to the aims of the state and of the ruling classes. In return, the working classes were encouraged into a sense of self-importance; they were part of the clearly superior Anglo-Saxon race that held dominion over much of the world's population. Also evident in this discourse, however, was anxiety that the working-class population was not up to its imperial responsibilities. Arguments about racial hierarchy among the peoples of the world meshed uneasily and in an unresolved way with fears about the racial character of the working classes themselves. Unable to do anything about the possibly degenerate 'racial make-up' of the students in the elementary school, school-book authors could only resort to exhortations and positive and negative role models of proper social behaviour taken from the 'inferior' races within the bounds of the empire.

An idealized notion of social harmony was also at the heart of civic rhetoric in elementary school readers. Working-class boys, regardless of whether they would actually ever acquire suffrage, were extolled to exercise 'good citizenship.' This was a gendered notion of citizenship that had little to do with the political franchise. It was, instead, an amalgam of masculinized duties and responsibilities that educators hoped working-class boys would aspire to uphold. Loyalty and a sense of duty to the nation and state were essential, but citizenship was to a large degree really just equated with nationality. Being a good citizen – being proud of the English heritage, loyal to English traditions and institutions, and dutiful to the needs of the nation and empire – was consequently formulated as being 'patriotic.' The role models used to promote good citizenship came from heroic events in English history, and were almost always the virile martial heroes who gave over their careers – and often their lives – to upholding the glory of their nation. Just as the working-class lad should not be blinded by any personal ambition that was antithetical to the needs of the state, so the martial heroes supposedly gave not a thought for their own reputation or fate.

Working-class girls were also brought into 'citizenship' by educational authors and curriculum planners, in a manner organized primarily around perceived gender differences and roles. Girls were taught to think of their own national duty in terms of their roles as wives and mothers to the English race. As both mothers and wives, English women were also tied symbolically to the English nation as the keepers of the 'home.' Theirs was a vitally important role. Through their intimate connection to the 'home,' women were placed at the core of patriotic sentiments and emotions. Home and hearth were used as intrinsic elements in English national iconography, particularly within the blandishments of English ruralism. Moreover, it was these mothers who would produce the next generation of English heroes, and so, increasingly, it was also projected that the working mother's duties would include conceiving and raising 'worthy' specimens of the English race. Educational effort was therefore expended in ensuring that working women knew as much about hygiene and 'efficient' domestic management as possible. However, the dictates of the prevailing social hierarchy in England at this time frustrated much of this effort, for undercutting this ideology of racial motherhood and the support of the domestic ideal for the working-class home was the need for the upper classes to have a surplus of well-trained domestic servants. Nevertheless, despite the evident disjunction between ideology and actual social practices, the working woman was encouraged to think of herself as having an eminently important place in national society.

The glue binding together these conceptions of social harmony and inclusion were the numerous patriotic symbols and national narratives that found common expression in school reading books and classroom practices. Romanticized explanations of political institutions and the unwritten constitution, the pivotal place of the monarch, the long-standing loyal service of the navy, and the emotive and symbolic meanings of the national flag were all elucidated through a variety of textual, oral, and visual means. By being encouraged to identify with these interconnected symbols and narratives, elementary schoolchildren were induced to feel and further nurture pride in those things that were signified as 'truly English' by professional educators. Significantly, many of these symbols and narratives fused older plebeian and radical traditions with contemporary concerns and attempted to channel the older values into a 'safer' direction – loyalty to the existing nation-state – and away from early radical-populist notions of the national mission. Thus, although liberal individualism and religion were never displaced entirely from the English elementary school, the thrust of the curriculum did move away from the essentially liberal and religious mode of mid-century – which emphasized character reformation, moral worthiness, personal salvation, and a view of society as the aggregate of responsible, morally upstanding individuals – and towards a more secular and collectivist or communitarian conception of the appropriate identity for the working masses. At mid-century religious deference and the dictates of liberal political economy had together been seen as the glue that bound the working class to those higher up in the social hierarchy. By the end of the century this was no longer the case, and a conception of the national 'citizenry' that identified itself closely with nation and state (and, hence, also the empire) was viewed as a reasonable alternative. And most important, the new vision looked to a reworked concept of the nation as the proper locus of the schoolchild's identity.

This overall transformation in the narrative and vocabulary of Englishness as they were deployed in elementary schooling between 1880 and 1914 was due to the complex interaction of three factors: the increasing professionalization of the disciplines from which the academic

authors were drawn; the changed manner in which elementary education was conceived of by these authors and by those concerned with
mass education generally; and the shifting nature of their own understanding of English national culture and identity. The reconstitution
of nationality under the rubric of Englishness used by professional
educators in the reading books written for elementary schoolchildren
in late-nineteenth and early twentieth-century England was ultimately
part of a subtle recasting of the national narrative. The old liberal
shibboleths were under pressure from a variety of sources – intellectual, political, social, economic – and this required a transformation of
national culture. Academic and educationalist intellectuals took it upon
themselves to impart their understanding of this national culture in
order to justify their disciplinary claims. As a result, they promulgated
the highly specific national genealogy that had developed since mid-
century in intellectual culture – a mythology about essential racial
origins – to schoolchildren even though a few of their colleagues were
coming to question and even discard these essentialist notions of racial inheritance in this same period. Moreover, the new national culture promoted in elementary schools depended on a range of symbols,
icons, and allegories that formed part of basic instruction in literacy.
Implicit to this national narrative and the vocabulary of identity that
accompanied it was an inclusionary vision of the social order, in which
the working classes had vital, if clearly subordinated places and middle-
class gender ideology was bolstered rather than challenged. The logical implication of the messages found in reading books at this time
was that national-imperial duty and responsibility were the unalter-
able consequences of the simple accident of English birth. The fact that
English citizenship was also somehow a 'question of race' strengthened the claim that these obligations were primordial and unchanging. Loyalty to nation was consequently a duty that 'naturally' superseded all other loyalties, such as to local community or class. National
origins and history, progress, and social harmony were thereby all
closely integrated within the ideals of national-imperial citizenship.

As the proponents of three academic disciplines at the centre of this
process – English literature, geography, and history – all jockeyed
with one another for the resources that would firmly establish them in
the mainstream of academic life, the success of each discipline seemed
dependent on convincing education officials that they should be a part
not just of the university curriculum, but also that they were important to the national elementary curriculum.[2] Ultimately, the pro-

fessionalization of authorship narrowed the range of opinions expressed in school books, and removed the idiosyncrasies and some of the more personal judgments found in earlier texts. Consequently, a circularity of ideas developed in which authors self-consciously drew on the work of their predecessors and contemporaries. In history readers this meant borrowing, in particular, from the historians E.A. Freeman, J.A. Froude, S.R. Gardiner, J.R. Green, J.R. Seeley, and W. Stubbs and repackaging their insights for a mass audience. In geography books, once the list-centred learning (wherein students were asked to memorize long lists of rivers, mountains, capes and bays, etc.) of the older mid-century texts came to be replaced by more descriptive narration in the readers of the 1890s, the work of G.G. Chisholm, A. Geikie, J.S. Keltie, C.P. Lucas, H.J. Mackinder, and H.R. Mill tended to predominate. Literature readers, meanwhile, continued to include a range of readings of widely varying quality taken from diverse historical periods. Even here, however, reader collections were increasingly being edited by the pioneering English literature professors, such as Sir Walter Raleigh, who drew examples from the coalescing 'canon' of the British literary heritage from Shakespeare to Tennyson and supplemented them with writings by contemporaries such as Haggard, Henty, and Kipling, finally packaged with introductions for elementary school consumption. 'National culture' was thereby increasingly being defined in school books by an academic elite bent on demonstrating its own importance to British society.

National Literacy and Imperial Propaganda

Much of the recent academic writing on late-Victorian culture and identities has attempted to demonstrate the importance of the wider empire and of imperialist ideas to domestic concerns. Pioneering in this welcome development has been the Manchester University Press 'Studies in Imperialism' series, edited by John M. MacKenzie. This series contains selections from a variety of scholars from diverse backgrounds. Unfortunately, however, far from being a synthesis or inter-disciplinary collection, most of the monograph volumes and the individual articles in the 'Studies in Imperialism' collections are discrete studies, relying heavily on the work of previous, similar-minded authors and perspectives from the same series. This has led some of the historians in this series to interpret the presence of imperialism within popular and educational culture mainly in light of John MacKenzie's general arguments about the transmission of imperial 'propaganda' – a term he defines as the 'transmission of ideas and values from one person, or group of persons, to another, with the specific intention of influencing the recipients' attitudes in such a way that the interests of its authors will be enhanced.'[3]

In one sense, of course, the term 'propaganda' does express succinctly what this study has demonstrated was going on in elementary classrooms. An elite group wrote the books and taught the teachers that would educate the masses, and this elite stamped its own views into these books and teaching practices. Fuelled by the logic of the concept of propaganda itself, however, the proponents of the 'imperialist propaganda' school have tried to positively identify the proselytizing individuals responsible for the spread of this ideology, and have argued for a process whereby imperialist rhetoric was to be picked up by educators and teachers in a form of social emulation.[4] John MacKenzie's assertion that the actual propagandists were bent on drawing the entire population into a fascination with elite values and concerns for their own selfish reasons seems, on the surface, a plausible position. Many historians following MacKenzie have attempted to demonstrate the varied but calculated means of transmitting this propaganda.[5] Typically, an attempt is made to connect prominent individuals and imperialist organizations – the Earl of Meath, Sir John R. Seeley, and the Tory nationalist leagues are usually the chief villains[6] – with the promotion of the ideas, values, and activities that are characterized as imperialist propaganda. And there is, indeed, abundant evidence of the activities of many imperialist advocacy groups in the late nineteenth and early twentieth centuries. In 1907, for example, the Lord Mayor received a letter from some thirty prominent 'notables of the empire' proposing the founding of an Empire Education Fund in order to 'bring maps, books and other sources of information within the reach of all classes, and thus create interest and enthusiasm, which will ultimately grow into a steady Imperial Patriotism.'[7]

Clearly, imperialist propagandists did believe that the mass of the population *should* think of themselves as having a stake in the imperial enterprise, but to suggest that this was done simply to justify the benefits that the empire accorded the imperialist elite actually downplays the pre-existing notions of national identity onto which imperialist ideas were grafted. Moreover, a major difficulty with this particular propaganda model is its concentration on the influence of only a few avowed propagandists. For the propaganda argument cannot explain either why there was so little effective dissent to these self-interested views, or why increasingly over this period there was so little variation in the approach and views of the materials being used in the classroom. The notion of 'propaganda' is surely a much too simplistic mechanism for explaining the production of educational or popular culture, and one that cannot convincingly justify why the views of these particular individuals were so apparently influential. It is premised, in fact, on two unproven and arguably fallacious assumptions: first, that propaganda from self-interested elite sources 'naturally' trickles down through society and is simply and willingly taken up and emulated by social 'inferiors,' and second, that educational and popular cultures are internally empty of the political-ideological currents of their time and yet are easily susceptible to ideological manipulation from propagandists from the 'outside.' The propaganda model falsely proposes, in other words, that educational and popular cultures are at first ideologically neutral but that through the efforts of a few individuals can become filled with the dictates of a selfish ideological creed.

The relationships between the production of educational and popular culture and various types of social ideology are surely far more complicated than this particular propaganda model allows. The links between popular educational culture and extracurricula organizations, to take but one example, were extremely complex, and while it is not denied here that propagandistic organizations had influence on popular education, it is certainly not justifiable to claim that imperial-nationalist values became incorporated into the content of elementary education entirely as a result of the campaigns of a few organizations and their prominent members, or even through the publication of their imperialist views in a few specific texts. This can be best demonstrated if we briefly examine the case of one of the Edwardian propagandistic groups, the Navy League, and its relationship to the elementary school system. The Navy League, founded in 1894, was an organization whose avowed purpose was the binding of the empire together through commitment to sea power and the elevation of naval issues above party politics.[8] The Navy League viewed popular education as a key to its aims and consequently tried repeatedly to have its specially written textbooks, pamphlets, and examination papers put into English elementary classrooms. Some education authorities, particularly in port towns such as Portsmouth – which had a long association with naval affairs and a reliance on navy contracts – likely accepted such books without any qualms.[9] However, in many other places these requests met with stiff resistance from local educational authorities, and from groups protesting against the Navy League's 'hidden agenda.' For example, the London County Council Education Committee in 1907 rejected the Navy League's offer of free books, pamphlets, and examination papers for use in class.[10]

The Navy League did manage to get its large empire wall maps put into many London schools, however, and some of texts and picture books, including *The British Navy, Past and Present*, while barred from classroom use, were authorized for inclusion in school libraries so that children might read them if they 'were so inclined.' In Bristol, initial school official reservations about the activities of the Navy League led to a flip-flop on the issue of sanctioning the use of their texts and other classroom materials. Pamela Horn asserts that despite the reservations of the school board, the Navy League's initiative to distribute its texts in Bristol schools went ahead in 1902.[11] However, she seems to have missed the fact that in 1903 the Bristol Education Committee rescinded its earlier decision and was publicly repudiating the activities of the Navy League in connection to its schools. In particular, the Bristol Education Committee objected to the activities of one representative of the Navy League, an Admiral Close, who boasted that he had delivered thirty speeches to area schools in 1902 – lectures that had been unauthorized by the committee and were considered unwelcome. Discussion over the issue dragged on through 1903, and although the committee did eventually authorize an annual prize essay scheme on the subject of the navy (by a close vote on the committee of sixteen for and twelve opposed), Navy League plans for the further distribution of textbooks and pamphlets for classroom use in 1903 were thwarted.[12]

The fact that the Navy League had some difficulty getting its materials included on the official curriculum of many schools (even when offered free of charge) highlights the reservations held by some educationalists, school authorities, and teachers towards the overtures of avowedly nationalist propagandists.[13] This does not mean that the views of these leagues and organizations were not endorsed by school officials and individual teachers: undoubtedly many teachers and educationalists supported such leagues – some were no doubt members – and as was demonstrated in Chapter 6 the story of the navy formed a prominent narrative in the classroom. The point is, however, that elected officials on school boards and, after 1902, on the local education authorities were often very conscious of the potential for public criticism of any perceived partisan or political biases in the official curriculum. For example, the London Education Authority, like its school board predecessor, was very anxious about possible public objections to the books it put on its requisition list. In 1907 the Books and Apparatus Subcommittee reported a heated meeting on 8 May 1907 in which it was recommended that Elizabeth Gaskell's novel *Mary Barton* be taken off the requisition list due to public complaints. Unfortunately, there is no record of the specific nature of the objection to this text, but this was obviously a controversial recommendation since the unusual step of recording all those who voted for and against the measure was taken. Despite the leadership of Sidney Webb in moving against the motion, it was carried, fourteen to ten.[14] Such an example highlights the fact that school boards and local education authorities were public forums, and the activities and decisions of these bodies could be scrutinized by all manner of groups and individuals. These authorities routinely considered letters and submissions of protest, particularly from trade unions and political clubs such as socialists and pacifists. As early chapters have detailed, book selection, from the very start of the school board era, had been a sensitive issue, provoking a flurry of protests in the early years regarding religious biases and continued concern over the educational merit of certain texts in later years. Moreover, as has also been noted, the school boards and local education authorities regularly censured commercial publishers for attempting to peddle their wares directly to the teacher.[15] Excessive 'jingoism' in texts or officially sanctioned school activities (especially Empire Day) prompted many complaints and protests around the turn of the century and after, and school officials had to take into consideration (though not necessarily yield to) such protests in their text selection decisions.[16]

School officials sometimes felt the need to remind their teachers of the delicate position in which they found themselves. The London School Board consultant W.H. Withers, for example, wrote in a 1901 memo to teachers about their choice of classroom history texts to be used in conjunction with the recently mandated history lessons: 'History lessons ought not to be made a vehicle either for partisan feeling in home affairs, or for international grudges in the discussion of international politics. The English spirit of fair play to opponents condemns alike the republican propaganda carried on in the schools of one great continental nation, and the anti-socialistic crusade which is maintained in the schools of another.'[17] Withers's concern with overt expressions of 'jingoism' in the selection of books, the topics to be taught, and the tone of classroom instruction does not in any way discount the existence of a pervasive nationalist influence in their views or in the elementary schools themselves; in fact, quite the reverse. In the passage above, used to argue against 'overly propagandistic texts,' the point is made through reference to English national stereotypes – the 'English spirit of fair play.' Moreover, a comparison of the content of books advocated by the propagandistic organizations with those texts and readers routinely and unproblematically approved for classroom requisition lists by school boards and local education authorities demonstrates that while the emphasis and tone of the texts may have differed, the core characterizations, the stereotypes deployed, the values promoted, and in fact much of the basic rhetoric were little different between the two.[18]

Approved texts only differed from 'propagandistic' ones in that they were published by 'respectable' commercial publishers and educational organizations; had 'professional' rather than amateur, self-interested, and 'sectarian' authors; and were consequently considered to be less tainted with political or partisan biases by public-opinion-wary school officials.[19] Thus, the Navy League's books were not objectionable because of their particular perspective – as we have seen, much of their perspective on the importance of the navy was already present in the curriculum – rather their avowedly partisan origins, and the symbolic importance of a public authority endorsing the use of materials prepared by a special interest group, threatened to upset the supposedly politically neutral and respectable status of rate-aided schools in the eyes of 'popular' public opinion. All this would suggest that the propaganda model, while certainly useful, is nevertheless much too narrow. The perspectives and values associated with nationalist rhetoric contained within school books actually fit within a very narrow continuum from as early as the mid-1880s, and virtually all the books used in the classroom – regardless of whether they were produced by an avowedly partisan group or commercial publisher – shared many of the same basic images, symbols, and narratives. It seems erroneous to suggest, then, that an imperial-nationalist perspective was brought into the national elementary curriculum through the efforts of a few propagandists. In the case of imperialist ideology, the propaganda model – with its attendant connotation of the conscious, wilful, cynical (and even knowingly duplicitous) promotion of ideas and values into popular culture – narrowly separates imperialism from its nationalist context. Instead of examining the imperialist ideology within popular culture only as the wilful and conscious process of elite justification, it has been a core argument of this study that it is far more useful to view imperialist ideas as an integral part of an evolving hegemonic nationalist ideology that was already a fundamental feature of the curriculum. Imperial-nationalism was a major constituent, in other words, of the parameters of the contemporary cultural hegemony.

Clearly much of what made up this cultural hegemony necessarily corresponded to the accepted truths of the educated middle classes. These *were* accepted truths because the works of supposedly disinterested academics were the basis of these truths. The tremendous influence of the historian, geographer, and other positivist academics on mid- and late-Victorian 'public culture' has been often noted.[20] As this study has argued, it was because these intellectuals were themselves in the process of professionalizing their academic disciplines – and, indeed, using the notion of professional specialization to justify their claims to be the authors of educational materials for all ages – that this discourse of national culture came to dominate the messages of school books. These nationalist ideas were highly subjective statements about the nature of perceived reality, which were, indeed, sometimes inconsistent and even contradictory, but which had long-term implications that would not have been fully perceived by either the individuals deploying them or those subject to them. Robert Colls and Philip Dodd, in their introductory essays to their 1986 collection *Englishness: Politics and Culture, 1880–1920*, explain how the members of the dominant English political culture created a distinctive interpretation of the national 'character' in this very period, primarily through the establishment of new national cultural institutions. But they rightly resist the temptation to assert that this reconstitution of national culture and redefinition of nationality had anything to do with 'social control.' As Colls notes:

Although there is certainly evidence to support the thesis that Englishness and the national culture were reconstituted *in order* to incorporate and neuter social groups – for example the working class, women, the Irish – who threatened the social order, it is unhelpful for two reasons to see the reconstitution as a simple matter of imposition of an identity by the dominant on the subordinate. First, the remaking of class, gender and national identity was undertaken at such a variety of social locations and by such a variety of groups that it is difficult to talk of any common intention ... The other reason why 'imposition' is too simple is that the establishment of hegemony involves negotiation and 'active consent' on the part of the subordinated.[21]

The authors of reading books were similarly immersed in this nationalist hegemony of their day: a hegemony that was evolving to the changed social and political conditions of the turn of the century. Thus, nationalist ideology operated within elementary educational culture in *both* a conscious *and* an unconscious manner: shaping, legitimating, rationalizing, and naturalizing the parameters of English identity that were determined by the newly established academic-cultural elite.

It would thus be erroneous to suggest that all the ideological messages that found their way into elementary school books were designed just to bolster the specific policies and agendas of a conspiratorial ruling elite: it would be more accurate to say that ideological messages were integral to Britain's mainstream educational outlook in this period. Whether the professional promoters of this outlook were blind to, or actively supported, the social prescriptions in their academic output is another question. As other scholars have demonstrated, some academics clearly recognized the social implications of their scholarship. Others, arguably, were merely following in the established footsteps of their disciplines. In this sense, the very professionalizing of the disciplines of history, geography, and English literature marked the parameters by which understandings of identity were constructed in the classroom. It remains here to say something about the effectiveness of the nationalist narratives and vocabulary of identity present in school books that were the product and sustainers of this hegemony; about, that is, the degree to which 'active consent' for these parameters was obtained.

The Impact of National Literacy

As was indicated in the introduction, the purpose of this study has been to suggest the way in which classroom reading set the conceptual boundaries and shaped the imaginative 'experience' of the mostly working-class children of the English elementary school. From current research in the field of political socialization we know that children begin to develop some understanding of their national identities between the ages of four and seven. At this age the process of identification seems to be achieved largely by means of symbols and by stereotyped contrasts with other nations: 'This sense of national identity has usually been expressed in the form of preferences: the Union Jack is the best flag, the USA is the best country.'[22] Clearly this age range corresponds to the period of schooling received by English children in elementary schools at the turn of the century, schooling – as this study has demonstrated – that was suffused with nationalist imagery and explanations. This contemporary evidence suggests, therefore, the potential importance of elementary education in the formation of an English national identity after 1880. Of course, neither contemporary research nor the dictates of theory will satisfy the demands of historians, who rightly question whether the same processes and effects on children of the very recent past hold true for the children of a hundred years ago and seek hard evidence to substantiate such claims. Despite the paucity of credible sources for such evidence, and although in no way definitive, some clues do exist that suggest the processes and effects of the period 1880 to 1914 were very similar to our own period.

First, we have evidence obtained from oral testimony and interviews. The problem here, of course, is that it is impossible to separate childhood understanding from subsequent meanings: what someone at the end of their life remembers about their childhood is necessarily conditioned by what happened in their life afterwards. With this caution in mind, what does the available evidence show? One scholar has made a statistical analysis of working-class testimony found at the Edwardian oral history archive at the University of Essex (444 interviews) on the topic of elementary education. Some 90 per cent of the working people who gave responses about their education said they had gained some 'benefit' from their education, and 'respondents most commonly credited their schools with a solid grounding in the three Rs, as well as geography, history and occasionally a foreign language.' Furthermore, only one out of seven had unhappy memories of their education.[23] Of course, this kind of analysis says nothing about the content of their education, or anything about what base concepts they took from their education. However, qualitative evidence from similar oral interviews does provide some evidence of the fundamental place of nationalist vocabulary in early education, as the following three excerpts of interviews with working-class individuals schooled prior to 1914 in Bristol indicate:

The best thing about school in them days was that they taught you right from wrong. They taught us we were the best nation in the world and must live up to it. We mustn't cause any trouble or bring disgrace on the country, because if we did anything wrong we should disgrace not just ourselves but the nation.[24]

They used to encourage us to be proud of the flag, salute the flag when we was at school. Yes, I was proud of being British. We was always taught to be proud of the Queen and King. We was the people of the world wasn't us?[25]

Now if you got a hold of all those history books we had at the time, they was all a load of flannel, about Edward the Peacemaker, Queen Victoria and Elizabeth the First ... And later on, when I getting on to fourteen, I started to read these historical books an' I took an interest in 'em. And I thought to myself at the time, well, what a load of rubbish we've been taught in the past.[26]

These three examples demonstrate the power of early education to shape attitudes, which might throughout life be accepted or, in the case of the last of these examples, later rejected. Of course, these few examples, even when multiplied many times as they could be, are hardly definitive. Stephen Humphries's *Hooligans or Rebels?* – a comprehensive oral history researched from all the available oral history archives available in the late 1970s, and which concentrates mostly on working-class resistance to the processes of schooling and socialization (and hence tends to overemphasize the accounts of those who consciously resisted or overturned in later life what they learned in school) – concedes 'that working-class children were generally much more responsive to lessons and activities that were inspired by imperialism than they were to any of the religious influence in the school.'[27] This would suggest that, on balance, the oral evidence that has been collected in no way disputes the claims of this study.

The evidence we have from autobiographies from this period is similarly of limited usefulness and again is certainly not definitive. Opinions in working-class autobiographies about the imperial-national content of education run the gamut from clearly having internalized what could be labelled a 'national-imperialist worldview,' to being fiercely hostile to it.[28] Of course, most individuals from the working class at this time who eventually published memoirs did so because they had managed to 'improve' themselves through entrepreneurship, politics, or trade union activities, or were unusually literate or talented. As a whole, they provide a skewed sample of the 'average' or common response. And while it would be difficult to find an autobiographical account that denied outright the existence of something called the English or British 'nation' or to find in autobiographies polemics against the very idea of the nation, this fact alone will not satisfy historians seeking evidence of popular mentalities. The memories of Walter Southgate of Bethnal Green, London, and Joseph Toole of Manchester, both of whom received elementary education in the 1890s, together provide some understanding of how their school instruction in national identity might have been mediated by the everyday concerns of working-class life. These two examples have been chosen not because they demonstrate all the 'correct' characteristics and values that might be expected if the process described in this book had been totally successful, but because they illuminate incidents about the power of schooling to set conceptual boundaries about the meaning of national identity.

Southgate and Toole both describe how during the Anglo–Boer War their teachers made special efforts to discuss imperial concerns, and particularly the affairs of South Africa. During the conflict Southgate and his friends played 'games like "English versus Boers," wore celluloid buttons in our lapels portraying our favourite generals like Buller, White, Baden-Powell and Lord Roberts. It only required the relief of Ladysmith or Mafeking to set the whole populace dancing, singing, waving flags, getting drunk and finishing of the celebrations with bonfires and fireworks.'[29]

Meanwhile, for Toole, also a child at the time, the South African war was a business opportunity:

In that war, as in all wars, the people had their great national heroes. Quick to perceive this, I purchased for a few pence a piece of timber, cut it in to the shape of a challenge shield ... covered it very neatly with a piece of black velvet, and secured a supply of lapel buttons upon which were beautifully painted portraits of the war heroes. I pinned these on to my velvet shield – my shop window – and stood on the pavement of Market Street, Manchester, offering to the passing public photographs of Lord Roberts, General Buller, White, Baden-Powell, Methuen, Kekewich and the rest.

The weather did not cause me any worry: rain or sleet made no matter, because I was doing a roaring trade. This was, of course, a passing fancy with the general public, and naturally could not last for long, but it served for the time being, and provided the consolation which earning your own honest living gives no matter how menial the job may be.[30]

For working-class children like Southgate and Toole, the war and the empire became the object of common school-yard games of the 'cowboys and Indians' variety. Cheap portraits of famous imperial warriors became the current fad in school-yard trading, or could become a way to make some money, and the news of British victories in a faraway place became the excuse for having a special celebration. Events in the empire were easily incorporated into the rhythm, the ordinariness, of everyday life.

Another passage from Southgate's memoirs highlights how the mere participation in what historians might rightly view as an attempt at overt imperialist indoctrination should be seen against the background of a more pervasive and subtle process of identity construction. When he was twelve Southgate joined an after-school drill brigade held at a local church hall. This was a group, no doubt, intent on instilling manly discipline and nationalist, imperial-patriotic virtues. Southgate describes how all the older boys were eager to join, but that

the upshot of that opening night was that every boy disregarded orders and words of command. They formed themselves into groups and marched round the hall singing all the popular music hall ditties with appropriate cockney wording and ribald phrasing unbecoming to a church hall. Their repertoire included *The British Grenadiers* to the words with which every school teacher of boys was conversant but which were unprintable. This was hardly what the missionaries had in mind and the lady at the small organ did her best to render *Onward Christian Soldiers* fortissimo, without success.[31]

The boys here willingly joined a propagandistic group, and engaged in the intended activity with gusto, but whatever ideological propaganda this activity was supposed to convey was mediated by the boys' own desires to have a good time and, more particularly, to have a good time on their own terms. The fact remains, however, that even as parody these boys had internalized aspects of the vocabulary of identity that this study has attempted to demonstrate was hegemonic in English society at this time. For the boys were savvy enough to 'send up' the earnest propagandists, they could use the symbols and language of that identity and modify it for the purposes of their own entertainment, but they had to have first understood much of the dominant meanings of the marching and the patriotic songs in order to poke fun at them. Similarly, Toole's patriotic portrait-pins were important to *him* not as a symbol of imperial pride and support, but because of the commercial opportunity they afforded. But he in no way questioned that middle, lower-middle class and even working people would *want* to buy such items: quite the reverse, as his business opportunity depended on his recognition of that desire. He may not have himself put much real emotional attachment to the symbols that he sold for profit, but he recognized that many others did find a patriotic appeal in them, enough indeed that his little scheme was a 'roaring' success.

These examples, and the many others that can be taken from autobiographical literature, demonstrate that negotiation and reconfiguration by the intended subjects of nationalist indoctrination were clearly part of the process. In Southgate's case, the boys, in an irreverent working-class parody of overtly imperialist militarism, appropriated regimented imperial rites. That many of these same lads would have likely signed up to serve their country and acted out this militarism for real during the First World War merely adds to the importance of proper contextualization when trying to assess the slippery nature of subjective meanings. Moreover, Toole's celebration of imperial-national heroes points to the importance of other active processes at this time: that is, to the commercialization of meanings and the role of consumption in the formation of identity. The point is, however, that before symbols and narratives can be reconfigured for another purpose in self-conscious and critical ways, some understanding of the original meaning is necessary. These examples demonstrate that the building of national identity worked (and continues to work) in complex and subtle ways that defy the label of propagandistic indoctrination, but was nonetheless dependent on the process of acquiring national literacy as described in this study.

Neil J. Smelser has recently argued against any general theory of nineteenth-century educational development based on the notion of 'nation building' by suggesting that educational efforts in the first half of the century were directed against active working-class citizenship.[32] He is certainly correct that prior to the 1880s the idea of the 'nation' was limited to a minority of the population (elite, middle-class, and 'respectable' artisan men). However, this clearly changed with the expansion of the franchise in 1884 and the broad changes of political culture during the late-Victorian and Edwardian years. The same political, intellectual, cultural, and economic forces that brought about the new relationship between state and society at the end of the century were also responsible for the reconfigured national identity promoted within the nation's elementary schools – one that sought to retain the basic status quo while simultaneously exhorting the existence of an inclusive national community. And, returning to the stated general purpose of this study that was outlined in the preface, it is in this tension between the rhetoric of the open and inclusive claims of the civic nation and the subtext of the essentially statist desires of the academic and educational establishment that we see the 'how' of nationalism in England at the turn of the twentieth century. The building of national identity through schooling at the turn of the century was clearly not the progressive 'nation building' that Smelser rightly critiques, but rather an attempted remoulding of the earlier liberal hegemony using a new language of the nation. While adult individual responses to the dictates of this refurbished hegemony might have differed – with some individuals clearly accepting some elements and rejecting others – classroom constructions of the ideas of the nation were ultimately successful enough to induce millions of working-class men and women to willingly sacrifice their lives and loved ones to the demands of the nation-state in the cataclysmic clash of rival nationalisms that erupted in 1914. This truly extraordinary fact seems to indicate that working-class schooling was a key part of a certain kind of 'nation building' after all.

Reading-Book Requisition and Approval Practices:

Excerpts from the Minutes of the School Board for London's Special Committee on the Selection of School Books[1]

Between 1880 and 1899 the system of book selection at the School Board for London did not change significantly. The only major change, in fact, was the establishment of a central depository for new books in 1891, which was intended to make book selection easier for teachers by having samples all the books that had been approved for use placed in one central location. However, the School Board's Books and Apparatus Subcommittee found the present system of a comprehensive requisition list, to which was added every new book that was approved by the board, increasingly cumbersome due to the huge expansion in book publishing over this period. Changes to the system were frequently called for by board members, and a Special Committee on the Selection of School Books was finally struck in 1899. The following passage – explaining the current practice – is an excerpt from the minutes of the meeting of this committee on 28 April 1899:

It is the [current] practice of publishers and others to forward specimens of their school publications or small apparatus to the Board. These specimens are submitted to the Books and Apparatus Sub-Committee, who recommend their approval or disapproval, as the case may be, to the School management committee.

When a book or any small apparatus is approved it is placed upon the Requisition List. This is a list of all books [etc.] which may be used in the schools of the Board, and from this list teachers are at liberty to make their own selection.[2]

The committee went on to explain that, in practice, the procedure for approving books involved two members of the Books and Apparatus

Subcommittee who reported to the clerk of the board on their observations of the book in question; these comments were then printed on the agenda of the subcommittee. It was, however, customary to put on the requisition list, without discussion, any book that was recommended by both members. Teachers could also apply for books not on the list directly through the subcommittee. Although the list was occasionally revised, rejection and retention was usually decided by the demand for the books. In their meeting of 28 April 1899, objections to the present system were raised by members of the special committee:

1. Too many books are placed on our requisition list. At present no less than 65 different sets of ordinary Readers, 45 of Upper Standard Readers, 26 of Historical Readers, 16 of Geographical Readers, 36 Arithmetical Books, etc.; and it is said that a large list gives a wider scope for the idiosyncrasies of different teachers. But it is obvious that a teacher, who is not likely to have much spare time, might spend many hours in the sample-room, and even then not find the best book, and that after all his selection would have to depend principally on the recommendation of others; such a situation seems to tend to a want of originality and so to defeat the main object which a large field of selection is held to attain.
2. It is too easy for an inferior book to find a place on the list ...
3. The present system makes the Board follow the lead of the publishers, instead of taking the initiative itself. The large purchasing power of the Board should enable it to exercise a greater degree of influence in the market than it does, and by advice and criticism the Board might do more to encourage the publishers to produce thoroughly satisfactory books.[3]

Following these observations, the special committee recommended some 'suggestions for improvement':

1. Limit the number of books – this would, so it was thought, induce keener competition amongst suppliers to produce better books. Books would be removed after a few years if not used, or if a better replacement was found.
2. doubtful books to be placed on a special 'suspended list' which would be revised every 6 months. More thorough criticism of books would be encouraged.
3. the L.S.B. should circulate to publishers a list of requirements which are to be considered indispensable for any books used by the L.S.B.[4]

These proposals were not agreed to at this time. All that was agreed to was an examination of how other large school boards adopted their books, and that teachers and publishers should be consulted on the possible changes. This information was presented at the meeting of 12 May 1899. The following list is a paraphrased sample compiled from the replies of some thirty-five school boards to inquiries made by the London School Board (the list has been shortened to reduce repetition; all of the various options on the full list are found here, in roughly the same proportion), demonstrating typical school board practices of book selection.[5]

- *Birmingham*: Board inspectors examined specimens of books and forwarded their recommendations to the Education Committee for approval.
- *Bolton*: Head teachers made selection; specimens were kept at the office for inspection.
- *Bradford*: Sample books periodically considered by a subcommittee; each member approved or rejected a book, and if a majority approved the book was placed on the approved list and the publishers informed.
- *Brighton*: Teachers made their own selections.
- *Bristol*: Publishers were asked to send in samples. Head teachers could ask for any book to be placed on the requisition list; these books were then examined by a special requisition committee; if book was approved it was put on the requisition list. Teachers had to select from the approved requisition list.
- *Hull*: Board ordered books requisitioned by head teachers, provided there had been no previous objections to the books. Books were discontinued from time to time by a decision of the committee.
- *Leeds*: Publishers sent books to the inspectors, who reported on them to the Education Committee, on whose recommendation the books were then approved and put on a list. The list was revised every few years.
- *Leicester*: A requisition list was periodically revised. Inspectors examined new books and recommended their adoption.
- *Liverpool*: All sample books were referred to the board's inspectors for examination. If approved, the book was added to the requisition list.
- *Manchester*: No requisition list. Teachers made their own selections subject to approval by the inspectors.
- *Nottingham*: Had an approved requisition list and a sample room. Teachers could suggest books for approval by the board.

- *Oldam*: A requisition list was based primarily on the recommendations of head teachers.
- *Portsmouth*: Another board that had a requisition list to which head teachers might make suggestions for additions.
- *Salford*: No requisition list. Teachers made selections but were subject to board inspector approval.
- *Sheffield*: Had an approved requisition list on the London model.
- *Sunderland*: The clerk of the board recommended all books.

Along with the school board survey, the committee asked for the opinion of London teachers on the best methods. Three headmasters and five headmistresses were consulted: 'There was a consensus of opinion in favour of the Requisition List. It was thought that it was unnecessary to have such a large number of sets of reading and other books on the list which are arranged in standards, and the number of sets of these books might be reduced.'[6] Publishers were also consulted and were found to be in favour of eliminating the list altogether and allowing teachers to choose their own texts. However, they did agree that the list was too long and included out-of-date and obsolete titles.

A final report on school-book selection was drawn up in draft form on 1 December 1899. Here are the key recommendations presented:

It is inexpedient to lay down any rule as to the number of books on different subjects which should be placed on the Requisition List. But it was agreed that the current list was unnecessarily large, and required careful revision with the object of removing all books out of date, or incorrect, or for which there is no demand ...

The Chair of the Committee was thereby empowered to move:

1. That the Books and Apparatus Sub-Committee of the School Management Committee be empowered, from time to time, to take the opinion of one or more Teachers on any books and apparatus proposed to be placed on the Requisition List ...
2. the List should be revised and updated,
3. to discontinue the 'allow if asked for' clause,
4. that teachers when applying for books not on the list may be called upon to state their reasons for their applications,
5. that the number of attendance prizes on the list be reduced.[7]

These recommendations were approved, the requisition list was updated, and the requisition system remained unchanged thereafter until the inter-war years.

Reading-Book Publication Figures for Selected Publishers

1. The Publishing House of Edward Arnold

The following are the number of copies of various reader sets – all of which were examined for this study – on order from the printer for Edward Arnold between 1896 and 1902. Some of these figures (compiled from Arnold publication records)[8] include a portion of a larger previous order still outstanding to the printer. It is impossible to know how big these orders might have been, though it is reasonably safe to say that they would have been *at least* as large as the next order, if not, in fact, somewhat greater. As they represent the number of books printed, these figures give an indication of the *expected* demand for these books (based on previous sales).

Arnold's Britannia Geography Readers I. Sept. 1896–July 1902: 24,028
Britannia Geography Readers II. Aug. 1896–May 1902: 27,000
Britannia Geography Readers III. Aug. 1896–July 1902: 23,000

Arnold's English Reader I. Apr. 1898–Apr. 1902: 15,077
English Reader II. Apr. 1899–July 1901: 11,000
English Reader III. July 1899–June 1901: 8,500
English Reader IV. Feb. 1899–Jan. 1900: 9,025
English Reader V. Feb. 1899–Apr. 1902: 6,000
English Reader VI. Oct. 1899–Jan. 1900: 5,000
English Reader VII. July 1902: 4,000

Arnold's Geography Readers I. Jan. 1899–Feb. 1902: 20,120
Geography Readers II. Oct. 1898–Dec. 1902: 29,090

Geography Readers III. Apr. 1898–Feb. 1902: 29,000
Geography Readers IV. Apr. 1898–Jan. 1902: 24,000
Geography Readers V. June 1898–Feb. 1901: 20,184
Geography Readers VI. June 1898–Feb. 1902: 12,000
Geography Readers VII. Sept. 1898–Dec. 1899: 6,000

King Alfred Reader I. May 1899–Nov. 1902: 40,099
King Alfred Reader II. June 1900–July 1902: 40,000
King Alfred Reader III. Aug. 1899–Nov. 1902: 30,000
King Alfred Reader IV. Sept. 1898–Jan. 1902: 30,000
King Alfred Reader V. Oct. 1899–May 1902: 20,000
King Alfred Reader VI. Nov. 1899–Jan. 1902: 15,000
King Alfred Reader VII. Nov. 1899: 10,000

Arnold's History Readers I. Jan. 1901–Jan. 1902: 10,500
History Readers II. Nov. 1900–Oct. 1901: 12,000
History Readers III. May 1898–May 1902: 30,131
History Readers IV. Aug. 1898–Oct. 1901: 24,030
History Readers V. Feb. 1898–Sept. 1902: 23,040
History Readers VI. Sept. 1898–Sept. 1902: 16,083
History Readers VII. May 1900–June 1901: 8,000

Arnold's Domestic Readers I. Oct. 1898–Mar. 1900: 10,071
Domestic Readers II. Oct. 1899: 9,135
Domestic Readers III. Sept. 1898–Jan. 1900: 7,000
Domestic Readers IV. Feb. 1899–Mar. 1902: 6,500
Domestic Readers V. Apr. 1900: 5,000
Domestic Readers VI. July 1901: 4,000

For comparison purposes, the following is the total publication numbers for a formal history text published by Edward Arnold in this period.

Oman's History of England. 1897–1902: 6,000

2. House of Longman and Company

Figures for Longman's books are taken from Impression Books – which indicate press runs rather than sales. Longman's Impression Books were organized via overlapping year, and thus it proved impractical to note months as well as years in dates of publication. The per-year breakdown of a few selected books is also provided in this list.[9]

New Geographical Readers I. 1888–1900: 165,000

1888	50,000
1891	40,000
1894	20,000
1897	35,000
1900	20,000

New Geographical Readers II. 1888–1900: 180,000
New Geographical Readers III. 1888–1900: 205,000
New Geographical Readers IV. 1888–1902: 200,000
New Geographical Readers V. 1888–1900: 120,000
New Geographical Readers VI. 1888–1902: 112,000
New Geographical Readers VII. 1888–1902: 44,000

Longman's New Reading Books I. 1885–1904: 720,000
Longman's New Reading Books II. 1885–1902: 610,000

1885	120,000
1888	150,000
1891	90,000
1894	80,000
1897	80,000
1900	40,000
1902	50,000

Longman's New Reading Books III. 1885–1902: 480,000
Longman's New Reading Books IV. 1885–1902: 395,000
Longman's New Reading Books V. 1885–1905: 245,000
Longman's New Reading Books VI. 1885–1900: 135,000

Longman's 'New Historical' Readers
Each reader in this series was produced on small press runs of between 5,000 and 10,000 every three years or so; the example provided here, Standard IV, is typical.

Std. IV. 'Sketches'

1882	10,000
1885	10,000
1891	5,000
1894	10,000
1897	20,000

Longman's Domestic Economy Readers
There were small press runs of between 10,000 and 20,000 for each standard every three years. The reader was printed only between 1895 and 1902. No more than 40,000 copies were produced per volume in the entire set-run.
Std. IV.
1894–7   20,000

Longman's Modern Geography Readers
Volumes are listed by name rather than volume number. Production seems to have stopped by 1886.

Introductory. 1882–1885: 4,000
Std. II. 1882: 10,000
British Isles. 1882–1885: 10,000
British Colonies. 1882–1885: 6,000
Europe and America. 1882–1885: 4,000
Asia and Africa. 1882–1885: 8,000

Longman's 'Ship' Historical Readers I. 1891–1905: 120,000
Longman's 'Ship' Historical Readers II. 1891–1905: 115,000
Longman's 'Ship' Historical Readers III. 1891–1905: 115,000
1891   15,000
1894   40,000
1897   20,000
1900   15,000
1905   25,000
Longman's 'Ship' Historical Readers IV. 1891–1905: 115,000
Longman's 'Ship' Historical Readers V. 1891–1905: 80,000
Longman's 'Ship' Historical Readers VI. 1891–1905: 57,000
Longman's 'Ship' Historical Readers VII. 1891–1905: 30,000

Longman's 'Ship' Literary Readers I. 1894–1905: 170,000
Longman's 'Ship' Literary Readers II. 1894–1905: 160,000
Longman's 'Ship' Literary Readers III. 1894–1905: 120,000
Longman's 'Ship' Literary Readers IV. 1894–1905: 130,000
Longman's 'Ship' Literary Readers V. 1894–1905: 100,000
1894   30,000
1897   30,000
1900   20,000

1905   20,000
Longman's 'Ship' Literary Readers VI. 1894–1905: 85,000
Longman's 'Ship' Literary Readers VII. 1894–1905: 17,500

For comparison purposes, the following are advanced history readers in the 'Epochs of History' series – used in some elementary schools, but mainly in higher-grade, secondary, grammar, and Public schools.

Oscar Browning, *Modern England*. 1880–1900: 34,000
1880   4,000
1882   5,000
1885   5,000
1888   6,000
1891   3,000
1894   3,000
1897   5,000
1900   3,000

Mandell Creighton, *Age of Elizabeth*. 1879–1905: c. 40,000
1879   2,000
1882   6,000
1885   2,000
1888   2,000
1891   c. 5,000
1894   c. 7,000
1902–5   c. 2,000 per year

3. House of Macmillan and Company

The following are statistics compiled from New Edition Books on the three mainstay reader series in the Macmillan catalogue between 1892 and 1899.[10]

Macmillan History Readers I. May 1895: 10,000
Macmillan History Readers II. Mar. 1894: 10,000
Macmillan History Readers III. Aug. 1893–Nov. 1899: 50,000
Macmillan History Readers IV. Apr. 1892–Nov. 1899: 63,000
Macmillan History Readers V. July 1892–Jan. 1898: 50,000
Macmillan History Readers VI. Apr. 1892–Dec. 1897: 60,000
Macmillan History Readers VII. Aug. 1895–June 1898: 20,000

Macmillan Geography Readers I. Oct. 1899: 5,000
Macmillan Geography Readers II. Nov. 1899: 5,000
Macmillan Geography Readers III. Jan. 1897–Nov. 1899: 15,000
Macmillan Geography Readers IV. Apr. 1897–Aug. 1898: 10,000
Macmillan Geography Readers V. Mar. 1896: 10,000
Macmillan Geography Readers VI. Mar. 1896: 10,000
Macmillan Geography Readers VII. Aug. 1895–June 1898: 12,500

Macmillan Literature Readers I. Feb. 1896–Sept. 1898: 20,000
Macmillan Literature Readers II. Feb. 1896–Sept. 1898: 20,000
Macmillan Literature Readers III. Aug. 1895–July 1896: 20,000
Macmillan Literature Readers IV. Aug. 1894–Feb. 1899: 25,000
Macmillan Literature Readers V. Aug. 1894–Feb. 1899: 25,000

Statistical Breakdown of Reader Sample Used in This Study

1. Nature of the Sample

The reader sample analysed for content in this study consists of reading books from some 162 different sets first published between 1880 and 1914. In addition, there are some forty-six readers and formal texts used both before and during the period of the sample, which were examined for the purposes of comparison. The actual sample breaks down into disciplinary categories as follows:

- History Readers: 167 texts examined from a total of 208 divided among 51 sets.
- Geography Readers: 143 texts examined from a total of 193 divided among 49 sets.
- Literature Readers: 107 texts examined from a total of 206 divided among 42 sets.
- Domestic Economy Readers: 15 texts examined from a total of 31 divided among 8 sets.
- Civics Readers: 14 texts examined from a total of 14 divided among 12 sets.
- Total Readers: 446 books from 162 different sets.

2. Reader Sample Breakdown by First Publishing Date

In Table 1, the reader sets used in the sample are arranged according to their date of first publication.

TABLE 1
Reader sets, by date of publication

Date	History	Geography	Literature	Other
1880–9	15	15	7	2
1890–9	17	15	10	11
1900–9	17	12	21	4
1910–14	2	7	4	3
Totals	51	49	42	20

3. Reader Sample Breakdown by Publisher

Table 2 indicates the publisher of the reader sets considered in the analysis. The first number in each category is the actual number of books from this publisher examined; the number in parentheses ( ) indicates the total number of books published in the sets examined; the number in square brackets [ ] indicates the number of different sets from which books from this publisher were examined. In those few occasions where readers of different subject types were part of the same set, they have been included in the literature category.

TABLE 2
Reader sets, by publisher

Publisher	History	Geography	Literature	Domestic science	Civics
Arnold	2 (7) [1]	16 (16) [3]	12 (15) [2]	2 (6) [1]	–
Black	6 (6) [3]	1 (1) [1]	7 (13) [3]	–	–
Blackie	29 (31) [7]	14 (26) [6]	11 (17) [4]	3 (5) [2]	2 (2) [2]
Blackwood	–	1 (1)	8 (13) [3]	–	–
Cambridge	8 (8) [1]	2 (7) [1]	1 (1)	–	–
Cassell	10 (10) [2]	3 (3) [1]	–	–	–
Chambers	26 (29) [7]	11 (14) [2]	1 (6) [1]	–	2 (2) [2]
Collins	7 (11) [2]	18 (26) [5]	9 (29) [4]	1 (7) [1]	–
Longman	19 (23) [6]	9 (9) [2]	14 (22) [4]	3 (7) [1]	–
Macmillan	7 (13) [2]	14 (19) [7]	10 (13) [4]	–	2 (2) [2]
Marcus Ward	1 (1) [1]	7 (16) [3]	4 (11) [2]	–	–
National Society	7 (11) [2]	1 (4) [1]	7 (7) [2]	4 (4) [1]	–
Nelson	5 (5) [2]	19 (22) [5]	12 (39) [8]	–	–

(continued)

TABLE 2 *(continued)*
Reader sets, by publisher

Publisher	History	Geography	Literature	Domestic science	Civics
Oliver & Boyd	–	2 (2) [2]	2 (7) [1]	–	–
Pitman	15 (20) [3]	12 (12) [3]	2 (6) [1]	–	2 (2) [2]
S.P.C.K.	6 (6) [2]	–	–	–	–
Others	19 (27) [10]	13 (15) [7]	7 (7) [3]	2 (2) [2]	6 (6) [4]
Total examined	167	143	107	15	14
Total in sets	(208)	* (193)	(206)	(31)	(14)
Total sets	[51]	[49]	[42]	[8]	[12]

Notes

Abbreviations

BRO   Bristol Record Office
CERC Church of England Records Centre, Bermondsey
GLRO Greater London Record Office
MCL   Manchester Central Library, Local Unit Archives
PP   *Parliamentary Papers*
PRO   Public Record Office, Kew

For the sake of simplicity, on second and subsequent citing in each chapter of a single volume in an anonymously published reading-book set, the title of the series is provided, followed by the date, volume, book or 'standard' number (in roman numerals), and the page reference given after the colon. For example: *Reader Title* II: 123–4.

Preface

1 Cynthia Herrup, 'Introduction to Special Issue on National Identity,' *Journal of British Studies* 31, no. 4 (October 1992): 307; Walker Conner, 'The Nation and Its Myth,' in Anthony D. Smith, ed., *Ethnicity and Nationalism* (New York 1992), 49.
2 Andy Green, *Education and State Formation* (London 1990), 3. See also the excellent recent studies on Spain and Alsace-Lorraine: Carolyn P. Boyd, *Historia Patria: Politics, History, and National Identity in Spain, 1875–1975* (Princeton 1997); Stephen L. Harp, *Learning to Be Loyal: Primary Schooling as Nation Building in Alsace and Lorraine, 1850–1940* (Delkalb 1998).

Introduction: Reading the Nation

1 Frans Coetzee, *For Party or Country: Nationalism and the Dilemmas of Popular Conservatism in Edwardian England* (London 1990); P.M. Kennedy and A. Nicholls, eds., *Nationalist and Racialist Movements in Great Britain and Germany* (London 1981).

2 On imperialist propagandists, see J.M. MacKenzie, *Propaganda and Empire* (Manchester 1985); and Robin Betts, 'A Campaign for Patriotism on the Elementary School Curriculum: Lord Meath, 1892–1916,' *History of Education Society Bulletin* no. 16 (1990): 38–45. On nationalism as a cultural phenomena, see Benedict Anderson, *Imagined Communities* (New York 1991), 9–46; Anthony D. Smith, *National Identity* (Harmondsworth 1991), 71–98; and Ernest Gellner, *Nations and Nationalism* (Oxford 1983).

3 Gerald Newman, *The Rise of English Nationalism* (New York 1987); Linda Colley, *Britons: Forging the Nation, 1707–1837* (New Haven, CT 1992); John Wolffe, 'Evangelicalism in Mid-Nineteenth-Century England,' in R. Samuel, ed., *Patriotism* I (London 1989): 188–200; Keith Robbins, 'Religion and Identity in Modern Britain,' in his *Religion and Identity in Modern Britain* (London 1993), 85–104; Catherine Hall, *White, Male, and Middle Class* (New York 1992), 205–54, and '"From Greenland's Icy Mountains, to Afric's Golden Sands": Ethnicity, Race and Nation in Mid-Nineteenth-Century England,' *Gender and History* 2 (1993): 224–6; Margot Finn, *After Chartism* (Cambridge 1993); Patrick Joyce, *Visions of the People* (Cambridge 1991).

4 H.T. Mark, *Modern Views on Education* (London n.d.), 33; Norman Lockyer, *Education and National Progress, Essays and Addresses, 1870–1905* (London 1906), 178; R.D. Haldane, *Education and Empire* (London 1902), 86.

5 Brian Simon, *Education and the Labour Movement* (London 1965), 147; R.J.W. Selleck, *New Education* (Oxford 1968), 174, 300–24. For just a few examples of this rhetoric, see S.S. Laurie, *Institutes of Education* (Edinburgh 1892), 3–4, 18; Hugh B. Philpott, *London at School: The Story of the School Board, 1870–1904* (London 1904), 57; Sir Norman Lockyer, *Education and National Progress: Essays and Addresses, 1870–1905* (London 1906), 229; the speech of J.H. Muirhead as reported by the *School Government Chronicle*, 9 February 1907, 169; F.J.C. Hearnshaw, 'The Place of History in Education,' *History* 1 (1912): 34–41; Lord Milner, *The Nation and the Empire* (London 1913), 171; John E. Gorst, *Education and Race Regeneration* (London 1913), 36–7.

6 F.H. Hayward, *The Primary Curriculum* (London 1909), 483.

7 J.G. Fitch, *Lectures on Teaching* (New York 1906), 97–8.

8 M.E. Sadler, 'Introduction,' in Sadler, ed., *Moral Instruction and Training in Schools* (London 1908), xvi, xxiv.

9 R.E. Hughes, *The Making of Citizens: A Study in Comparative Education* (London 1907), 4. See also Henry Holman, *Education: An Introduction to Its Principles and Their Psychological Foundations* (London 1896), 11–12, 465–8.

10 E. Lyulph Stanley, *Our National Education* (London 1899), 139–40.

11 T. Raymont, *The Principles of Education* (London 1904), 14–15. Emphasis in original. For similar sentiments, see Amos Henderson, *Some Notes on Teaching* (Nottingham 1903), 73.

12 Carolyn Steedman, *Childhood, Culture and Class in Britain: Margaret McMillan, 1860–1931* (London 1990), 3–13, 62–81, 173–88.

13 For school books, see G.M.D. Howat, 'The Nineteenth-Century History Textbook,' *British Journal of Educational Studies* 13 (1965): 147–59; V. Chancellor, *History for Their Masters* (Bath 1970); J.M. Goldstrom, *The Social Content of Education* (London 1972); F.A. Glenndening, 'School Textbooks and Racial Attitudes, 1804–1911,' *Journal of Educational Administration and History* 2 (1973): 33–43; MacKenzie, *Propaganda and Empire*, 174–97; and most recently, Katherine Castle, *Britannia's Children* (Manchester 1996).

14 See the *Report of the Board of Education, 1899–1900*, vol. III and appendices, Cd. 330 [*PP* XIX.1] (1900), 6–7, 18–19, 170. On the perceived widespread inadequacy of formal history instruction, see the *Royal Commission Appointed to Inquire into the Workings of Elementary Education Acts (England and Wales)*, Third Report, C. 5158 [*PP* XXX.1] (1887), 891. On the cost-inefficiency of textbooks, see Gordon R. Batho, 'History Text-Books, 1870–1914: A Note on the Historical Association Collection at Durham,' *History of Education Bulletin* no. 33 (1984): 16.

15 David Vincent, *Literacy and Popular Culture* (Cambridge 1989), 73–94; Alec Ellis, *Books in Victorian Elementary Schools* (London 1971), 103–5.

16 H. Dunn and J.T. Crossley, *The Daily Lesson for the Use of Schools and Families* (London 1840), Book no. III: 103; and Book no. I: 8. Quoted in Goldstrom, *Social Content*, 124–5.

17 *National Reading Books Adapted to the Government Code* Standards I–IV (London 1857–68).

18 The National Society book depository reported a substantial increase in requests for readers after initial uncertainty about levels of government funding; see CERC, *Fifty-Fourth Report of the National Society* (1865), 9; Ellis, *Books*, 105.

19 British and Foreign School Society, *The Revised Lesson Book for Standard II of the Revised Code of the Committee on Education* (London 1864), preface.

20 Ibid., 44.
21 William Francis Collier, *Nelson's School Series: Pictures of English History for Junior Pupils* (London 1864), 69.
22 Dunn's *Principles of Teaching or the Normal School Manual*, 9th ed. (London 185?), quoted in Goldstrom, *Social Content*, 151.
23 Ibid., 128–9.
24 On the parameters of the debate on literacy in the London Board Schools, see Gretchen Galbraith, *Reconstructing Childhood, Books and Schools in Britain, 1870–1920* (New York 1997), 121–34. On more general developments in this area, see Vincent, *Literacy and Popular Culture*, 53–94.
25 *Report of the Royal Commission Appointed to Enquire into the Workings of Elementary Education Acts (England and Wales)*, Final Report, C. 5329 [*PP* XXXVII, I] (1888), 17.
26 'Reading with fluency and expression' and 'reading with intelligence' were phrases first included in the requirements of the higher standards in the codes of 1875 and 1879. See *Report of the Committee of Council on Education*, C. 1513-II [*PP* XXIV.1, 673] (1874–5), cxlix; and also C. 2342 [*PP* XXIII.1] (1878–9), 373.
27 *Report of the Committee of Council on Education*, C. 3312.I [*PP* XXIII.1] (1881–2), 132.
28 *Cassell's Stories from English History* (London 1884), 13.
29 *English History Reading Books: Old Stories* (London 1882), 93–4.
30 *Chambers's Geography Readers* (London 1883), I: 60.
31 *Arnold's English Readers* (London 1893), V: 15–16. Emphasis in original.
32 Figures for Arnold's and Longman's publications were compiled from archival sources. See Appendix B.
33 MCL, M65/1/12/1, Manchester School Board Proceedings of Subcommittees I, 'Instruction of Pupil Teachers Subcommittee,' 13 March 1890, 314. Some 300 copies of Cyril Ransome's *Short History of England* and 300 copies of J.M. Meiklejohn's *New Geography* were purchased for pupil teachers by the Manchester School Board in this year.
34 The school board rate (the money owed by each householder to the local authority for the provision of board schools) for Manchester in 1892 was 5d, while London was 1s, Bristol 7.5d, Sheffield 9d, and Bradford 7d. Rural boards and voluntary schools tended to have even less resources than the board of a major city such as Manchester. For a list of school board rates and a discussion, see *Reynolds Newspaper*, 10 January 1892, 4.
35 MCL, M65/1/5/16, Manchester School Board School Managers Committee, 'Report on the Cost of Books and Stationary,' 15 July 1895.

36 GLRO, SBL 188, School Board for London, 'Special Purpose Committee on Selection of Schoolbooks' (1899), 4, 26–8.

37 PRO, Ed. 14/96, 12 November 1912. This and an earlier report on the teaching of English, Ed. 14/95, 10 August 1908, confirm that a variety of cheap readers made up the vast majority of books available for use in class.

38 For example, BRO, Eastville Board School for Boys, Bristol, Logbook, October 1888, 22; Westbury on Tyrm Board School for Girls, Bristol, Logbook, 1900, 157–8.

39 Simon Eliot, 'Some Patterns and Trends in British Publishing, 1800–1919,' *Occasional Papers of the Bibliographical Society* 8 (London 1994): 48; Simon Nowell-Smith, *The House of Cassell, 1848–1958* (London 1958), 108.

40 See the reviews of Longman and Cassell readers in *School Board Chronicle*, 14 June 1873, 429–30, and 11 September 1881, 262. Harold Cox and John E. Chandler, *The House of Longman, 1724–1824* (London 1925), 37–8; Nowell-Smith, *House of Cassell*, 108–10; Roy Yglesias, 'Education and Publishing in Transition,' in Asa Briggs, ed., *Essays in the History of Publishing* (London 1974), 359–77. For Longman's publication figures, see Appendix B.

41 John A.H. Dempster, 'Thomas Nelson and Sons in the Late Nineteenth Century: A Study in Motivation, Part 1,' *Publishing History* 13 (1983): 67.

42 I. Norrie, *Mumby's Publishing and Bookselling in the Twentieth Century* (London 1982), 55.

43 David Keir, *The House of Collins* (London 1952), 211.

44 Bryan Bennett and Anthony Hamilton, *Edward Arnold: 100 Hundred Years of Publishing* (London 1990), 11–15.

45 CERC, *National Society Annual Reports*, vols. 69–103 (1880–1914).

46 Peter Sutcliffe, *The Oxford University Press: An Informal History* (Oxford 1978), 19–24.

47 M.H. Black, *Cambridge University Press, 1584–1984* (Cambridge 1984), 158–60; BRO, Marlborough Hill National School (mixed), Gloucester, Logbook, 1905, 157.

48 See the open letter of complaint sent to A.H.D. Acland, the vice president of the Committee of Council on Education, from publishers Edward Arnold, Bell and Sons, Cassell and Co., National Society, Gill and Sons, Longman's, Green and Co., Macmillan and Co., Marcus Ward, Philip and Son, et al., regarding recent changes in the Education Code and the effects these changes would have on reader and textbook production, printed in the *School Guardian*, 25 March 1895, 248.

49 For London, see GLRO, SBL 682, School Board for London, 'Minutes of the Meeting of the Books and Apparatus Subcommittee,' 15 March 1889;

SBL 188 'Special Committee,' 1 December 1899; London County Council Education Committee, 'Minutes: Books and Apparatus Subcommittee Report,' no. 16, 3 July 1907, 2084. For Bristol, see BRO, MB/F2, Bristol School Board, 'Requisition Committee Minutes,' June 1901, 15. For Manchester, see MCL M428, Manchester County Council Education Committee, 'Elementary Education Subcommittee Minutes,' no. 3, 1 December 1903, 220–1.

50 See Appendix A.

51 Galbraith, *Reconstructing Childhood*, 123.

52 Articles and book reviews in the *School Board Chronicle* frequently point to the importance of professional qualifications. Moreover, see specifically the letters in *School Guardian* 20 (1895): 429, and the exchange regarding the professional qualifications of 'civics' reader authors in every issue of the *Schoolmaster* XLVIII, between 5 October 1895 and 2 November 1895.

53 Chancellor, *History for Their Masters*, 29.

54 Michael Apple and L. Christian-Smith, *The Politics of the Textbook* (New York 1991), 3. On reading school-book ideology, see Michael Apple, *Curriculum and Ideology* (New York 1990); Allan Luke, *Literacy, Textbooks and Performance* (London 1988); John Ahier, *Industry, Children and the Nation* (Brighton 1988).

55 Raymond Williams, *The Long Revolution* (London 1961), 50–9.

56 Dina Copelman, *London's Women Teachers* (London 1996); Alison Oram, *Women Teachers and Feminist Politics, 1900–1939* (Manchester 1996).

57 Joan W. Scott, 'The Evidence of Experience,' *Critical Inquiry* 17 (Summer 1991): 797.

Chapter 1: Citizen Authors and the Language of Citizenship

1 See Derek Heater, *Citizenship: The Civic Ideal in World History, Politics and Education* (London 1990).

2 C. Cook and J. Stevenson, *Longman's Handbook of Modern British History, 1714–1980* (New York 1983), 62.

3 O. Newland, *The Model Citizen* (London 1907), 14. For an Edwardian discussion of citizenship, see W.F. Trotter, *The Citizen and His Duties* (London 1907), 7–8.

4 James Welton, *Principles and Methods of Teaching* (London 1906), 227; Earl of Meath, 'Duty and Discipline in the Training of Children,' in Meath et al., eds., *Essays on Duty and Discipline* (London 1910), 8.

5 J.M. MacKenzie, 'The Imperial Pioneer and Hunter and the British Masculine Stereotype in Late Victorian and Edwardian Times,' in

J.A. Mangan and J. Walvin, eds., *Manliness and Morality: Middle-Class Masculinity in Britain and America* (London 1987); J.A. Mangan, *The Games Ethic and Imperialism* (London 1986), and *Athleticism in the Victorian and Edwardian Public School* (London 1981). For a caution about seeing masculinity constructed solely in these terms, see M. Roper and J. Tosh, eds., *Manful Assertions* (London 1991), 8; and for a nuanced and balanced corrective to earlier views, see Paul R. Deslandes, 'Masculinity, Identity and Culture: Male Undergraduate Life at Oxford and Cambridge, 1850–1920' (PhD dissertation, University of Toronto 1996).

6 *Whitehall Literary Readers* IV (London 1895), 195.

7 H.E. Malden, *The Life and Duties of a Citizen* (London 1894), 128. Emphasis in original.

8 *King Alfred Readers* VI (London 1900), 99–100.

9 Linda Simpson, 'Education, Imperialism and National Efficiency in England, 1895–1905' (PhD dissertation, Glasgow University 1979), 15–50, 91–136.

10 E.J.T. Brennan, *Education for National Efficiency: The Contribution of Sidney and Beatrice Webb* (London 1975); G.R. Searle, *The Quest for National Efficiency* (London 1971); R.J.W. Selleck, *The New Education* (Oxford 1968); Brian Simon, *Education and the Labour Movement, 1870–1920* (London 1965).

11 Sir Norman Lockyer, *Education and National Progress: Essays and Addresses, 1870–1905* (London 1906), 229; Laurie Magnus, ed., *Essays in National Education* (London 1901), 22.

12 Earl of Meath et al., eds., *Our Empire, Past and Present* (London 1901), 49, 103; and see also the Earl of Meath and the Countess of Meath, *Thoughts on Imperial and Social Subjects* (London 1906), 246.

13 Right Rev. Bishop J.F.C. Welldon, 'The Early Training of Boys in Citizenship,' in Meath et al., eds., *Essays on Duty and Discipline*, 4, 7, 8–9.

14 For some of the more strident of the innumerable examples, see Meath, 'Duty and Discipline in the Training of Children,' in Meath et al., eds., *Essays on Duty and Discipline*; T.H. Manners Howe, 'Save the Boys,' ibid.; Capt. G.F. Ellison, *Home Defence* (London 1898), 102; Lord Milner, *The Nation and Empire* (London 1913), 171–2; Lord Roberts, *A Nation in Arms: Speeches on the Requirements of the British Army* (London 1907), v–vi.

15 Matthew Hendley, '"Help Us to Secure a Strong, Healthy, Prosperous and Peaceful Britain": The Social Arguments of the Campaign for Compulsory Military Service in Britain, 1899–1914,' *Canadian Journal of History* 30 (August 1995): 261–88; Anne Summers, 'Militarism in Britain before the Great War,' *History Workshop Journal* no. 2 (1976): 104–23; MacKenzie, 'The Imperial Pioneer and Hunter,' 189.

16 James Bryce, *The Hindrances to Good Citizenship* (London 1909), 6–7, 121.
17 Dr W. Boyd, *Education in Citizenship: The Modern Teacher* (London 190?), 224.
18 L.H. Hobhouse, *Social Evolution and Political Theory* (London 1928), 184. Hobhouse's own lecture at Columbia University in 1911 made this inference in reference to the Old Age Pensions Act of 1908. See also T.H. Marshall, 'Citizenship and Social Class,' in his *Class, Citizenship and Social Development* (Westport, CT 1973), 87.
19 S.S. Laurie, *Institutes of Education* (Edinburgh 1892), 3.
20 H.E. Oakley, HMI report for Manchester, quoted in J.S. Hurt, 'Drill, Discipline and the Elementary School Ethos,' in P. McCann, ed., *Popular Education and Socialization in the 19th Century* (London 1977), 180.
21 W. Turnbull, Chief HMI, Northeastern Division, in *the Report of the Board of Education, 1900–1,* vol. II, Appendix to Report, Cd. 756 [PP XIX., xx. 1] (1901), 126.
22 Selleck, *New Education,* 40, 46, 60–3.
23 Cheryl Walsh, 'The Incarnation and the Christian Socialist Conscience in the Victorian Church of England,' *Journal of British Studies* 34, no. 3 (1995): 353.
24 K.S. Inglis, *Churches and the Working Classes in Victorian England* (London 1963), 251.
25 J.M. Goldstrom, 'The Content of Education and the Socialization of the Working-Class Child, 1830–1860,' in McCann, ed., *Popular Education,* 98.
26 R.E. Hughes, *The Making of Citizens* (London 1902); *The Democratic Ideal in Education* (London 1903); *School Training* (London 1905). See the reviews of these books by Welton in the *International Journal of Ethics* 13 (1902–3): 505–7, and 16 (1905–6): 251–2.
27 Hughes, *The Making of Citizens,* 11, 63, and *The Democratic Ideal in Education,* 18.
28 Hughes, *School Training,* 3.
29 Hughes, *The Democratic Ideal in Education,* 30–4.
30 Hughes, *School Training,* 27, 107–10.
31 Hughes, *The Democratic Ideal in Education,* 40.
32 Hughes, *School Training,* 36, 110.
33 T. Raymont, *The Principles of Education* (London 1904), 14–15.
34 Sophie Bryant, *The Teaching of Morality in the Family and the School* (London 1907), 137.
35 *Suggestions for the Consideration of Teachers and Others Concerned in the Work of Public Elementary Schools* (HMSO 1909–10), 5, 97.

36 For one of the first recommendations for 'civics,' see *The Final Report of the Commissioners Appointed to Inquire into the Workings of the Elementary Education Acts (England and Wales)*, C. 5485 [*PP* XXXVII] (1888), 13. The *Report of the Board of Education, 1905–6*, Cd. 3270 [*PP* XXVIII.85] (1906), 25–7, provides some indication of the state of instruction in 'civics' and 'morality' by that date. On the production of citizenship readers, see the National Society official paper, the *School Guardian*, 5 December 1896, 947; and the exchange in the National Union of Teachers organ, the *Schoolmaster*, 5 October 1895, 553; 12 October 1895, 598; 19 October 1895, 642; 26 October 1895, 671; 2 November 1895, 613.

37 Preface by W.E. Forster to H.O. Arnold-Forster's *The Citizen Reader* (London 1886).

38 Selleck, *New Education*, 325; Simon Nowell-Smith, *The House of Cassell, 1848–1958* (London 1958), 73.

39 W. Beach Thomas, ed., *The Citizen Books* III (London 1908), 5; Malden, *Life and Duties*, preface.

40 J. Edward Parrot, *The Waterloo Citizen Reader* (London 1893), 26.

41 H.L. Withers, 'Memorandum on the Teaching of History in the Schools of the London School Board,' reprinted in Withers, *The Teaching of History and Other Papers* (Manchester 1904), 200.

42 *Report of the Board of Education, 1910–11*, Cd. 6116 [*PP* XXI] (1912), 10–14, 16, 23; *Third Report of the Royal Commission Appointed to Enquire into the Workings of Elementary Education Acts (England and Wales)*, C. 5158 [*PP* XXX, I] (1887), 891; *Revised Education Code for 1882*, C. 3152 [*PP* L.511] (1882); and GLRO, *London County Council Report on the Teaching of History in London* (1911), 11.

43 J. Gill, *Introductory Textbook to School Education and Method* (London 1858), 17.

44 J. Currie, *Principles and Practice of Common School Education* (London 1861), 438–43.

45 L. Playfair, *Subjects of Social Welfare* (London 1889), 288; A.W. Newton, *The English Elementary School* (London 1919), 116; F.H. Spencer, *An Inspector's Testament* (London 1938), 97–8; *Reports of the Committee of Council on Education, 1872–3*, C. 812-I (1873), 48, 60; ibid., *1874–5*, C. 1265-I (1875), 50, 74–5; ibid., *1875–6*, C. 1513-I (1876), 328, 398–9.

46 *Educational Times*, January 1878, 10; Seymour's Elementary Series, *Concise History of England* (London 1879), 13.

47 J. Lubbock, *Addresses, Political and Educational* (London 1879), 76–7.

48 *Second Report of the Commission Appointed to Enquire into the Workings of the Elementary Education Acts (England and Wales)*, C. 5056 [*PP* XXIX] (1887), 46.

49 *School Board Chronicle*, 30 March 1872, 198, and 1 March 1873, 56, 66. See also PRO, Ed. 9/17 (S433) for the long series of complaints about religious and political bias in schools in correspondence to the Board of Education after 1870.

50 *Educational Times*, May 1887, 137. The later debate took place in several numbers of the *Educational Times* in 1900, with J.J. Findlay looking to the example of Germany and the United States, and Fitch decrying the use of patriotism for nationalistic ends. See also Valerie Chancellor, *History for Their Masters* (Bath 1971), 113.

51 J. Fitch, *Lectures on Teaching* (London 1885), 113.

52 David Salmon, *The Art of Teaching* (London 1898), 213.

53 John Landon, *The Principles and Practice of Teaching and Class Management* (London 1894), 405.

54 A.H. Garlick, *A New Manual of Method* (London 1896), 258. Italics in original.

55 T.A. Cox and R.F. Macdonald, *The Suggestive Handbook of Practical School Method* (London 1896), 358.

56 J. Gunn, *Class Teaching and Management* (London 1895), 136–7; G. Collar and C. Crook, *School Management and Methods of Instruction (with special reference to elementary schools)* (London 1900), 182; Amos Henderson, *Some Notes on Teaching* (Nottingham 1903), 73; Welton, *Principles and Methods of Teaching*, 226; J.W. Adamson, ed., *The Practice of Instruction: A Manual of Method* (London 1907), 251; F.H. Hayward, ed., *The Primary Curriculum* (London 1909), 83.

57 Joseph H. Cowham, *A New School Method: For Pupil Teachers and Students* (London 1894), 349.

58 Originally printed in Board of Education, *Suggestions for the Consideration of Teachers and Others Concerned in the Work of the Public Elementary Schools*, Cd. 2638 [*PP* LX] (1905), 61–4. The section on history was reprinted, unedited, as Board of Education Circular no. 599, *The Teaching of History* (1908), and reprinted again, with revisions, as Circular no. 833, *Suggestions for the Consideration of Teachers and Others Concerned in the Work of Public Elementary Schools: History* (1914).

59 Board of Education, *Suggestions*, 46.

60 Board of Education, Circular no. 833, pp. 1–8.

61 Ibid., 5.

62 Collar and Crook, *School Management*, 183; Cowham, *New School Method*, 346; Henderson, *Notes*, 75–7; Landon, *Principles and Practice*, 404–5.

63 W.H. Woodward, *Essays on the Teaching of History* (London 1901), 74.

64 *School Government Chronicle*, 11 January 1908, 51.

65 Sara Cone Bryant, *How to Tell Stories to Children* (London 1910), 17; Septimus Rivington, *The Publishing Family of Rivingtons* (London 1919), 89–96; see also M. Plant, *The English Book Trade: An Economic History* (London 1974), 457–8, 464.

66 J.M. Goldstrom, *The Social Content of Education* (London 1972), 8–38; Chancellor, *History for Their Masters*, 22.

67 See the series preface to the *Raleigh History Readers* (London 1896).

68 Reba Soffer, *Discipline and Power: The University, History and the Making of an English Elite, 1870–1930* (Stanford 1994), 171–2.

69 Peter H. Slee, *Learning and Liberal Education* (Manchester 1986), 162–3.

70 Richard Symonds, *Oxford and Empire: The Last Lost Cause* (New York 1986); Deborah Wormell, *Sir John Seeley and the Uses of History* (Cambridge 1980), 111; Phillipa Levine, *The Amateur and the Professional: Antiquarians, Historians and Archaeologists in Victorian England, 1838–1886* (Cambridge 1986), 161; Brian Doyle, *English and Englishness* (London 1989), 24–8; James R. Ryan, 'Visualizing Imperial Geography: Halford Mackinder and the Colonial Office Visual Instruction Committee, 1902–11,' *Ecumene* 1, no. 2 (1994): 157–8; Anthony Kearney, 'English Versus History: The Battle for Identity and Status, 1850–1920,' *History of Education Society Bulletin* 48 (1991): 22–9.

71 *School Board Chronicle*, 13 January 1883, 44.

72 Bryant, *How to Tell Stories*, 40–1.

73 Hayden White, 'The Historical Text as Literary Artifact,' in *Tropics of Discourse* (Baltimore 1992), 81–100.

74 J.S. Bratton, *The Impact of Victorian Fiction* (London 1981), 29.

75 Board of Education, *Suggestions*, 47. For a theoretical discussion of the discursive construction of national identity, see Benedict Anderson, *Imagined Communities* (New York 1991).

76 *Chambers's Summary of English History* (London 1904), 62.

77 *Cassell's Historical Course for Schools* I (London 1884), 181–2.

78 J.M. MacKenzie, *Propaganda and Empire* (Manchester 1984), 199–226; J.A. Mangan, 'Grit of Our Forefathers,' in J.M. MacKenzie, ed., *Imperialism and Popular Culture* (Manchester 1986), 113–39.

79 I am indebted to Graham Dawson, 'The Blond Bedouin: Lawrence of Arabia, Imperial Adventure and the Imagining of English-British Masculinity,' in Roper and Tosh, eds., *Manful Assertions*, esp. 119–20, for the conceptual framework of this paragraph. See also Kelly Boyd, 'Knowing Your Place: The Tensions of Manliness in Boys' Story Papers, 1918–1939,' also in Roper and Tosh, eds., *Manful Assertions*, 145–67; Patrick A. Dunae, 'Boys' Literature and the Idea of Race,' *Wascana Review* (Spring 1977): 84–107; and MacKenzie, *Propaganda*, 199–226.

80 Martin Green, *Dreams of Adventure: Deeds of Empire* (New York 1979), 3, and also Patrick Brantlinger, *Rule of Darkness: British Literature and Imperialism, 1830–1914* (Ithaca 1988).

81 BRO, Eastville Board Boys School, Bristol, Logbook, 1892, 78; Greenbank Council School (Girls), Bristol, Logbook, 1906, 54; St Philip's National Boys School, Bristol, Logbook, 1904, 16. GLRO, Grove St. Board School, Girls Dept., London, Logbook, 1897, 40; Cobold Rd., Mixed Board School, Chelsea, Logbook, 1900, 45. MCL, St Barnabas Board School, Manchester, Logbook, 1902, 206.

82 Robert H. MacDonald, *The Language of Empire: The Myths and Metaphors of Popular Imperialism* (Manchester 1994), 37.

83 Malden, *Life and Duties*, 189–90. For nearly identical remarks, see Oscar Browning, *The Citizen: His Rights and Responsibilities* (London 1893), 10–11; C.H. Wyatt, *The English Citizen* (London 1894), 212; and J. St Loe Strachey, *The Citizen and the State* (London 1913), 123.

84 Arnold-Forster, *Citizen Reader*, 24–5, 133. Emphasis mine.

85 Rev. C.S. Dawe, *King Edward's Realm* (London 1902), 219.

86 MacKenzie, *Propaganda*, 5. Douglas Johnson presents an interesting analysis of the political purposes to which Gordon's death was used by the late-Victorians in his 'The Death of Gordon: A Victorian Myth,' *Journal of Imperial and Commonwealth History* 10, no. 3 (May 1982): 285–310.

87 *Longman's New Historical Readers* IV (London 1888), 193.

88 *Chambers's Alternative History Readers* IV (London 1898), 160.

89 Arnold-Forster, *Citizen Reader*, 5–26.

90 C.F. Behrman, *Victorian Myths of the Sea* (Athens, GA 1981), 96.

91 BRO, 'Syllabus for 1892–3,' Eastville Board (later Council) Boys School, Logbook, 1892, 78; 'Syllabus and Notes on Curriculum,' St Philip's National Boys School, Logbook, 1904, 16; 'Syllabus for 1906–7,' St George's School Board, Greenbank (later Council) Girls School, Logbook, 1906, 150–3. GLRO, 'Notes on Lessons,' Drayton Park, Holloway Rd., Board School, Boys, Logbook, 1894, 1, and 1898, 82; 'Notes on Lessons and Recitation,' Grove St. Board School, Girls Dept., Logbook, 1902, 150.

92 *Tower History Readers* VI (London 1911), 101.

93 *The King Alfred Readers* III (London 1900), 43.

94 *Raleigh History Readers* V: 166; *Chambers's Alternative History Readers* V (London 1898), 145.

95 Arnold-Forster, *Citizen Reader*, 96.

96 *Cassell's Historical Course for Schools: Simple Outline of English History* (London 1884), 168.

97 John Finnemore, *Famous Englishmen* I (London 1901), 3–5.

98 See Chancellor, *History for Their Masters*, 39–43.
99 Newland, *Model Citizen*, 15–16.
100 Arnold-Forster, *Citizen Reader*, 102.
101 *The King Alfred Readers* I (London 1900), 15–16.

Chapter 2: The Syntax of National Identity

1 See F. York Powell, *Longman's New Historical Readers* IV (London 1888), 6.
2 *Cassell's Historical Course for Schools: Simple Outline of English History* (London 1884), 181.
3 Anne McClintock, 'Family Feuds: Gender, Nationalism and the Family,' *Feminist Review* (Summer 1993): 61–7; George Mosse, *Nationalism and Sexuality* (London 1985).
4 For instance, *The Warwick History Readers* (London 1895–6); *The Britannia Geography Readers* (London 1896).
5 For example, the first two volumes of Blackie's *Complete History Readers* (London 1904) contained a total of five illustrations of women (Boadicea, Elizabeth I, Victoria, Florence Nightingale, and Elizabeth Fry) out of a grand total of forty-eight illustrations depicting historical figures. And, from an admittedly cursory survey of the illustrations in the books of the overall sample, this series seemed to *overrepresent* women in comparison to the vast majority of the others.
6 Catherine Hall, *White, Male and Middle Class* (New York 1992), 207; John Wolffe, 'Whose Jerusalem: Evangelicalism and Nationalism in Nineteenth Century England,' *Christianity and National Consciousness* (Leicester 1987), 41.
7 Peter J. Bowler, *The Invention of Progress* (Oxford 1989); J.W. Burrows, *A Liberal Descent: Victorian Historians and the English Past* (Cambridge 1981); Rosemary Jann, *The Art and Science of Victorian History* (Columbus 1985); J. Kenyon, *The History Men: The Historical Profession in England since the Renaissance* (London 1983); Phillipa Levine, *The Amateur and the Professional: Antiquarians, Historians and Archaeologists in Victorian England, 1838–1886* (Cambridge 1986).
8 R. Colls, 'Englishness and the Political Culture,' in Robert Colls and Philip Dodd, eds., *Englishness: Politics and Culture* (London 1986), 31.
9 Margot Finn, '"A Vent Which Has Conveyed Our Principles": English Radical Patriotism in the Aftermath of 1848,' *Journal of Modern History* 64, no. 4 (December 1992): 637–59; Gregory Claeys, 'Mazzini, Kossuth, and British Radicalism, 1848–54,' *Journal of British Studies* 28 (1989): 225–61.
10 Stedman Jones, *Languages of Class* (Cambridge 1983), esp. 90–178; Patrick Joyce, *Visions of the People* (Cambridge 1991); James Vernon, *Politics and the*

People (Cambridge 1993); James Vernon, ed., *Rereading the Constitution* (Cambridge 1996).

11 Margot Finn, *After Chartism* (Cambridge 1993), 227.

12 Joyce, *Visions of the People*, 27–55.

13 On the rise of a professional ethic among a growing segment of the middle class, see Harold Perkin, *The Rise of Professional Society: England since 1880* (London 1989); on the importance of the universities in the politics of this eventual development, see Christopher Harvie, *The Lights of Liberalism* (London 1976).

14 Joyce, *Visions of the People*, 190–1.

15 For example: Osmund Airy, *Text-Book of English History* (London 1891); Mandell Creighton, *The Shilling History of England* (London 1881); C.S. Fearenside, *A School History of England* (London 1904); C.R.L. Fletcher and R. Kipling, *A School History of England* (Oxford 1911); S.R. Gardiner, *A Student's History of England* (London 1892); C. Oman, *History of England* (London 1895); C. Ransome, *Elementary History of England* (London 1890); T.F. Tout, *History of Britain* (London 1906); F. York Powell and T. Tout, *History of England* (London 1900).

16 For instructive comments by school officials on the content and approval of readers, and on the sometimes tense relationship between local education boards and publishers, see GLRO, SBL 681, School Board for London, *Minutes of the Meeting of the Books and Apparatus Subcommittee*, 19 June 1885; SBL 188, School Board for London, *Minutes of Special Committee on the Selection of School Books*, meetings of 28 April 1899 and 12 May 1899; London County Council Education Committee, *Minutes: Books and Apparatus Subcommittee Report*, 3 July 1907; BRO, MB/F2, Bristol School Board, *Requisition Committee Minutes*, June 1901. For author and publisher comments on these issues, see the prefaces to Longman's *'Ship' Historical Readers* (London 1893); *Chambers's 'New Scheme' History Readers on the Concentric Plan* (London 1901–5); *Chambers's Alternative Geography Readers* (London 1899); John Finnemore, *Black's School Series: The Story of the English People – A Simple Introductory Historical Reader* (London 1905); and *The Complete History Readers* (1902–6).

17 A.H. Garlick, *A New Manual of Method* (London 1896), 263.

18 E.H. Spalding, *Piers Plowman Series* (London 1914), preface to series, v–vii.

19 *Chambers's Historical Readers* III (London 1882), 187. See also *Chambers's 'New Scheme' Readers: Advanced History of England* (London 1904), 275.

20 H.E. Malden, *The Life and Duties of a Citizen* (London 1894), 2.

21 *The Raleigh Geography Readers* VI (London 1899), 28–9.

22 Oscar Browning, *Epochs of Modern History Series: Modern England, 1815–1885* (London 1891), preface.

23 *Cassell's Historical Course for Schools: Simple Outline*, 182.

24 See John Burrow, *A Liberal Descent* (Cambridge 1981), for a comprehensive deconstruction of the Whig master narrative in Victorian historiography.

25 E.H. Goodwin, response to a paper delivered at the North of England Education Conference, *School Government Chronicle* 79 (1908): 51. See also Garlick, *A New Manual of Method*, 262–3, on the attractions for young children of romance with special reference to Magna Carta.

26 S.R. Gardiner, *English History Reading Books: Outline of English History* (London 1881), 63.

27 *Chambers's Alternative History Readers* IV (London 1898), 61; *Chambers's 'New Scheme' History Readers, Preparatory History of England* (London 1901), 45; and *Chambers's Alternative Geography Readers* V (London 1899), 74–6. The other monuments noted in reverent terms in readers were Trafalgar Square and, of course, Westminster – 'the Mother of all Parliaments.'

28 Mary Hancock, *King Edward History Readers: The Story of England, 55 BC to 1904* (London 1904), 52. For examples of vitriolic attacks on the character and rule of King John, see *Chambers's 'New Scheme' History Readers: Stories from British History* 2 (London 1905), 41; Finnemore, *The Story of the English People*, 51; *Cambridge Historical Readers: Junior* (Cambridge 1911), 82–6.

29 *Raleigh History Readers* IV (London 1896), 63.

30 *Cassell's Historical Course for Schools: Simple Outline*, 71–2.

31 *Cassell's Historical Course for Schools: Class History of England* (London 1884), 10.

32 *Chambers's Historical Readers* II: 114; S.R. Gardiner, *English History Reading Books: Historical Biographies* (London 1884), 4.

33 *The Warwick History Readers: Stories from English History to 1485* (London 1895), 120.

34 *Tower History Readers* III (London 1910), 111.

35 *Cambridge History Readers: Junior* (Cambridge 1911), 94; see also Newland's discussion of the growth of Parliament, *The Model Citizen* (London 1910), 72.

36 *Cambridge History Readers: Junior*, 86–7; see also *Raleigh History Readers* IV: 63.

37 *Cassell's Historical Course for Schools: Class History*, 134.

38 *Warwick History Readers: Stories from English History to 1485*, 124–5.

39 *King Edward History Readers* VI (London n.d.), 125; Gardiner, *English History Reading Books: Historical Biographies*, 17.

40 T.F. Tout, *Longman's Historical Series* I (London 1903), 67–70.

41 *Cambridge Historical Readers: Junior*, 91; *Warwick History Readers, Stories from English History to 1485*, 125.

42 *Cassell's Historical Course for Schools: Class History*, 112.

43 M. Creighton, *Longman's Life of Simon de Montfort* (London 1895), 1; *Cambridge Historical Readers: Junior*, 94.

44 *Chambers's 'New Scheme' History Readers: Advanced History of England* (London 1904), 61.

45 Tout, *Longman's Historical Series for Schools* I: 67; Finnemore, *The Story of the English People*, 54.

46 S.R. Gardiner, *An Easy History of England* (2nd Course, Std. VI and VII), printed as one of *Longman's New Historical Readers* (London 1888), 55; *Chambers's Alternative History Readers* IV: 61.

47 Rev. D. Morris, *Senior Standard History Readers* I (London 1883), 116.

48 For example, see G.R. Gleig's *School History of England* (London 1859), 121–31. Throughout the 1870s the Society for the Promotion of Christian Knowledge's New Reading Series severely criticized Edward I's 'terrible acts of injustice and cruelty' in his dealings with the Welsh and Scots. See their revised reader *English History* (London 1881), 47–8.

49 *Warwick History Readers* IV: 125.

50 Gardiner, *English History Reading Books: Historical Biographies*, 42, and *English History Reading Books: Outline*, 71–2.

51 For some examples, see Joseph Cowham, *A New School Method: For Pupil Teachers and Students* (London 1894), 346–8; John Landon, *The Principles and Practice of Teaching and Class Management* (London 1894), 395; John Gunn, *Class Teaching and Management* (London 1895), 135; L.C. Miall, *Thirty Years of Teaching* (London 1897), 12. For the use of this approach in historical and geographical accounts of the empire, see J.M. MacKenzie, *Propaganda and Empire* (Manchester 1984), 179, and Peter Burroughs, 'John R. Seeley and British Imperial History,' *Journal of Imperial and Commonwealth History* 1 (1972–3): 192.

52 See Valerie Chancellor, *History for Their Masters* (Bath 1970), 67–89.

53 *Chambers's National History Readers* IV (London 1897), 55, 60–2.

54 Rev. C.S. Dawe, *King Edward's Realm* (London 1902), 28–31.

55 Royal Standard Series, *Clough's Reign of Elizabeth* (London 1899), 7.

56 *New Era Geography Readers: Our Imperial Heritage* (London 1903), 7; C.H. Wyatt, *The English Citizen: His Life and Duty* (London 1894), 170; *English History Reading Books* I (London 1881), 192; *Chambers's Alternative History Readers* IV: 25–33, 124.

57 *Cambridge Historical Readers* II (Cambridge 1911), 16.

58 Fredric Jameson *The Political Unconscious* (Ithaca 1982), 82–3, 254.
59 Rev. Dr Brewer, *My First Book of History of England: A Catechism for Very Young Children Is Subjoined* (London 1864), 41.
60 Ibid., 44. Male monarchs' private lives were also judged by this and other mid-century texts, and were found inappropriate to basically middle-class notions of personal conduct. These kings were also commented on as having 'flaws of character.'
61 New Reading Series, *English History* (London 1881), 138; Gardiner, *English History Reading Books: Outline*, 192–3; *The Warwick History Readers* IV: 80–3; *King Edward History Readers: Stories from Modern English History* (London 1904), 49–56; *Cambridge Historical Readers: Junior*, 157–69.
62 This speech, or excerpts from it, appeared in nearly every history reader covering the Elizabethan period. This version comes from *The Warwick History Readers: Simple Stories* II (London 1895), 65.
63 Gardiner, *English History Reading Books: Outline*, 182.
64 *The Patriotic Historical Readers* II (London 1898): 26–8; *The Warwick History Readers* II: 65–6.
65 *Longman's New Historical Readers* VI: 98; Gardiner, *English History Reading Books: Outline*, 182; *Chambers's Historical Readers* III (London 1882), 91; *The Patriotic Historical Readers* II: 26; *The Warwick History Readers* II: 65.
66 *The Warwick History Readers* VII: 8.
67 *The Warwick History Readers* IV: 80; *Chambers's National History Readers* IV: 55.
68 Royal Standard Series, *Clough's Reign of Elizabeth*, 7.
69 *Chambers's Alternative History Readers* IV: 125.
70 Dawe, *King Edward's Realm*, 59.
71 *Chambers's Alternative History Readers* IV: 157; *Raleigh History Readers* IV: 208. Whole chapters were often devoted to Raleigh. See, for example, *King Edward History Readers: Stories from Modern English History* (London 1904); *Cassell's Historical Course for Schools: Stories from English History*; *Chambers's National History Readers* IV (London 1897); *The Warwick History Readers* IV and VI; Blackie's *The Complete History Readers* II (London 1904).
72 Like Raleigh, Drake tended to get an entire chapter devoted to him in the early standard's reading books, and often large section of chapters in the later ones. Examples include *Chambers's Alternative History Readers* IV; *Raleigh History Readers* IV; *King Edward History Readers: The Story of England, 55 BC–1904*; *Senior Standard History Readers* I (London 1883); *Chambers's 'New Scheme' Readers: Stories from British History* 1 (London 1905); *English History Reading Books: Historical Biographies*; *Chambers's National History Readers* IV; John Finnemore, *Famous Englishmen* (London

1901); *The Warwick History Readers* Books II, IV, and VI; *The Complete History Readers* II; and George Bosworth, *Narrative Geography Readers* 2 (London 1910).

73 *Raleigh History Readers* IV: 188–90.

74 See, for example, *The Westminster Reading Books* V (London 1891); *The Warwick History Readers*; and *Macmillan's New History Readers* I (London 1905).

75 PRO, Ed. 14/95, Report on the Teaching of English in London Elementary Schools, 10 August 1908, appendices, and Ed. 14/96, Report on the Supply and Use of Books in London Elementary Schools, November 1912, 2.

76 *The Warwick History Readers*, 2: 70; *Cambridge Historical Readers: Primary*, 134.

77 *Chambers's Historical Readers* III (London 1882), 175; *Cassell's Historical Course for Schools: Stories from English History*; *The Patriotic Historical Readers* II: 28.

78 *Cassell's Historical Course*, 124.

79 Landon, *Principles and Practice*, 406, and F.H. Hayward, *The Primary Curriculum* (London 1909), 28.

80 *The Warwick History Readers* II: 68.

81 *Raleigh History Readers* IV: 193.

82 Finnemore, *Famous Englishmen*, 3.

83 *Cambridge Historical Readers: Junior*, 157.

84 Dina Copelman, *London's Women Teachers* (London 1996), 124.

85 Morris, *Historical Readers* V: 160–2.

86 *Chambers's 'New Scheme' History Readers* V (London 1901), 128, 137.

87 John Finnemore, *Famous Englishmen* II (London 1902), 2–17. The depiction of Charles I's rule as that of a 'despotic tyrant' was found in the majority of history readers, even in those accounts that were generally unsympathetic to Cromwell; see *The Warwick History Readers* II: 78–80; *Chambers's National History Readers* IV: 119; *The Patriotic Historical Readers* II: 62; *Chambers's Alternative History Readers* V: 14; Mary Hancock, *King Edward History Readers: Stories from Modern English History* (London 1904), 61–3.

88 *Chambers's Alternative History Readers* V: 23; *Raleigh History Readers* V (London 1896), 34; *The Warwick History Readers* IV: 172–3; Hancock, *King Edward History Readers*, 63.

89 *Chambers's 'New Scheme' History Readers, History of England*, 138.

90 Christopher Hill, 'The Norman Yoke,' in John Saville, ed., *Democracy and the Labour Movement* (London 1954), 11–66; E.P. Thompson, *The Making of the English Working Class* (Harmondsworth 1968), 84–110; Finn, *After Chartism*, 34–50.

91 Malden, *Life and Duties*, 52.
92 *The Quarterly Magazine of the Bristol Pupil Teachers Centre* (March 1901): 33.
93 Ibid., 53.
94 O. Newland and R.L. Jones, *The Model Citizen*, Scots edition (London 1910), 104.
95 Walter Bagehot, *The English Constitution* (London 1973), 82–120.
96 David Cannadine, 'The Context, Performance and Meaning of Ritual: The British Monarchy and the "Invention of Tradition," c. 1820–1977,' in Eric Hobsbawm and Terence Ranger, eds., *The Invention of Tradition* (Cambridge 1983), 120.
97 C.S. Dawe, *Queen Victoria and Her People* (London 1897), 183; *King Edward History Readers: The Story of Our Own Times* (London 1903), 22; J.H. Rose, *Raleigh History Readers* VI (London 1897), 15.
98 Malden, *Life and Duties*, 53.
99 *Raleigh History Readers* IV: 24.
100 *Chambers's National History* III (London 1897), 26. See also *Arnold's History Readers* VII (London 1895), 7, for a detailed description of Victoria's descent from the Anglo-Saxon king Egbert.

Chapter 3: Ethnicity and National Belonging

1 Eric Hobsbawm has argued that similar processes were evident all over Europe at this time; see his 'Mass Producing Traditions: Europe, 1870–1914,' in Eric Hobsbawm and Terence Ranger, eds., *The Invention of Tradition* (Cambridge 1983), 263–307.
2 John Willinsky, *Learning to Divide the World: Education at Empire's End* (Minneapolis 1998), and *Empire of Words: The Reign of the OED* (Princeton 1994); Robert Colls and Philip Dodd, eds., *Englishness: Politics and Culture* (London 1986).
3 Frans Coetzee, *For Party or Country: Nationalism and the Dilemmas of Popular Conservatism in Edwardian England* (Oxford 1990); P. Kennedy and A. Nicholls, *Nationalist and Racialist Organizations in Britain and Germany* (Cambridge, MA 1981), 7; Robert Colls, 'Englishness and the Political Culture,' in Colls and Dodd, eds., *Englishness*, 48–52.
4 *The Avon Geographical Readers* V (London 1895), 102.
5 A.J. Herbertson, *Oxford Geographies* II (Oxford 1908), 150.
6 *Collins' Wide-World Reader* III (London 1901), 74.
7 Herbertson, *Oxford Geographies* II: 116–17.
8 For *patria*, see A.D. Smith, *National Identity* (Harmondsworth 1991), 10. For the distinction between ethnic and civil nationalisms, see Hans Kohn, *The*

Idea of Nationalism (New York 1967), 455–576; Elie Kedourie, *Nationalism* (London 1986), 74; Peter Alter, *Nationalism* (London 1994), 8–12; Michael Ignatieff, *Blood and Belonging* (London 1993).

9 See P. Scott, *Knowledge and Nation* (Edinburgh 1990), 44–8.

10 Stephen Harp, *Learning to Be Loyal* (Dekalb 1998), 13.

11 Catherine Hall, *White, Male and Middle Class* (London 1992), 25–6.

12 On anthropological and 'scientific racism,' see John Burrow, 'Evolution and Anthropology in the 1860s: The Anthropological Society of London, 1864–1871,' *Victorian Studies* 7 (1963): 137–54; John S. Haller, *Outcasts from Evolution: Scientific Attitudes of Racial Inferiority, 1859–1900* (Urbana 1971); Ronald Rainger, 'Race, Politics and Science: The Anthropological Society of London in the 1860s,' *Victorian Studies* 22 (1978): 51–70. On philology and European romantic and nationalist thought, especially the philological explorations of Benjamin Thorpe and John Kemble in the 1830s, see Hans Aarsleff, *The Study of Language in England, 1780–1860* (Princeton 1967), 182–203, and Reginald Horsman, *Race and Manifest Destiny* (Cambridge, MA 1981), 37–8. On the development of evolutionary and social Darwinistic thought, see Greta Jones, *Social Darwinism and English Thought: The Interaction between Biological and Social Theory* (Sussex 1980).

13 See N. Stepan, *The Idea of Race in Science: Great Britain, 1800–1960* (London 1982), xv; Christine Bolt, *Victorian Attitudes to Race* (London 1971), 143–6, 207; D.A. Lorimer, *Colour, Class and the Victorians* (Leicester 1978), 14; Michael Banton, *Racial Theories* (Cambridge 1987), xiv.

14 Michael Banton, *The Idea of Race* (Cambridge 1977), 46–9; Philip D. Curtin, *The Image of Africa* (Madison 1964), 378–80; M.D. Biddiss, 'The Politics of Anatomy: Dr Robert Knox and Victorian Racism,' *Proceedings of the Royal Society of Medicine* 69 (1976): 245–50; L.P. Curtis, Jr, *Anglo-Saxons and Celts* (New York 1968), 56; Reginald Horsman, 'Origins of Racial Anglo-Saxonism in Great Britain before 1850,' *Journal of the History of Ideas* 37, no. 3 (1976): 405–8; Paul Rich, 'The Long Victorian Sunset: Anthropology, Eugenics and Race in Britain, c. 1900–48,' *Patterns of Prejudice* 18, no. 3 (1984): 3–17.

15 Burrow, 'Evolution and Anthropology'; Rainger, 'Race, Politics and Science'; and George Stocking, 'What's in a Name? The Origin of the Royal Anthropological Institute, 1837–1871,' *Man* 6 (1971): 369–90; Jones, *Social Darwinism*, 10–24; Haller, *Outcasts from Evolution*, 77, 210; J.W. Burrow, *Evolution and Society: A Study in Victorian Social Theory* (London 1966), and Peter J. Bowler, *The Invention of Progress* (Oxford 1989), 59–71.

16 For Arnold, see Rosemary Jann, *The Art and Science of Victorian History* (Columbus 1985), 1–32; A. Dwight Culler, *The Victorian Mirror of History* (New Haven, CT 1985), 74–89. On the complexities of Kingsley's racial

thought, see Michael Banton, 'A Nineteenth-Century Racial Philosophy: Charles Kingsley,' in Banton, *The Idea of Race*, 63–88. Finally, see Carlyle's *On Heroes and Hero Worship* (1841) and the two articles, 'Occasional Discourse on the Negro Question,' and 'Occasional Discourse of the Nigger Question,' published in *Fraser's Magazine* in 1849 and 1853, and reprinted in E.R. August, ed., *Carlyle: The Nigger Question, Mill: The Negro Question* (New York 1971).

17 Disraeli's speech to the House of Commons, 1 February 1849, quoted in H. Odom, 'Generalisations on Race in Nineteenth Century Physical Anthropology,' *Isis* 63 (1967): 9.

18 Benjamin Disraeli, *Tancred* (London 1887 edition), 148–50; C. Dilke, *Greater Britain* (Philadelphia 1869: two volumes in one edition), I: 109 and II: 345.

19 Bowler, *Invention of Progress*, 41; C.J.W. Parker, 'The Failure of Liberal Racialism: The Racial Ideas of E.A. Freeman,' *Historical Journal* 24, no. 4 (1981): 825–46; J.W. Burrow, *A Liberal Descent* (Cambridge 1981); Jann, *Art and Science of History*, 116–17, 149–53, 175–276; Hugh MacDougall, *Racial Myth in English History: Trojans, Teutons and Anglo-Saxons* (Montreal 1982), 98–103. Seeley used rhetoric emphasizing 'blood' ('the strongest tie') and the 'ethnological unity' of the colonial empire in his *The Expansion of England* (London 1911 edition), 13, 59.

20 James R. Ryan, 'Visualising Imperial Geography: Halford Mackinder and the Colonial Office Visual Instruction Committee, 1902–1911,' *Ecumene* 1, no. 2 (1994): 157–76.

21 Anthony Brundage, *The People's Historian* (Westport, CT 1994); G.M.D. Howat has traced the broad influence of Green on the production of history texts in 'The Nineteenth-Century History Textbook,' *British Journal of Educational Studies* 13 (1965): 147–59.

22 John M. MacKenzie, *Propaganda and Empire* (Manchester 1984), 184–6; J.S. Bratton, 'Of England, Home and Duty: The Image of England in Victorian Edwardian Fiction,' in John M. MacKenzie, ed., *Imperialism and Popular Culture* (Manchester 1986), 73–93; J.A. Mangan, 'Images for Confident Control,' in J.A. Mangan, ed., *Imperial Curriculum* (London 1993), 13; Patrick Brantilinger, 'Victorians and Africans: The Genealogy of the Myth of the Dark Continent,' in Henry Louis Gates, Jr, ed., *Race, Writing and Difference* (Chicago 1986), 197–215; Patrick A. Dunae, 'Boys' Literature and the Idea of Race,' *Wascana Review* (Spring 1977): 84–107; Edward Said, *Orientalism* (New York 1978), and *Imperialism and Culture* (New York 1993).

23 Catherine Hall, 'The Economy of Intellectual Prestige: Thomas Carlyle, John Stuart Mill, and the Case of Governor Eyre,' *Cultural Critique* 12 (Spring 1989): 167–96, and 'Ethnicity, Race and Nation in Mid-Nineteenth-

Century England,' *Gender and History* 5, no. 2 (1993): 224–6; Bolt, *Victorian Attitudes*, 75–108, 157–205; Bernard Semmel, *The Governor Eyre Controversy* (London 1962).

24 Paul R. Deslandes, '"The Foreign Element": Newcomers and the Rhetoric of Race, Nation and Empire in "Oxbridge" Undergraduate Culture, 1850–1920,' *Journal of British Studies* 37 (January 1998): 54–90.

25 Valerie Chancellor, *History for Their Masters* (Bath 1970), 25.

26 See the letter from a National School teacher recommending Yonge's work in the *School Guardian*, 5 March 1898, 176.

27 Sheldon Rothblatt, *The Revolution of the Dons: Cambridge and Society in Victorian England* (London 1968), esp. 250; Reba Soffer, *Discipline and Power: The University, History, and the Making of an English Elite, 1870–1930* (Stanford 1994); Gordon Batho, 'History Text-Books, 1870–1914: A Note on the Historical Association Collection at Durham,' *History of Education Society Bulletin* no. 33 (1984): 10; Howat, 'Nineteenth-Century History Textbook,' 151. For coherent scholarly treatments of this process, see P. Levine, *The Amateur and the Professional* (Cambridge 1986); D.N. Livingston, *The Geographical Tradition: Episodes in the History of a Contested Enterprise* (Oxford 1992); T.W. Freeman, 'The Royal Geographical Society and the Development of Geography,' in E.H. Brown, ed., *Geography: Yesterday and Tomorrow* (Oxford 1980), 1–99; D.J. Palmer, *The Rise of English Studies* (London 1965); Brian Doyle, *English and Englishness* (London 1989). For contemporary views on this process, see J.W. Allen, *The Place of History in Education* (London 1909); Thomas Hodgkin, *The Teaching of History in Schools* (London 1908); R.L. Archer, W.J. Lewis, and A.E. Chapman, *The Teaching of Geography in Elementary Schools* (London 1910).

28 *School Board Chronicle* 27 (June 1882): 606. For a typical example of the kind of cursory review of readers, see the glowing survey of C.M. Yonge's National Society *English History Reading Books*, and the somewhat less glowing review of the matched geography series in the *School Board Chronicle* 257 (May 1881): 453.

29 For example, see the religious objections raised in the review of Bullock's *Modern European History for Schools and Private Students* by D.C.L. in the *School Board Chronicle* in October 1871 and March 1872.

30 Review in *Educational Times* quoted by Chancellor, *History*, 114. Chancellor claimed 'some slight evidence that reviewers of history textbooks were eager to praise authors who were notably patriotic in their attitudes towards the end of the nineteenth century.'

31 See, for example, H.O. Arnold-Forster, *The Citizen Reader* (London 1887), 119–29; M.T. Yates, *Arnold's English Readers* IV (London 1893), 11; H.E.

Malden, *The Life and Duties of a Citizen* (London 1894), 1; *Blackie's Tropical Readers* (London 1897), 184; *King Edward History Readers* VII (London 1903), 16; *Collins' School Series, Over Land and Sea: England and Wales* (London 1906), 194.

32 Hall, *White, Male and Middle Class*, 206.

33 Walker Conner, 'The Nation and Its Myth,' in A. Smith, ed., *Ethnicity and Nationalism* (New York 1992), 54.

34 Malden, *Life and Duties*, 1.

35 J. St Loe Strachey, *The Citizen and the State: Industrial and Social Life and the Empire* (London 1913), 126.

36 See, for example, the following sets: *Macmillan's Geography Readers* (London 1900); *Royal School Series, Highroads of Geography* (London 1900); *Collins' Wide-World Readers* (London 1901).

37 John Landon, *The Principles and Practice of Teaching and Class Management* (London 1894); Joseph Cowham, *A New School Method* (London 1894), esp. 285–6.

38 J. Gunn, *Class Teaching and Management* (London 1895), 125, 134.

39 F.H. Hayward, ed., *The Primary Curriculum* (London 1909), 107–9.

40 Cowham, *New School Method*, 341.

41 GLRO, Christ Church National Girls School, Cancell Rd., Brixton, Logbook, 1888, 229.

42 A few of the innumerable examples from a wide variety of schools should suffice here: BRO, Westbury on Trym Board School for Girls, Bristol, Logbook, 1900, 157–8; Eastville Board School for Boys, Bristol, Logbook, 1902, 196; GLRO, Manchester St. Board School for Girls, Kings Cross, London, Logbook, 1905, 86–9; MCL, Birley St. Council School, Boys Dept., Manchester, Logbook, 1903, 22; Fallowfield British School, Manchester, Logbook, 1886, 277, and 1893, 384; Longsight Municipal School (Wesleyan), Manchester, Logbook, 1880, 170.

43 BRO, St Philip's National School for Boys, Bristol, Logbook, 1904, 14.

44 See, for example, *Chambers's Historical Readers*, 'English Code,' 4 vols. (London 1882–8), and 'Scotch Code,' 3 vols. (Edinburgh 1888); *Macmillan's New History Reader*, English Code, 4 vols. (London 1901), and Scottish Code, 3 vols. (London 1905); Osman H. Newland, *The Model Citizen*, English edition (London 1907), and Scottish edition (London 1910).

45 Osman Newland, for example, explained worldwide British success to the nature of Anglo-Saxon characteristics and the development of the English race, especially in the struggle for peculiarly English democratic liberties; *The Model Citizen*, Scottish edition, 72. See also Oscar Browning, ed., *Pitman's King Edward History Reader* (London n.d.), 242; T.F. Tout, *A First*

Book of British History I (London 1903), 15; Archibald Geikie, *An Elementary Geography of the British Isles* II (London 1888); *Britannia Geography Readers* II (London 1896), 223.

46 Horsman, 'Origins,' 387–410; MacDougall, *Racial Myth*, 31–70; Christopher Hill, 'The Norman Yoke,' in *Puritanism and Revolution: Studies in the Interpretation of the English Revolution of the 17th century* (Harmondsworth 1968), 58–125; Asa Briggs, 'Saxons, Normans, and Victorians,' in *The Collected Essays of Asa Briggs* II (Brighton 1985), 215–35.

47 Horsman, 'Origins,' 390, and *Race and Manifest Destiny*, 38–9. See Sharon Turner, *The History of the Anglo-Saxons from the Earliest Period to the Norman Conquest*, 3 vols. (London 1799–1805), and Scott's influential classic, *Ivanhoe* (London 1817). See MacDougall, *Racial Myth*, 92–6, for a discussion of Turner, and Alice Chandler, *A Dream of Order: The Medieval Ideal in Nineteenth-Century English Literature* (Lincoln 1970), 25–51, and Culler, *The Mirror*, 20–31, for instructive treatments of Scott.

48 Horsman, *Race and Manifest Destiny*, 40–1.

49 BRO, Nellie Luke, 'Harold,' *The Quarterly Magazine of the Bristol Pupil Teachers Centre* (December 1902): 19–20.

50 G.R. Green, *Short History of the English People* (London 1881), 1–2, 6–7.

51 *The Warwick History Readers* 6 (London 1895), 10; F. York Powell, *English History Reading Books: Old Stories from British History* (London 1882), 9–10; *Chambers's Geographical Readers* IV: 8–10; *Royal English History Readers, Simple Stories of English History* II (London 1891), 52; A.L. Stronach, *Royal English Class Books: Simple History of English Literature* (London 1899), 12; Ella Armitage, *English History Reading Books: Richard I and Edward I* (London 1881), 112; *Chambers's Geographical Reader* VII: 68; *Britannia Geography Readers* II: 223.

52 *The Young Students' English History Reading Book* (London 1881), 36, 10.

53 *Chambers's National History Readers: Scheme A* III (London 1897), 31; *Collins' School Series, The Patriotic Historical Readers* I (London 1898), 54; T.F. Tout, *Longman's Historical Series for Schools* I (London 1903), 11–12; *Cambridge Historical Readers: Intermediate*, 5.

54 *Longman's New Geography Readers* IV (London 1886), 5; *Chambers's Alternative History Readers* V (London 1898), 65; *Chambers's 'New Scheme' Readers: Stories from English History* (London 1901), 88.

55 M.T. Yates, *Arnold's Geography Readers* IV (London 1894), 14.

56 *Chambers's Historical Readers* IV (London 1882), 56; *Chambers's Geographical Reader* IV (London 1884), 8–10; *Cambridge Historical Readers: Intermediate*, 5. Curtis argues that in English culture in general 'the racialist hue' of the antithesis of Anglo-Saxon and Celt became greater at the end of the

century with the development of more scientific theories about race, and that the 'Irish Question' was both a symptom and a contributing cause of race-consciousness in England; *Anglo-Saxons and Celts*, 15. Curtis's point is certainly borne out to a certain degree in school reading books, though only rarely was explicit anti-Irish sentiment expressed in elementary texts (unlike Fletcher and Kipling's 1911 *History of England*, a formal text intended for secondary and Public schools, which *was* overt in its dismissal of the Irish) and never any of the caricature that he presents in *Apes and Angels* (Newton Abbot 1971).

57 *The Young Students' English History Reading Book*, 22. For nearly identical comments on the enduring qualities of Anglo-Saxon 'forefathers,' see *Chambers's Summary of English History* (London 1904), 62.

58 *Chambers's Geographical Reader* V (London 1883), 14.

59 H.O. Arnold-Forster, *Things New and Old, or Stories from English History* I (London 1893), 25.

60 *English History Reading Books: Old Stories from British History*, 9–10.

61 Stronach, *Simple History of English Literature*, 13.

62 Oscar Browning, *The Citizen: His Rights and Responsibilities* (London 1893), 23.

63 W. Beach Thomas, *The Citizen Books* III (London 1909), 7.

64 *Chambers's Historical Readers* III (London 1882), 134.

65 S.R. Gardiner, *English History Reading Books: Historical Biographies* (London 1881), preface.

66 *Chambers's Historical Readers* III: 25.

67 J. Finnemore, *Black's School Series: The Story of the English People – A Simple Introductory Historical Reader* (London 1905), 45–6.

68 *King Edward History Readers* VI (London 1901), 6.

69 J.C. Nesfield, *English Grammar Past and Present* (London 1898), 225. See also Richard Morris, *Elementary Lessons in Historical English Grammar* (London 1893), 1–27.

70 *Chambers's 'New Scheme' Readers: Stories from English History*, 158. This strategy also appeared in some grammars: Henry Froude's *The King's English* (Oxford 1906), 1, prescribed that 'as a general rule, good writers prefer the Saxon word to the Romance' since 'the writer whose percentage of Saxon words is high will generally be found to have fewer words that are out of the way, long or abstract.'

71 G. Armitage-Smith, *The Citizen of England* (London 1895), 7–8.

72 *Chambers's 'New Scheme' Readers: Advanced History of England* (London 1904), 45.

73 *Raleigh History Readers* IV (London 1896), 47.

74 Chambers's 'New Scheme' Readers: Preparatory History of England, 55 BC to Present Time (London 1901), 32–3.

75 J.M.D. Meiklejohn, The British Empire: Its Geography, Resources, Commerce, Land-ways, and Water-ways (London 1891), 6–7; see also Browning, The Citizen, 137.

76 Arnold-Forster, Citizen Reader, 14. Emphasis mine.

77 Warwick History Readers 7 (London 1896), 246; King Edward History Readers V (London 1902), 212.

78 Chambers's Alternative Geography Readers VII (London 1899), 8.

79 Malden, Life and Duties, 196–7.

80 Chambers's Geographical Reader III (London 1883), 7–8.

81 Newland, The Model Citizen, Scottish edition, 183–4. Typically, the German Empire and Germans in general tended to fare better in the texts than did Russia and Russians. For an example, see Collins' Wide-World Reader III: 74, 83.

82 Browning, The Citizen, 174.

83 Seeley's The Expansion of England was clearly important in the development of this narrative; see Colls and Dodd, Englishness, 44; and MacKenzie, Propaganda and Empire, 179. However, Froude, Freeman, and Green were equally important in that they recast the Whig historical narrative within racial discourse.

84 J. Finnemore, Black's Simple Introductory Reader (London 1905), 154.

85 Thomas, Citizen Books 1: 25–6.

86 Malden, Life and Duties, 4.

87 Newland, Model Citizen, 222.

88 Paul Rich, Race and Empire in British Politics (Cambridge 1986), 12–13; J.A. Mangan, 'Introduction,' in J.A. Mangan, ed., Making Imperial Mentalities (Manchester 1990), 3–4.

89 School Guardian, 27 April 1895, 333–4, and 4 May 1895, 351–2. Emphasis in original.

90 A.H. Garlick, A New Manual of Method (London 1896), 217.

Chapter 4: Imagining the Racial 'Other' Within

1 Katherine Castle, Britannia's Children (Manchester 1996), 6; John Willinsky, Learning to Divide the World: Education at Empire's End (Minneapolis 1998), 2–4.

2 See the various contributions in J.A. Mangan, ed., The Imperial Curriculum (London 1993).

3 J.M. MacKenzie, Propaganda and Empire (Manchester 1984).

4 Gareth Stedman Jones, *Outcast London* (Harmondsworth 1976), 128; G.R. Searle, *The Quest for National Efficiency* (Oxford 1971), 96.

5 D.A. Lorimer, *Colour, Class and the Victorians* (Leicester 1978), 202, 13–16.

6 Victor Kiernan, *The Lords of Human Kind: Black Man, Yellow Man and White Man in an Age of Empire* (London 1969), 316–17; Robert Colls and Philip Dodd, eds., *Englishness: Politics and Culture* (London 1986), 46–7; P. Mason, *Prospero's Magic: Some Thoughts on Class and Race* (London 1962), 18–20.

7 George Sims, *How the Poor Live and Horrible London* (London 1889), 3.

8 *The Bitter Cry of Outcast London: An Inquiry into the Condition of the Abject Poor* (London 1883), 4. For a perceptive analysis of Sims's articles and Mearns's *The Bitter Cry* and the furore they raised, see Anthony S. Wohl, *The Eternal Slum: Housing and Social Policy in Victorian London* (Montreal 1977).

9 Joseph H. Cowham, *New School Method: For Pupil Teachers and Students* (London 1894), 340.

10 Archibald Geikie, *The Teaching of Geography* (London 1887), 4; J. Gunn, *Class Teaching and Management* (London 1895), 134.

11 A.H. Garlick, *A New Manual of Method* (London 1896), 217. See also the letter from the Royal Colonial Institute arguing the importance of teaching imperial geography in the *School Board Chronicle* 29 (March 1883): 250. For an educationalist critique of the 'common custom' of devoting time to imperial geography, see R.L. Archer, W.J. Lewis, and A.E. Chapman, *The Teaching of Geography in Elementary Schools* (London 1910), 43.

12 *School Guardian*, 1 September 1900, 697–8.

13 J.W. Adamson, *The Practice of Instruction: A Manual of Method* (London 1907), 227.

14 James Welton, *Principles and Methods of Teaching* (London 1906), 281.

15 Archer et al., *Teaching of Geography*, 4, 43.

16 Ibid., 56.

17 Geikie, *Teaching of Geography*, 4–5; Gunn, *Class Teaching*, 124; L.C. Miall, *Thirty Years of Teaching* (London 1897), 58; David Salmon, *The Art of Teaching* (London 1898), 197; Amos Henderson, *Some Notes on Teaching* (Nottingham 1903), 66–71.

18 James R. Ryan, 'Visualising Imperial Geography: Halford Mackinder and the Colonial Office Visual Instruction Committee, 1902–1911,' *Ecumene* 1, no. 2 (1994): 169.

19 A good example is the first volume of *Longman's New Geography Readers* I (London 1886), which is divided into sections according to areas of the world using the following titles: 'the Far South – Black Men; the Far East – Brown Men; the Farthest East – Yellow Men; the Far West – Red Men.'

20 *Collins' School Series: Over Land and Sea: Europe* (London 1905), 29, 34.

21 The ideological function of stereotypical images, particularly as it relates to imperialism, is discussed usefully in J.A. Mangan, 'Images for Confident Control: Stereotypes in Imperial Discourse,' in *Imperial Curriculum*, 6–22. For an older but still solid discussion, see Kiernan's *Lords of Human Kind*.

22 *Black's Literary Readers* I (London 1906), 68; *Collins' Wide-World Reader* V (London 1901), 12–13.

23 *Chambers's Geographical Readers* VI (London 1884), 122; *Avon Geographical Reader* I (London 1896), 118; *Raleigh Geography Readers* VI (London 1899), 5, 199, 221; C.S. Dawe, *The Growth and Greatness of Our World-Wide Empire* (London 1899), 282; *The Globe Geography Readers*, Junior (London 1911), 176.

24 Archer et al., *Teaching of Geography*, 56, 73. On the use of narrative pictures and the stimulation of the imagination in the teaching of geography, see also Gunn, *Class Teaching*, 124; Garlick, *New Manual*, 217.

25 George Bosworth, *Narrative Geography Readers* I (London 1910), 26–7.

26 Mangan, 'Images for Confident Control,' 6–7.

27 John Ahier, *Industry, Children and the Nation* (Falmer 1988), 169–70.

28 Bosworth, *Narrative Geography Readers*, I: 27–8; *Longman's New Geography Readers* I (London 1886), 86; *Avon Geographical Reader* I: 118; *Black's Literary Readers* I (London 1906), 67.

29 W. Beach Thomas, *The Citizen Books* I (London 1908), 26. Victor Kiernan has pointed to the prevalence of this self-confirming image of the dependent, infantilized native in his *Lords of Human Kind*, 233.

30 Mangan, 'Images for Confident Control,' 7–8.

31 M.T. Yates, *Arnold's Geography Readers* II (London 1894), 102–5.

32 Castle, *Britannia's Children*, 123–30.

33 *Longman's New Geography Readers* I: 103.

34 Castle, *Britannia's Children*, 134–60.

35 Kiernan, *Lords of Human Kind*, 33.

36 Edward Said, *Orientalism* (New York 1978), 41–5.

37 *Raleigh History Readers* VII (London 1898), 164.

38 *The English Citizen: His Rights and Responsibilities* III (London 1883), 7.

39 *The Raleigh Geography Readers* VI: 21–4; *Macmillan's Geographical Series* V (London 1890), 3, 36.

40 *Britannia Geography Readers* III (London 1896), 49; *The Raleigh Geography Readers* VI: 25; *Warwick History Readers* V (London 1895), 199.

41 *Britannia Geography Readers* III: 49.

42 *The English Citizen* III: 6; *Macmillan's Geographical Series* V: 5; H. George, *Historical Geography of the British Empire* (London 1904), 214.

43 *The Raleigh Geography Readers* VI: 25, 28–9.

44 Ibid., 23.

45 *Collins' School Series: Over Land and Sea: England and Wales* (London 1906), 9; Royal School Series, *Highroads of Geography*, III *South Britain* (London 1910), 11; *Collins' Alternative Geography Readers*, I *The World* (London 1900), 114.

46 Archer et al., *Teaching of Geography*, 73.

47 Cowham, *New School Method*, 286–7.

48 Archer et al., *Teaching of Geography*, 9.

49 *Chambers's Historical Readers* IV (London 1882), 197; *The English Citizen* III: 10; *Raleigh Geography Readers* VI: 27; *Raleigh History Readers* V (London 1896), 121; *Chambers's 'New Scheme' History Readers: Stories from English History*, 146.

50 Katherine Castle, 'The Imperial Indian,' in Mangan, ed., *Imperial Curriculum*, 26, and *Britannia's Children*, 20–5.

51 *Stories from English History*, 98.

52 Castle, 'The Imperial Indian,' 31–2.

53 *The Warwick History Readers* V: 194. For other examples of this language, see *Chambers's Historical Readers* IV (London 1882), 197; Charlotte Mason, *London Geographical Readers* V (London 1891), 68; *Chambers's 'New Scheme' History Readers: Stories from English History*, 146; *Chambers's 'New Scheme' History Readers: Stories from British History* I (London 1905), 108.

54 *Stories from British History* I: 111.

55 Homi K. Bhabha, 'The Other Question – The Stereotype and Colonial Discourse,' *Screen* 24 (1983): 23.

56 *Chambers's Geographical Readers* IV: 179; *Longman's New Geography Readers* IV: 195–6; *The Avon Geographical Readers* VI (London 1895), 186–8; *Warwick History Readers* V: 212; *Chambers's Alternative Geography Readers* VI (London 1898), 60–1; *Raleigh Geography Readers* VI: 31, 136–7; *Royal Osborne Geography Readers* VI (London 1900), 156.

57 *The Avon Geographical Readers* IV A (London 1895), 186–8.

58 *Longman's New Geography Readers* IV: 196; *The Avon Geographical Readers* VI: 160.

59 *Chambers's Geographical Reader* IV: 179.

60 *Royal Geography Readers* V (London 1882), 45; *Chambers's Geographical Readers* VI: 82; *The Royal Star Readers* IV (London 1887); *Raleigh Geography Readers* VI: 201.

61 *The Avon Geographical Readers* VI: 140; *Royal Osborne Geography Readers* VI: 139; *Black's Literary Readers* III (London 1906), 115; *Longman's New Geography Readers* IV: 161; *Chambers's Geographical Readers* IV: 162; *Chambers's Alternative Geography Readers* VI (London 1898), 46, 49; *Raleigh Geography Readers* VI: 31, 136–7; *Royal Osborne Geography Readers* VI: 139; *Black's Literary Readers* III: 115; *Pitman's New Era Geography Handbooks: The British Empire* (London 1905), xi; *Collins' School Series: Over Land and Sea: The British Empire* (London 1906), 17.

62 *Chambers's Geographical Readers* IV: 162.

63 *Raleigh Geography Readers* VI: 139.

64 *The Warwick History Readers* V: 212.

65 *Royal Osborne Geography Readers* VI: 156, 139.

66 *Raleigh Geography Readers* VI: 136–8.

67 *Collins' School Series: Over Land and Sea: The British Empire*, 173, 28. For similar statements, see *Longman's New Geography Readers* IV: 161; H.B. George, *A Historical Geography of the British Empire* (London 1904), 188; *The Citizen Books* I: 27; and 'The Australian Commonwealth,' *Geographical Teacher* II, no. 1 (1901): 3.

68 *Black's Literary Readers* III: 115–18.

69 *The Citizen Books* I: 26.

Chapter 5: 'The Home of the Race'

1 Nelson's Royal School Series, *Highroads of History* (London 1909), 55. See also John Ahier's analysis of this book in his *Industry, Children and the Nation* (London 1988), 83–4.

2 J. Edward Parrott, *The Waterloo Citizen Reader* (London 1893), 9–10, 12–13.

3 H.O. Arnold-Forster, *The Citizen Reader* (London 1887), 18.

4 On familial metaphor, see Lynn Hunt, *The Family Romance of the French Revolution* (Berkeley 1992). For an account of early modern anatomical images of the organization of society, see Ernst H. Kantorowicz, *The King's Two Bodies* (Princeton 1957).

5 See J.A. Mangan, *The Games Ethic and Imperialism* (New York 1986); J.M. MacKenzie, ed., *Imperialism and Popular Culture* (Manchester 1986); J.A. Mangan and James Walvin, eds., *Manliness and Morality: Middle-class Masculinity in Britain and America, 1800–1940* (Manchester 1987); J.M. MacKenzie, *The Empire of Nature: Hunting, Conservation and British Imperialism* (Manchester 1990); Robert H. MacDonald, *The Language of Empire: Myths and Metaphors of Popular Imperialism, 1880–1918* (Manchester 1994). For a powerful critique of this sort of treatment of masculinity, see Peter Roper and John Tosh, eds., *Manful Assertions* (London 1991), 8.

6 Laura Tabili, 'We Ask for British Justice': Workers and Racial Difference in Late Imperial Britain (Ithaca, NY 1994), 10.

7 On this point I concur with George L. Mosse's observations in his book Nationalism and Sexuality: Respectability and Abnormal Sexuality in Modern Europe (New York 1985), that the development of nationalism and 'respectable' bourgeois sexual and gender roles were intrinsically linked. ·

8 See Ellen Ross, Love and Toil (New York 1993), and also Jane Lewis, 'The Working-Class Wife and Mother and State Intervention, 1870-1918,' in her edited volume, Labour of Love (Oxford 1986).

9 Britannia Geography Readers II (London 1898), 12; Chambers's Alternative History Readers IV (London 1898), 31; The Warwick History Readers VII (London 1896), 246; School Guardian, 1 September 1900, 697–8.

10 H. Osman Newland and Russell L. Jones, The Model Citizen (London 1910), 223.

11 MacDonald, Language of Empire, 51.

12 School Guardian, 1 September 1900, 697. See also 'Geography and Empire,' Journal of Education (January 1905): 21; School Government Chronicle 75 (January 1906): 74–5; School Government Chronicle 77 (February 1907), 169; R.L. Archer, W.J. Lewis, and A.E. Chapman, The Teaching of Geography in Elementary Schools (London 1910), 43; F.J.C. Hearnshaw, 'The Place of History in Education,' History 1, no. 2 (1912): 34–41; W.H. Webb, 'History, Patriotism, and the Child,' History 2, no. 5 (1913): 53–4; 'History and the National Life,' History 3, no. 2 (1914): 63–7.

13 Macmillan's New History Readers (London 1905), 1.

14 Royal Standard Series, Highroads of Geography III (London 1910), 11.

15 The Britannia Geography Readers III (London 1896), 5.

16 M.T. Yates, Arnold's English Readers IV (London 1893), 17.

17 M.T. Yates, Arnold's Geography Readers III (London 1894), 6–8.

18 Britannia Geography Reader II: 12–13.

19 Cassell's Historical Course for Schools: Stories from English History (London 1884), 13.

20 King Edward History Readers: The Story of Our Own Times, 1837–1901 (London 1903), 7.

21 New Era Geography Readers: Our Imperial Heritage (London 1903), 8.

22 Royal Osborne Geography Readers VI (London 1900), 7.

23 Longman's New Readers IV (London 1885), 143.

24 H.O. Arnold-Forster, Things New and Old: or Stories form English History II (London 1893), 131–3.

25 J. Edward Parrott, The Waterloo Citizen Reader (London 1893), 24–5.

26 G.F. Boswell, ed., Cambridge Historical Readers, Intermediate (Cambridge 1911), 47; Rev. C.S. Dawe, Queen Victoria and Her People (London 1897), 183.

27 John Landon, *Principles and Practice of Teaching and Class Management* (London 1894), 404; *Arnold's Geography Readers* V (London 1894): 7; M.T. Yates, ed., *Arnold's English Readers* IV.

28 For excellent treatments of the distinctly English (rather than British) form of romantic idealization of the countryside, see Martin Wiener, *English Culture and the Decline of the Industrial Spirit* (Cambridge 1981), and David Lowenthal, 'British National Identity and the English Landscape,' *Rural History* 2 (1991): 205–30.

29 Ahier, *Industry*, 83.

30 This is particularly evident in readers like that of Edith Elias, *This England of Ours* (London 1914), which along with sections on 'our race,' 'our dress,' 'our cities,' 'our railways,' and 'our weather,' devoted considerable space to 'our rivers,' 'our mountains,' 'our forests,' 'An English Village,' and 'An English Farm.' A large section in the centre of the book was devoted to explaining 'why a hedge is one of the first things a foreigner visiting our English village is sure to admire.'

31 Ahier, *Industry*, 83.

32 T.F. Tout, *Longman's Historical Series for Schools* II (London 1902), 52.

33 *King Edward History Reader: The Evolutionary History of England* (London 1904), 32.

34 Spalding and Wragg, *Piers Plowman Readers* V (London 1914), 89.

35 Arnold-Forster, *Citizen Reader*, 104.

36 G. Guest, *A Social History of England* (London 1913), 175.

37 See Ahier, *Industry*, 110–11.

38 Guest, *Social History*, 177–8; John Finnemore, *Social Life in England* (London [1912] 1932 shortened single-volume edition), 231–6, 254–7; *The English Homeland* (London n.d.), 145; Arnold-Forster, *Citizen Reader*, 178; *Chambers's Alternative History Readers* V: 173.

39 Patricia Branca, *Silent Sisterhood: Middle Class Women in the Victorian Home* (Pittsburgh 1975); Anna Davin, 'Imperialism and Motherhood,' *History Workshop Journal* no. 20 (1978); Judith Schneid Lewis, *In the Family Way: Childbearing in the British Aristocracy, 1760–1860* (New Brunswick, NJ 1986); Ross, *Love and Toil*.

40 L. Davidoff and C. Hall, *Family Fortunes: Men and Women of the English Middle Class, 1780–1850* (Chicago 1987).

41 John Tosh, 'Domesticity and Manliness in the Victorian Middle Class: The Family of Edward White Benson,' in Roper and Tosh, *Manful Assertions*, 45.

42 Nelson's Royal School Series, *The Royal Star Readers* VI (London 1887), 9.

43 *The Young Student's English History Reading Books* (London 1881), 22.

44 Davin, 'Imperialism and Motherhood,' 9–65; Jane Lewis, *The Politics of Motherhood* (Montreal 1980); Joanna De Groot, '"Sex" and "Race": The Construction of Language and Image in the Nineteenth Century,' in Susan Mendus and Jane Rendall, eds., *Sexuality and Subordination: Studies of Gender in the Nineteenth Century* (London 1989), 89–128.

45 L. Davidoff, 'Class and Gender in Victorian England,' *Feminist Studies* 5 (1979), reprinted in J. Newton, M. Ryan, and J. Walkowitz, eds., *Sex and Class in Women's History* (London 1983), 24–7, 40–1, 46–8. See also Davidoff and Hall's discussion of marriage in *Family Fortunes*, 322–43.

46 De Groot, '"Sex" and "Race,"' 98.

47 See Dina Copelman, *London's Women Teachers* (London 1996); Alison Oram, *Women Teachers and Feminist Politics, 1900–1939* (Manchester 1996); Patricia Hollis, *Ladies Elect: Women in English Local Government, 1865–1914* (London 1989), esp. 471–3; Judith Moore, *A Zeal for Responsibility: The Struggle for Professional Nursing in Victorian England, 1868–1883* (New York 1988); Ellen Jordan, '"Making Good Wives and Mothers"? The Transformation of Middle-Class Girls' Education in Nineteenth-Century Britain,' *History of Education Quarterly* 31, no. 4 (1991): 439–62; Barry H. Bergen, 'Only a Schoolmaster: Gender, Class, and the Effort to Professionalize Teaching in England, 1870–1910,' *History of Education Quarterly* 22, no. 1 (1982): 1–21.

48 Tosh, 'Domesticity and Manliness,' 67. See also Peter Cominos, 'Late Victorian Sexual Respectability and the Social System,' *International Review of Social History* 8 (1963): 18–48 and 216–50; David Newsome, *Godliness and Good Learning* (London 1961), esp. 196; and J.M. MacKenzie, 'The Imperial Pioneer and Hunter and the British Masculine Stereotype in Late Victorian and Edwardian Times,' in Mangan and Walvin, eds., *Manliness and Morality*.

49 Claudia Nelson, *Invisible Men: Fatherhood in Victorian Periodicals, 1850–1910* (Athens, GA 1995), 4.

50 T.A. Cox and R.F. Macdonald, *The Suggestive Handbook of Practical School Method* (London 1896), 368; see, for similar examples, M.L.V. Hughes, *Citizens to Be* (1915), 149; J. Welton, *Principles and Methods of Teaching* (1906), 226–9; *Board of Education: Suggestions for the Consideration of Teachers* (1905), 62.

51 Ellen H. Richards, *The Cost of Living as Modified by Sanitary Science: Lectures on Domestic Science* (New York 1900), 4–5.

52 Ibid., 15. Italics in original.

53 *Arnold's Domestic Readers* VI (London 1894), 10.

54 Charles E. Hecht, ed., *Rearing an Imperial Race: Report of the Second Guildhall Conference on Diet, Cookery and Hygiene* (London 1913), xxviii.

55 Sara A. Burstall, *The Story of Manchester High School for Girls, 1871–1911* (Manchester 1911), 13.

56 Sara A. Burstall, 'The Proper Use of the Lecture System and the Text-book,' in the Historical Association, Leaflet no. 19, *The Methods of Teaching History in Schools* (London 1910), 4.

57 See Davin, 'Imperialism and Motherhood,' 28 (esp. footnote 75).

58 *School Government Chronicle* 81 (January 1909): 1219.

59 John Gillis, *Youth and History* (New York 1974), esp. 105–41.

60 Bernard Bosanquet, 'The Duties of Citizenship,' in *Aspects of the Social Problem* (London 1895), 10.

61 William Finlayson Trotter, *The Citizen and His Duties* (London 1907), 67.

62 Booth's study of *London Labour* is the most famous and most comprehensive, but there was also a vast 'urban travel' literature in this period as well. See Gillis, *Youth and History*, and Stephen Humphries, *Hooligans or Rebels?* (Oxford 1981).

63 William Morrison, *Juvenile Offenders* (London 1896), 29.

64 Mary G. Barnett, *Young Delinquents: A Study of Reformatory and Industrial Schools* (London 1913), 10–11.

65 Gillis, *Youth and History*, 13–17, 33–57. This period of forced adolescence was seen to be quite successful for middle-class youth, but probably much less so for those from the working class. See J. Springhall, 'Building the Character of the British Boy,' in Mangan and Walvin, eds., *Manliness and Morality*.

66 Nelson, *Invisible Men*, 200. Several scholars suggest that much of the recasting of domestic ideology in this period was done with a definite eye towards retarding the development of first-wave feminism, and amid concern over the large-scale expansion of women into the workforce after 1890. See Thane and McKay, 'The Englishwoman,' in Robert Colls and Philip Dodd, eds., *Englishness: Politics and Culture* (London 1986), 193, 213, 223–4; Shelley Pennington and Belinda Westover, *A Hidden Workforce* (London 1989), 8; and Jordan, '"Making Good Wives and Mothers"?' 439–62.

67 Carol Dyhouse, 'Towards a "Feminine" Curriculum for English Schoolgirls: The Demands of Ideology, 1870–1963,' *Women's Studies International Quarterly* 1 (1978): 301.

68 Lewis, 'The Working-Class Wife and Mother and State Intervention, 1870–1918,' in her *Labour of Love*, 102–3.

69 H.E. Malden, *The Life and Duties of a Citizen* (London 1894), 4.

70 *Arnold's Domestic Readers* VI: 13.

71 Annmarie Turnball, 'Learning Her Womanly Work: The Elementary School Curriculum, 1870–1914,' in Felicity Hunt, ed., *Lessons for Life: The Schooling of Girls and Women, 1850–1959* (Oxford 1987), 99.

72 See Ravenhill's article in *The School Government Chronicle* 81 (January 1909): 73.

73 Turnball, 'Learning Her Womanly Work,' 94.

74 See Carolyn Steedman, *Past Tenses* (London 1992), 119–26; and Ross, *Love and Toil*.

75 Carol Dyhouse, *Girls Growing-up in Edwardian Britain* (London 1981), 82–3. See the evidence to the Cross Commission of Miss Fanny Calder, Honourary Secretary of the Liverpool Training School of Cookery: *Second Report of the Royal Commission Appointed to Inquire into the Workings of the Elementary Education Acts*, C. 5056 [*PP* XXIX, I] (1887), 479–89; GLRO, School Board for London, SBL 709 *Minutes of Subcommittee on Domestic Subjects*, July 1899, 103, 398; *Report of the Board of Education, 1899–1900*, Cd. 328 [*PP* XIX.1] (1900), 330.

76 Pennington and Westover, *A Hidden Workforce*, 8. For a clear example of contemporary recognition of this fact, see the exhortations made by the boosters of the National Association for the Promotion of Housewifery in Reginald Brabazon, Earl of Meath, *Some National and School Reforms* (London 1887).

77 C. Dyhouse, '"Good Wives and Little Mothers": Social Anxieties and the Schoolgirl's Curriculum, 1890–1920,' *Oxford Review of Education* 3 (1977): 21–35, and 'Social Darwinistic Ideas and the Development of Women's Education in England, 1880–1920,' *History of Education* 5 (1976): 41–58; Davin, 'Imperialism and Motherhood'; Lewis, *Politics of Motherhood*; Ross, *Love and Toil*.

78 Alice Ravenhill in *School Government Chronicle* 81 (January 1909): 72; Havelock Ellis, *The Problem of Race-Regeneration* (London 1911), 30; Mary Scharlieb, *Womanhood and Race-Regeneration* (London 1912), 25–37; John E. Gorst, *Education and Race Regeneration* (London 1913), 27–36.

79 Thane and McKay, 'The Englishwoman,' 202–3; Davin, 'Imperialism and Motherhood,' 14–18; Lewis, *Politics of Motherhood*, 16.

80 A.H.D. Acland, *The Education of Citizens* (London 1883), 19.

81 See Davin, 'Imperialism and Motherhood,' 10–11. For an early example of the racial motherhood discourse, see Dr Alice Ker, *Motherhood: A Book for Every Woman* (Manchester 1891).

82 Davin, 'Imperialism and Motherhood,' 10, 13.

83 J.N. Clark, *Education in a Market Town: Horncastle, 1329–1970* (London 1976), 59, 79; Turnball, 'Learning Her Womanly Work,' 84; see Felicity Hunt, *Gender and Policy in English Education* (Toronto 1991), 139–41, for a

summary of the Board of Education's attempt to extend this policy into the inter-war period.

84 The total average attendance for all voluntary schools in this year was just under 2,500,000; while the total average attendance for all board schools was only slightly less, at 2,144,000. *Report of the Board of Education 1900* (Appendix III: Statistics of Schools on Annual Grant list), 6–7.

85 Hunt, *Gender and Policy*, 98–9, 105; Bergen, 'Only a Schoolmaster,' 5, 13.

86 *Report of Committee of Council on Education, 1885–6*, C. 4849. I [*PP* XXIV.1] (1886), 109–20.

87 PRO, Ed. 14/37, School Board for London, Management Minute on Instruction in Cookery, 9 March 1883.

88 Dyhouse, *Girls*, 90.

89 Turnball, 'Learning Her Womanly Work,' 95.

90 *Report of the Board of Education, 1912–1913*, Cd. 7341 [*PP* XXV] (1914), 88–9.

91 *Report of the Board of Education, 1910–1911*, Cd. 6116 [*PP* XXI] (1912), 18.

92 Hunt, *Gender and Policy*, 124. Volume III of *The Teacher's Encyclopedia* (London 1911) noted that financial arithmetic was the 'arithmetic of citizenship,' 17.

93 Davin, 'Imperialism and Motherhood'; Lewis, *Politics of Motherhood*; Hunt, *Gender and Policy*, 139–40.

94 *Report of the Inter-Departmental Committee on Physical Deterioration*, Cd. 2175 [*PP* XXXII 1] Vol. I (1904), 61–2.

95 PRO, Ed. 11/60, memo dated 8 August 1905.

96 *School Training for the Home Duties of Women*, Pt. III, Cd. 2963 [*PP* XXVIII, 437] (1906), iii; and PRO, Ed. 12/41, minute, 3 November 1907.

97 *Report of the Inter-Departmental Committee on Physical Deterioration*, I: 38–9; Lewis, *Politics of Motherhood*, 90–1.

98 Lewis, *Politics of Motherhood*, 90. Such recommendations confidently assumed that most men preferred less educated women.

99 Dyhouse, 'Towards a "Feminine" Curriculum,' 302–3.

100 Lewis, *Politics of Motherhood*, 91. Some of the recommendations in support of the 1904 report were suggested by the National League for Physical Education and Improvement, which can be found in PRO, Ed. 24/279, 'Note on Deputation,' 27 February 1906.

101 PRO, Ed. 11/51, Circular 758.

102 Ibid., 1, 7–8, 10. See also the summary in PRO, Ed. 11/150, 'Lessons on Mother-craft to Schoolgirls,' 21 July 1923.

103 Lewis, *Politics of Motherhood*, 93–5.

104 Catherine Dodd, 'Primary Education of Girls,' in Spencer Wilkinson, ed., *The Nation's Needs: Chapters on Education* (London 1903), 56, 63, 69.

105 Alice Ravenhill, 'Hygiene and Household Economics in Education,' in Wilkinson, ed., *Nation's Needs*, 91–106.
106 Newsholme and Scott, *Domestic Economy* (London 1894), 202, quoted in Dyhouse, 'Towards a "Feminine" Curriculum,' 301.
107 Lilian Whitling and Mrs Pillow, 'The Teaching of Domestic Science,' in A. Laurie, ed., *The Teacher's Encyclopedia* II (London 1911), 170.
108 Cassell's *Penny Book for Mothers* (1911), quoted in Davin, 'Imperialism and Motherhood.'
109 Alice Ker, *Motherhood* (1896 edition), 11. Ker was a teacher at the Manchester School of Domestic Economy.
110 Fanny Heath, *Pattern-Making by Paper Folding* (London 1900); T.M. James, *Longman's Complete Course of Needlework, Knitting and Cutting Out* (London 1903); Amy J. Reeve, *Practical Home Millinery* (London 1903); Margaret Swanson and Ann MacBeth, *Educational Needlecraft* (Glasgow 1910).
111 Dyhouse, *Girls*, 83.
112 For an analysis of the illogical and mind-numbing instruction of needlework, for example, see Turnball, 'Learning Her Womanly Work,' 87–92.
113 Dyhouse, *Girls*, 89.
114 Board of Education, Circular 750, quoted in ibid.
115 Dyhouse, 'Towards a "Feminine" Curriculum,' 298.
116 For example, *Arnold's Domestic Economy Readers*; *Longman's Domestic Economy Readers*. Specific course textbooks were prepared as well: Annie Butterworth, *Manual of Household Work and Management* (London 1899); E.E. Mann, *Liverpool School of Cookery Recipe Book* (London 1901); M.A. Rotheram, *Household Cookery Recipes* (London 1907).
117 *Good Things, Made, Said and Done for Every Home and Household* (Leeds 1895), 13.
118 E. Rice, *A Text-Book of Domestic Economy* (London 1910), 77.
119 *Arnold's Domestic Readers* VI: 10, 13.
120 Anna Davin, '"Mind that you do as you are told": Reading Books for Board School Girls, 1870–1902,' *Feminist Review* 3 (1979): 89–98. Davin convincingly demonstrates the degree to which gender prescriptions were encoded within the social ideology offered to children in school books, but her focus on the early years of the board schools (all but one of her examples are from books published in the early 1870s) leads her away from any consideration of the way in which nationalist imaginings intersected with gender ideology, particularly in the later years of the nineteenth century.
121 Ibid., 94.

122 Jarrold, *New Code Reading Books*, II (1871), quoted in ibid., 95.
123 Thane and McKay, 'The Englishwoman,' 192–3.

Chapter 6: Narratives and Rituals of National Belonging

1 Eric Hobsbawm, *Nations and Nationalism* (Cambridge 1992), 45; see also Eric Hobsbawm and Terence Ranger, eds., *The Invention of Tradition* (Cambridge 1983), especially 1–14 and 263–307.
2 W.H. Davenport Adams, *England on the Sea: Or the Story of the British Navy, Its Decisive Battles and Great Commanders* I (London 1885), quoted in C.F. Behrman, *Victorian Myths of the Sea* (Athens, OH 1977), 111.
3 Arthur Marder, *The Anatomy of British Sea Power* (London 1940), 44–5; Bernard Semmel, *Liberalism and Navy Strategy* (London 1986); and Christopher Lloyd, *The Nation and the Navy* (London 1954).
4 *The Avon Geographical Reader* VI (London 1895), 12.
5 *The Avon Geographical Reader* III (London 1895), 186; *Raleigh History Readers* VII (London 1896), 265.
6 *Chambers's Geographical Readers* VII (London 1886), 8; H.O. Arnold-Forster, *The Citizen Reader* (London 1887), 96; *Avon Geographical Reader* III: 186; *Chambers's Alternative History Readers* VII (London 1899), 181; *Tower History Readers* III (London 1910), 55.
7 *Chambers's Alternative History Readers* IV (London 1898), 25.
8 For a general discussion of the popularity of Alfred in the nineteenth century, see Asa Briggs, 'Saxons, Normans and Victorians,' in *The Collected Essays of Asa Briggs* II (Brighton 1985), 215–35.
9 *The Catholic Child's History of England* (Manchester 1890), 26; *Chambers's Alternative History Readers* IV: 33; *Raleigh History Readers* IV (London 1896), 33; *The Patriotic Historical Readers* V (London 1898), 184; *Collins' Wide-World Reader* II (London 1901), 7–8.
10 *Tower History Readers* III: 61.
11 *Chambers's Alternative History Readers* IV: 25, 31, 33.
12 C.H. Wyatt, *The English Citizen: His Life and Duty* (London 1894), 170; *Collins' Wide-World Reader* II: 8.
13 H. Hayens, *Ye Mariners of England*, quoted in Behrman, *Victorian Myths*, 27. Hayens's book was a common prize book in elementary schools. See GLRO, London County Council Education Committee Minutes, 'Books and Apparatus Subcommittee Report,' May 1907 (prize book listing), 1214.
14 Examples include: *Chambers's Geographical Readers* VII: 8; *London Geographical Readers* IV (London 1898): 9, 12; Rev. C.S. Dawe, *King Edward's Realm* (London 1902), 9–10; MacDougall's *The English Homeland* (London

n.d.), 21, 27. See also the fulsome account of the English sailor's genealogically acquired character traits in J. Cuthbert Hadden, *The Boy's Book of the
Navy* (London 1911), 49.

15 *The Patriotic Historical Readers* III (London 1898), 37–8.

16 John Finnemore, *Famous Englishmen* I (London 1901), 5, 13, 17.

17 H. Osman Newland, *The Model Citizen* (London 1907), 180; see also J.M.
MacKenzie, *Propaganda and Empire* (Manchester 1984), 183.

18 GLRO, Paragon School, New Kent Rd. Boys School, London, Logbook,
1901, 94, and Christ Church National School, Forest Hill, Boys Dept.,
Logbook, 1901, 98. BRO, Westbury on Tyrm, Bristol, Girls Board School,
Logbook, 1901, 259. MCL, Longsight Municipal School (Wesleyan, mixed),
Manchester, Logbook, 1901, 495. A major new series of general reading
books, *The King Alfred Readers* 8 vols. (London 1901), was issued to
commemorate the Alfred Millenary as well.

19 *The Warwick History Readers* (London 1895), VII: 246. This poem also
appeared in such varied books as *The Westminster Reading Books* VI
(London 1891) and *Nelson's Literature Readers* I (London 1906).

20 GLRO, Ancona Road Board School, Plumstead, Girls Dept., Logbook, 24
May 1907, 140; Christ Church National School, Forest Hill, Boys Dept.,
Logbook, 22 May 1908, 264. MCL, Abbott Street Board School, Girls Dept.,
Logbook, October 1881, 90–3.

21 P.T. Palgrave, *The Children's Treasury of Lyrical Poetry*, and *The Children's
Treasury of English Song*, Part One in both editions (London 1889), 31–2;
Songs of England's Glory (London 1902), 8–9.

22 *Songs of England's Glory*, 133–4.

23 Paul Rich, *Race and Empire in British Politics* (Cambridge 1986), 21–5.

24 Pamela Horn, 'English Elementary Education and the Growth of the
Imperial Ideal, 1880–1914,' in J.A. Mangan, ed., *Benefits Bestowed?*
(Manchester 1987), 44–5.

25 *School Government Chronicle* 77 (May 1907): 421.

26 'The Teaching of Patriotism,' *School Guardian* 21 (5 December 1896):
947–8.

27 For Lord Meath's flag-raising efforts, and the objections raised by various
groups, see Meath, *Memories of the Nineteenth Century* (London 1923), 328,
332; and the *School Government Chronicle* 77 (29 June 1907): 578. For
analysis of this campaign, see Horn, 'English Elementary Education,' 45;
and J.O. Springhall, 'Lord Meath, Youth, and Empire,' *Journal of Contemporary History* 5, no. 4 (1970): 97–111.

28 See the *Times*, 25 May 1905. By 1919 all but a handful of education
authorities in Britain supported the movement; see Horn, 'English
Elementary Education'; Springhall, 'Lord Meath'; and Anne Bloomfield,

'Drill and Dance as Symbols of Imperialism,' in J.A. Mangan, ed., *Making Imperial Mentalities* (Manchester 1990), 75–6.

29 See for examples from London, GLRO, Christ Church National School, Forest Hill, Girls Dept., Logbook, 24 May 1906, 237; Eglington Rd. Board School, Boys Dept., Logbook, 17 May 1907, 82; Grove St. Board School, Girls Dept., Logbook, 24 May 1907, 240; Our Lady of Victories, Warwick Rd. Catholic School, Boys, Logbook, 24 May 1907, 203; Christ Church National School, Forest Hill, Boys Dept., Logbook, 22 May 1908, 264; Halford Rd., North End Rd., Board School, Girls Dept., Logbook, 22 May 1908, 407; Ancona Road Board School, Plumstead, Girls Dept., Logbook, 24 May 1912, 194. For Manchester, see MCL, Upper Jackson St. Board School, Hulme, Girls Dept., Logbook, 22 June 1897, 82; St Barnabas Board School, Mixed, Logbook, 22 June 1897, 111, and January 1901, 187. For Bristol, see BRO, St Silas's School, Logbook, 24 May 1909, which is quoted in Horn, 'English Elementary Education.'

30 For some examples from school records from London of this practice, see GLRO, Calvert Rd. Board School, Girls Dept., Logbook, 22 May 1908, 164; Eglington Rd. Board School, Boys Dept., Logbook, 22 May 1908, 94; Kilburn Lane, Kensal Green, Board School, Boys, Logbook, 22 May 1908, 79; Paragon School, New Kent Rd. Boys, Logbook, 22 May 1908, 378; Our Lady of Victories, Warwick Rd. Catholic School, Boys, Logbook, 24 May 1909, 268.

31 GLRO, Halford Rd., North End Rd., Board School, Girls Dept., Logbook, 22 May 1908, 407.

32 See the stream of letters and articles in the *School Government Chronicle*. For instance, there were exchanges on the topic in the 11 May 1907 and 8 June 1907 issues (vol. 77).

33 *School Government Chronicle* 77 (29 June 1907): 578.

34 *King Edward History Readers: The Story of Our Own Times* (London 1903), 16.

35 J. St Loe Strachey, *The Citizen and the State* (London 1913), 222–3; George Bosworth, *Narrative Geography Readers* II (London 1910), 141–2. See also Arnold-Forster, *Citizen Reader*, 119.

36 Bosworth, *Narrative Geography Readers* II: 144.

37 *Collins' School Series: Over Land and Sea: England and Wales* (London 1906), 194.

38 Arnold-Forster, *Citizen Reader*, 132.

39 Yates, *Collins' Alternative Geography Readers* II: 7. See also Yates's comments in the *Graphic Science and Geography Readers* (London 1900).

40 *Raleigh History Readers* VII (London 1898), 265.

41 M. Yates, *Arnold's English Readers* IV (London 1893), 11. In this reader there are two distinct sections on the Union Jack, 'The Union of Our Flag' and 'The Flag of England.'

42 H.E. Malden, *The Life and Duties of a Citizen* (London 1894), 1–2.

43 Arnold-Forster, *Citizen Reader*, 121.

44 St Loe Strachey, *Citizen and State*, 223.

45 Bosworth, *Narrative Geography Readers* II: 140; *Chambers's Alternative Geography Readers* VII: 8.

46 Malden, *Life and Duties*, 1–2; Arnold-Forster, *Citizen Reader*, 129.

47 Bosworth, *Narrative Geography Readers* II: 142–4.

48 *Collins' School Series: Collins' Wide-World Reader* I (London 1901), 116.

49 Ibid.

50 *Collins' School Series: Over Land and Sea: England and Wales* (London 1906), 202.

51 Ibid., 203.

52 Yates, *Collins' Alternative Geography Readers* II: 7.

53 Arnold-Forster, *Citizen Reader*, 14.

54 St Loe Strachey, *Citizen and State*, 219.

55 Newland and Jones, *Model Citizen*, Scottish edition, 223.

56 Arnold-Forster, *Citizen Reader*, 130.

57 J.S. Hurt, 'Drill, Discipline and the Elementary School Ethos,' in Paul McCann, ed., *Popular Education and Socialization in the Nineteenth Century* (London 1977), 169.

58 *Reports on the Training of Pauper Children* (1839), quoted in ibid., 169–70.

59 See the *Report of the Committee of Council on Education, 1869–70*, C. 165 [PP XXII.1] (1870), cxxxvi; *Minute Modifying Provisions of New Code*, C. 1192 [PP LVIII.73] (1875); and also *Hansard Parliamentary Debates*, 3rd Series, vol. 223 (1875), cols. 1203–4.

60 Hurt, 'Drill, Discipline and the Elementary School Ethos,' 171. Alan Penn's excellent study, *Targetting Schools: Drill, Militarism and Imperialism* (London 1999), was published too late for its findings to be incorporated in this study. It does, however, support the general argument made here.

61 F.M. Normon (Commander, R.N.), *The Schoolmasters' Drill Assistant: A Manual of Drill for Elementary Schools* (London 1871), 3.

62 E. Chadwick, *The Health of Nations* vol. I (London 1887), 194.

63 *School Board Chronicle* 36 (24 July 1886), 92.

64 P.C. McIntosh, *Physical Education in England since 1800* (London 1952), 146–8.

65 PRO Ed. 22/3B, *Model Course of Physical Training* (HMSO 1901); Board of Education, *Syllabus of Physical Exercises for Use in Public Elementary Schools*

(HMSO 1909), vii; T. Chesterton, 'Physical Education under the School Board for London,' Committee of Council on Education, *Special Reports on Educational Subjects*, vol. II (1898), 186–201.

66 The 1902 code specified the use of the manual *Infantry Drill, 1902*. See McIntosh, *Physical Education*, 139–40. For the use of dummy rifles, see Sir Norman Lockyer, *Education and National Progress: Essays and Addresses, 1870–1905* (London 1906), 241.

67 *Hansard Parliamentary Debates* 4th Series, vol. 79 (1900), col. 410, and vol. 81 (1900), col. 831.

68 Numerous proposals to increase the amount of military drill can be found in the *School Board Chronicle* 63 (1900), and Lord Meath's campaign for compulsory drill in elementary schools can be seen in his letters to the *Morning Post* from November 1898 through February 1899.

69 PRO, Ed. 22/36, July 1902, copy of letter from J.K. Kenny, Adjutant General.

70 T. Chesterton, *The Theory of Physical Education in Elementary Schools* (London 1910), 118.

71 C. Dukes, 'Health and Physical Culture,' in P.A. Barnett, ed., *Teaching and Organisation* (London 1903), 362.

72 G.M. Campbell, 'Physical Training,' in J. Adams, ed., *The New Teaching* (London 1918 edition), 357. For other similar statements, see John Gorst, *The Children of the Nation* (London 1906), 1; W.P. Welpton, *Primary Artisan Education* (London 1913), ix; C. Jackson, *Outlines of Education in England* (London 1913), 86–9; M.H. Spalding, 'The Case for the Swedish System,' in Adams, ed., *New Teaching*, 378.

73 Hugh B. Philpott, *London at School: The Story of the School Board, 1870–1904* (London 1904), 116.

74 Ibid., 118.

75 London County Council, *Report of Proceedings: Eighth Annual Conference of Teachers, 1906* (London 1906), 2.

76 *School Government Chronicle* 75 (13 January 1906): 74–5.

77 Carolyn Steedman, *Childhood, Culture and Class in Britain: Margaret McMillan, 1860–1931* (New Brunswick, NJ 1990), 67.

78 *English History Reading Books: Illustrated English History* III: 283–4.

Conclusion: 'For Home, Country, and Race'

1 F.B. Toms, *Royal Artillery Gibraltar Christmas Pantomime: 'The Babes in the Woods and Robin Hood'* (Gibraltar 1898), 19.

2 PRO, Ed. 14/95, 'Report on the Teaching of English in London Elementary Schools,' 10 August 1908, and 'Minute to Selby-Biggs re: instruction,' 17 June 1908. GLRO, London County Council, *Report on the Teaching of History* (1911), and *Report on the Teaching of Geography* (1913). For the insistence of the professionals in these disciplines that they have a part to play in elementary education, see J.J. Findlay, *The Training of Teachers* (Manchester 1903); Halford J. Mackinder, *The Scope and Methods of Geography and the Geographical Pivot of History* (London 1904, reprinted 1969); James Bryce, *The Historical Association*, Leaflet no. 4, *The Teaching of History in Schools* (1907); 'Discussion following Papers,' *The Historical Association*, Leaflet no. 19, *The Methods of Teaching History in Schools* (London 1910).

3 J.M. MacKenzie, *Propaganda and Empire* (Manchester 1984), 4.

4 MacKenzie, *Propaganda and Empire*, 6.

5 Robin Betts, 'A Campaign for Patriotism on the Elementary School Curriculum: Lord Meath, 1892–1916,' *History of Education Society Bulletin*, no. 16 (1990): 38–45; MacKenzie, *Propaganda and Empire*, 173–98; J.A. Mangan, 'The Grit of Our Forefathers,' in John M. MacKenzie, ed., *Imperialism and Popular Culture* (Manchester 1986), 110–27; see also the articles in J.A. Mangan, ed., *Making Imperial Mentalities* (Manchester 1990), and J.A. Mangan, ed., *Benefits Bestowed? Education and British Imperialism* (Manchester 1987), especially, in this last collection, Pamela Horn's essay, 'English Elementary Education and the Growth of the Imperial Ideal: 1880–1914,' 39–55.

6 Betts, 'Campaign for Patriotism'; Managan, ed., *Benefits Bestowed?*; and Anne Bloomfield, 'Drill and Dance as Symbols of Imperialism,' in Mangan, ed., *Making Imperial Mentalities*, 74–95. For an earlier but similar approach, see J.O. Springhall, 'Lord Meath, Youth, and Empire,' *Journal of Contemporary History* 5, no. 4 (1970): 97–111.

7 *School Government Chronicle* 77 (20 April 1907): 370.

8 'Objects of the Navy League,' in *Minutes of the Proceedings at the Navy League Conference* (London 1898).

9 For the relationship between civil authorities and the navy in Portsmouth, see K. Lunn and R. Thomas, 'Naval Imperialism in Portsmouth, 1905–1914,' *Southern History* 10 (1988): 145–6.

10 GLRO, London County Council, *Education Committee Minutes: Books and Apparatus Subcommittee Report* (May 1907), 1219.

11 Horn, 'English Elementary Education,' 46 and footnote 42. She cites the Bristol School Board records for July 1901 and April 1902, but appears not

to have consulted the records for the Education Committee after the school board was abolished.

12 BRO, MB/S04/1, *Bristol Education Committee Minutes* (1903), 32, 107.

13 See the comments made by London teachers on this subject, in GLRO, School Board for London, SBL 682, 15 March 1889. For Manchester, see MCL, M65/1/5/16, *Minutes of School Mangers Committee*, 13 December 1894, 60. This reluctance also applied to the requests of other nationalist organizations for military training in schools and to the proposals of local socialist and pacifist organizers. See PRO, Ed. 24/408, Letters from the Education Department to H.O. Arnold-Forster, July 1905, and BRO, MB/S03/4, *Bristol Education Committee Minutes*, Special Committees, Series A, 1905, 3; Series B, 1906, 87.

14 GLRO, London County Council, *Education Committee Minutes, Books and Apparatus Subcommittee*, no. 11, May 1907, 1234.

15 See the nationwide survey on methods of book selection conducted by the School Board for London, GLRO, SBL 188, *Minutes of the Special Committee on the Selection of Schoolbooks* (reprinted as Appendix A), 12 May 1899, 10. Voluntary schools had less formal procedures, although the Anglican National Schools tended, on the whole, to be supplied with official National Society books and materials.

16 BRO MB/S03/4, *Bristol Education Committee Minutes*, Series A, 6 January 1906, record of letters from Bristol socialists complaining about the introduction of Empire Day observance. The letters argue that such an event would encourage 'false ideals of national egoism, worship of war, conquest and militarism, with its consequent racial hatred.' For similar letters sent to the London Educational authorities, see GLRO, London County Council, *Education Committee Minutes*, meeting of 3 July 1907, 2116. Pamela Horn notes that, in London, groups opposed to the London County Council's celebration of Empire Day suggested that a Peace Day also be observed; Horn, 'English Elementary Education,' 50.

17 GLRO, SBL 1419, London School Board Memo on the Teaching of History (with addenda), 18 July 1902, 7.

18 See my unpublished dissertation, 'English Elementary Education and the Construction of National Identity, 1880–1914' (PhD dissertation, University of Toronto 1996).

19 On the minimal role of the state in book selection and censorship, see Alec Ellis, *Books in Victorian Elementary Schools* (London 1971), 31–3.

20 Peter J. Bowker, *The Invention of Progress: The Victorians and the Past* (Oxford 1989); John Willinsky, *Learning to Divide the World: Education at Empire's End* (Minneapolis 1998).

21 'Introduction,' Robert Colls and Philip Dodd, eds., *Englishness: Politics and Culture, 1880–1920* (London 1986), 2. Emphasis in original.

22 Derek Heater, *Citizenship: The Civic Ideal in World History, Politics and Education* (London 1990), 189–90. See also J. Torney-Purta and J. Schwille, 'Civic Values Learned in School: Policy and Practice in Industrialized Countries,' *Comparative Education Review* 30, no. 1 (1986); J.V. Torney, A.N. Oppenheim, and R.F. Farnen, eds., *Civic Education in Ten Countries: An Empirical Study* (Stockholm 1975), esp. 29.

23 Jonathan Rose, 'Willingly to School: The Working-Class Response to Elementary Education in Britain, 1875–1914,' *Journal of British Studies* 32, no. 2 (1993): 28.

24 From an interview with Florence Mullen, born 1899, housewife and factory operative. Quoted in S. Humphries, 'Schooling and the Working Class in Bristol, 1870–1914,' *Journal of Southern History* 1 (1979): 184.

25 From an interview with Bill Woods, born 1902, Bristol, and who worked all his life as a labourer. Quoted in Stephen Humphries, *Hooligans or Rebels?: An Oral History of Working-Class Childhood and Youth, 1889–1939* (Oxford 1981), 42.

26 From an interview with Fred Mattock, born 1895, Bristol, tram and bus conductor. Quoted in ibid., 43.

27 Humphries, *Hooligans or Rebels?* 41.

28 The sample used for this conclusion includes: Philip Ballard, *Things I Cannot Forget* (London 1937); Kathleen Dayus, *Her People* (with introduction by John Rudd, London 1982); Harry Fletcher, *A Life on the Humber: Keeling to Shipbuilding* (London 1975); Grace Foakes, *My Part of the River* (London 1974); Bud Flannagan, *My Crazy Life* (London 1961); Clara Grant, *Farthing Bundles* (London 1930); Wal Hannington, *Never on Our Knees* (London 1967); Rowland Kenney, *Westering: An Autobiography by Rowland Kenney* (London 1939); Joy Lakeman, *Them Days: From the Memories of Joan Bellan* (Padstow, Cornwall 1982); Alice Bond, *Life of a Yorkshire Girl* (Hull 1981); Robert Roberts, *A Ragged Schooling* (London 1982); C.H. Rolph, *Living Twice: An Autobiography* (London 1974); Walter Southgate, *That's the Way It Was: A Working Class Autobiography, 1890–1950* (London 1982); Arthur Sturgess, *A Northamptonshire Lad* (Northampton 1982); Joseph Toole, *Fighting through Life* (London 1934); Frederick Willis, *Peace and Dripping Toast* (London 1950); Katherine Woodward, *Jipping Street* (London 1983).

29 Southgate, *That's the Way It Was*, 32.

30 Toole, *Fighting through Life*, 14.

31 Southgate, *That's the Way It Was*, 39.

32 Neil J. Smelser, *Social Paralysis and Social Change: British Working Class Education in the Nineteenth Century* (Berkeley 1991), 360.

Appendices

1 GLRO, SBL 188, *Minutes of Special Committee on the Selection of School Books,* (1899), 3–20.
2 Ibid., 3.
3 Ibid., 4.
4 Ibid.
5 The survey from which this list is compiled can be found in ibid., 10.
6 Ibid., 13.
7 Ibid., 20.
8 Corporation of London Record Office, Guildhall Library, MS. 29072, *Edward Arnold Publication Books,* vol. 1: 14, 15, 16, 43–5, 147, 149–55, 157, 159, 161, 163, 165, 167–91, 199, 203, 205, 207, 209, 244–6, 250, 252, 303, 305, 307, 309–14, 427–40, 474, 670, 823, 825–9, 831, 871.
9 University of Reading Archives, Longman Papers, *Impression Books,* vols. H26, H27, H28, H29, H30, H31, H32, H33, H34, H35.
10 British Library, *Add. Mss.* 55909, 55910, 55911, 55912, *Macmillan New Edition Books,* 4 vols., January 1892–December 1899.

Select Bibliography

Only archival sources and the classroom reading materials used in the preparation of this monograph are listed below. For references to contemporary books, teachers' manuals, and periodicals, and all secondary sources used, please consult the notes for each chapter.

I. Archival Sources

Public Record Office, London

Education File Series: Ed. 3; Ed. 9; Ed. 10; Ed. 11; Ed. 12; Ed. 14; Ed. 22; Ed. 24; Ed. 91; Ed. 92.

Church of England Record Centre, Bermondsey, London

National Society Annual Reports, vols. 69–103, 1880–1914.
National Society Finance Committee Minutes, vols. 7–8, 1884–1912.
National Society Standing Committee Minutes, vols. 8–10, 1880–1910.

Macmillian and Company Archive at the British Library, Manuscript Collection, London

Add. Mss. No. 55260–55269 General Correspondence, 1891–1914.
Add. Mss. No. 55354–55355 Letter Books, 1893–6.
Add. Mss. No. 55909–55918 Edition Books, 1892–1910.

Records of Edward Arnold and Company (Hodder and Stoughton Archive) at the Corporation of London Record Office, Guildhall Library, London

Ms. 29072 Publication Book, vol. 1, 1890–1902.
Ms. 29076 Stock Books, vols. 1–3, 1890–1910.
Ms. 29078 Copyright Record Books, vols. 1–4, 1890–1912.

Records of Longman, Green and Company at Reading University Archives

H24.–H36. Impression Books, 13 vols. 1879–1907.
Copyright Ledgers, No. 7 and No. 8. 1865–1909.
Longman Catalogue of Educational Works. 1910.

Bristol Record Office

School Board Minutes and Documents: MB/S/03; MB/S/04; MB/F2.
Bristol School Board Triennial Reports, 1889–1903.
Education Committee Printed Minutes, 1903–1914. Series A, B, and C.
Acc. 38773/11–17S Examination Papers, 1899–1912.
Acc. 40364 Bateman Papers: Kingswood Wesleyan Day School, 1896–1900.
Acc. 40542 St Mark's School, papers and logs.
Acc. 40556 Bristol School Board Newspaper reports.
Bristol Pupil Teachers' Centre Quarterly Magazine, vols. 1–9, November 1900–
    September 1909.
Bristol Area School Logbooks for 12 Elementary Schools, 1885–1910.

Greater London Record Office

School Board and Council Education Committee Records: SBL 188; SBL 681–
    2; SBL 709; SBL 861; SBL 1350; SBL 1419; LCC 1.a.a.
London County Council, *Report on the Teaching of English in London.* 1909.
London County Council, *Report on the Teaching of Geography in London.* 1911.
London County Council, *Report on the Teaching of History in London.* 1911.
London Area School Logbooks for 40 Elementary Schools, 1880–1914.
Middlesex Rural School Board Records and Logbooks: MCC/SB/1; MCC/
    SB/2; MCC/SB/3; MCC/SB/4; MCC/SB/7; 3 Logbooks, 1863–1898.

Manchester Central Library, Local Unit

Manchester School Board Records, including minutes: M65/1; M428/1–4.
Proceedings of the Elementary Education Subcommittee, 4 vols. 1903–1914.
Manchester Area School Logbooks for 15 Schools, 1880–1914.

II. United Kingdom Parliamentary Papers

Parliamentary Commissions and Reports

Report of the Commissioners Appointed to Enquire into the State of Popular
   Education in England. 2794-1-VII. 1861.
Copyright Commission. The Royal Commissions and the Report of the Commission-
   ers. C. 2036. 1878.
Reports of the Royal Commission Appointed to Enquire into the Workings of
   Elementary Education Acts (England and Wales).
   1st Report. C. 4863. 1886.
   2nd Report. C. 5056. 1887.
   3rd Report. C. 5158. 1887.
   Final Report, Minutes of Evidence, Index. C. 5329. 1888.
   Appendices. C. 5485. 1888.
Special Reports on Educational Subjects.
   1st Report. C. 8447. 1897.
   2nd Report. C. 8943. 1898.
Special Reports on Educational Subjects.
   Vol. 9. *Education in Germany.* Cd. 836. 1902.
   Vol. 16. *School Training for the Home Duties of Women.* Cd. 2963. 1906.
Report of the Inter-Departmental Committee on Physical Deterioration. Vol. I.
   Report and Appendix. Cd. 2175. 1904.
Revised Elementary Education Codes. 1862–99.
Reports of the Committee of Council on Education. 1861–97.
Reports of the Board of Education. 1900–14.

Board of Education Publications

Board of Education Circulars. Bound together in PRO, Ed. 142/35–41.
General Report by Mr H. Ward, H.M.I., Divisional Inspector, Upon Elementary
   Education in Lancashire and Cheshire, 1913–1914. HMSO. 1915.
Suggestions for the Consideration of Teachers and Others Concerned in the Work of
   Public Elementary Schools. HMSO. 1909–10.
Suggestions for the Consideration of Teachers and Others Concerned in the Work of
   Public Elementary Schools. A reprint of Cd. 2638 (1905). HMSO. 1912.
Syllabus of Physical Exercises for Use in Public Elementary Schools. HMSO. 1902,
   1904, 1905, and 1909.
Regulations for Secondary Schools. Report No. 561. HMSO, 1907.

The Teaching of History in Secondary Schools. Report No. 599. HMSO. 1908.
The Teaching of English in Secondary Schools. Report No. 753. HMSO. 1910.
Curricula of Secondary Schools. Report No. 826. HMSO. 1913.
Suggestions for the Teaching of History. Report No. 833. HMSO. 1914.
Suggestions for the Teaching of Geography. Report No. 834. HMSO. 1914.
Memorandum on Teaching in Secondary Schools. Report No. 869. HMSO. 1914.

III. Readers and Textbooks

The place of publication is London unless otherwise indicated. Dates refer to the edition consulted. The following format variations were used when listing the readers: if a series was published over a period of years a dash has been used between the earliest and latest dates; if several editions of the same series have been examined, the dates of each later edition are followed by a comma. The number of volumes indicated in the citation refers to the number of volumes consulted, not necessarily to the total number in the series. Lastly, the symbol '*' denotes formal textbooks, while the symbol '+' denotes texts used prior to 1870.

Abbott, Rev. E.A., and J.R. Seeley. *English Lessons for English People.* Seeley & Co. 1906.
Adams, John. *Blackwood's Literature Readers.* 4 vols. Blackwood & Sons. 1903.
Airy, Osmund. *Text-Book of English History.* Longmans. 1891.*
Alford, Henry. *The Queen's English.* W. Ibster & Co. 1874.
Allison, M.A. *A Guide to English History and Biography.* Jarrold & Sons. 1857.
Armitage-Smith, G. *The Citizen of England.* Chambers. 1895.
Arnold's Domestic Readers. 2 vols. Edward Arnold. 1894.
Arnold's English Readers. 4 vols. Edward Arnold. 1893.
Arnold's Geography Readers. 7 vols. Edward Arnold. 1894.
Arnold's History Readers. 2 vols. Edward Arnold. 1895.
Arnold's Scottish Geography Readers. 6 vols. Edward Arnold. 1899.
Arnold-Forster, H.O. *The Citizen Reader.* Cassell & Co. 1887.
Arnold-Forster, H.O. *Things New and Old: Stories from English History.* 7 vols. Cassell & Co. 1895.
Avon Geographical Readers. 4 vols. Pitman & Sons. 1892–8.
Avon Historical Readers. 2 vols. Pitman & Sons. 1892–8.
Baker, W.G. *Blackie's Comprehensive School Series Geographical Reader.* Blackie. 1881.
Bartlett, Barbara. *Allman's Penny School Series: History of England; Natural History; Geography of the British Empire and Colonies; Domestic Economy for Girls.* T.J. Allman. 1872.

Black's Literary Readers. 3 vols. Adam & Charles Black. 1906.

Black's School Geography. Adam & Charles Black. 1897.

Black's Sentinal Readers. Vol. 1. Adam & Charles Black. 1912.

Black's Supplementary Readers. 3 vols. Adam & Charles Black. 1908–9.

Blackie's Class Books of Geography. 3 vols. Blackie & Co. 1900.

Blackie's Complete History of England. 4 vols. Blackie & Co. 1896.

Blackie's Continental Geography Readers. 3 vols. Blackie & Co. 1901.

Blackie's Continuous Readers. 4 vols. Blackie & Co. 1910.

Blackie's Domestic Economy Readers. 2 vols. Blackie & Co. 1895.

Blackie's Geographical Readers. 2 vols. Blackie & Co. 1884.

Blackie's Historical Readers. 4 vols. Blackie & Co. 1883.

Blackie's Model Readers. 2 vols. Blackie & Co. 1908.

Blackie's Scottish Supplementary Readers. Vol. 1. Blackie & Co. 1909.

Blackie's Tropical Readers. 4 vols. Blackie & Co. 1897–1911.

Blackwood's Education Series Literary Readers. 3 vols. Wm. Blackwood. 1883, 1886.

Blackwood's Literature Readers. 1 vol. Wm. Blackwood. 1899.

Blandford, H. *An Elementary Geography of India.* Macmillan. 1890.*

Bosworth, George. *Narrative Geographical Readers.* 2 vols. Macmillan. 1910.

Brewer, E.C. *My First Book of Geography.* Cassell, Petter, & Galpin. 1864.+

Brewer, E.C. *My First Book of History.* Cassell, Petter, & Galpin. 1864.+

Britannia Geography Readers. 3 vols. Edward Arnold. 1896.

Browning, Oscar. *The Citizen: His Rights and Responsibilities.* Blackie & Sons. 1893.

Browning, Oscar. *Epochs of English History: Modern England.* Longmans. 1891.

Butler, Henry. *The Etymological Spelling Book and Exposition.* Simpkin & Co. 1865.+

Callcot, Lady. *Little Arthur's History of England.* John Murray. 1900.+

Cambridge Geography Texts. 2 vols. Cambridge: University Press. 1912.

Cambridge Historical Readers. 8 vols. Cambridge: University Press. 1911, 1915, 1927.

Cassell's Historical Course for Schools. 3 vols. Cassell & Co. 1884.

Cassell's Modern School Series. Vol. 1. Cassell & Co. 1885.

Cassell's New Geographical Readers. 3 vols. Cassell & Co. 1895.

Catholic Child's History of England. Robert Washbourne. 1890.

The Century Historical Readers. 2 vols. Blackie. 1890.

Chambers's Alternative Geography Readers. 4 vols. Chambers. 1898–9.

Chambers's Alternative History Readers. 4 vols. Chambers. 1898.

Chambers's Geographical Readers. 7 vols. Chambers. 1883–6.

Chambers's Historical Readers. 4 vols. Chambers. 1882–8.

Chambers's Historical Readers. Scotch [sic] Code. 3 vols. Edinburgh. Chambers. 1888.

Chambers's National History Readers: Scheme A. 6 vols. Chambers. 1897.
Chambers's New Scheme History Readers. 6 vols. Chambers. 1901–5.
Chambers's Summary of English History. Chambers. 1904.
Chambers's 20th Century Geography Manuals. 7 vols. Chambers. 1903.
Clough's Reign of Elizabeth. Royal Standard Series. Ralph, Holland & Co. 1899.*
Cockran, J.F. *Concise History of England.* Constable. 1859.+
Collier, W.F. *Collier's Great Events of History.* Nelson & Sons. 1888.*
Collins' Alternative Geography Readers. 3 vols. Collins. 1900.
Collins' Graphic School Series. 2 vols. Collins. 1907.
Collins' New Biographical Series. 3 vols. Collins. 1909.
Collins' Wide-World Geography Readers. 5 vols. Collins. 1901.
The Complete History Readers. 7 vols. Blackie & Son. 1902–6.
Creighton, Mandell. *Longman's Historical Biographies.* Vol. 1. *Life of Simon de Montfort.* Longman, 1895.
Creighton, Mandell. *The Shilling History of England.* Longman, 1881.*
Curtis, J.C. *Outlines of English History.* Simpkin, Marshall & Hamilton. 1901.*
Cutts. *Turning Points of English History.* Society for the Promotion of Christian Knowledge. 1889.
Daniel, Rev. C. *The Grammar, History and Derivation of the English Language.* National Society Depository. 1896.*
Davies, A.M. *Macmillan's Practical Geography of British Isles.* Macmillan. 1909.*
Dawe, Rev. C.S. *King Edward's Realm.* Educational Supply Association. 1902.
Dawe, Rev. C.S. *The Growth and Greatness of Our World-Wide Empire.* Educational Supply Association. 1899.
Dawe, Rev. C.S. *Queen Victoria and Her People.* Educational Supply Association. 1897.
Dunn, Henry, and John Thomas Crossley. *The Daily Lesson Books for the Use of Schools and Families.* 4 vols. British & Foreign School Society. 1840–2.+
Elias, Edith L. *This England of Ours.* G.G. Harrapt & Co. 1914.
English History Home Lesson Books. 4 vols. National Society's Depository. 1882.
English History Reading Books. 5 vols. Society for the Promotion of Christian Knowledge & National Society's Depository. 1881, 1885.
Fearenside, C.S. *A School History of England.* Clive. 1904.*
Finnemore, J. *Black's School Series: Story of the English People.* 2 vols. Adam & Charles Black. 1905.
Finnemore, J. *Boys and Girls of Other Days.* National Publishing. 1898.
Finnemore, J. *Chambers Supplementary Readers: Children of Empire.* 2 vols. Chambers. 1905.
Finnemore, J. *Famous Englishmen.* 2 vols. Adam & Charles Black. 1901.
Finnemore, J. *Social Life in England.* 2 vols. Adam & Charles Black. 1912.

First Reading Book. Parts 1–4. Society for the Promotion of Christian Knowledge. 1854.+

Flanagan, Rev. T. *A Short Catechism of English History.* Derby. 1845.+

Fletcher, C.R.L., and R. Kipling. *A School History of England.* Oxford: Clarendon Press. 1911.*

Froude, Henry. *The King's English.* Oxford: Clarendon Press. 1906.*

Gardiner, S.R. *1st Course Standard History Readers.* 4 vols. Longman. 1887–8.

Gardiner, S.R. *A Student's History of England.* Longman. 1892.*

Garnett, R. *Nelson's Literature Readers.* 4 vols. Nelson and Son. 1906.

Gasquet, F.A. *The Abbey History Readers.* 4 vols. George Bell and Sons. 1902–3.

Gill's History of England in Lessons for Home Use. Gill & Sons. 1870.

Gill's Illustrated Series of Readers. 3 vols. Gill & Sons. 1871.

Gill's Imperial Series Standard Geography. Gill & Sons. 1878.*

Gleig, Rev. George R. *School History of England.* Society for the Promotion of Christian Knowledge. 1859.+

Glover, William. *A Little Book on the Cardinal Virtues. Including a Chapter on Citizenship.* Chambers. 1914.

Good Things. Made, Said, and Done for Every Home and Household. Leeds: Goodall, Backhouse & Co. 1895.

Harris's First Book. Reading Made Completely Easy. J.S. Otley Publishing. 1870.

Hassall, A. *The Making of the British Empire.* Blackie. 1896.*

Henty, G.A. *The Sovereign Reader.* Blackie. 1887.

Herbertson, A.J. *The Junior Geography.* Oxford: Clarendon Press. 1908.

Heroic Reader. Jarrold. 1897.

Hewitt, James. *Geography of the British Colonies and Dependencies.* Vol. 1. National Society. n.d.

Heywood, J. *Heywood's Manchester Readers.* 3 vols. Manchester: John Heywood. 1871.

Holborn Series of Reading Books. Vol. 1. Educational Supply Association. 1884.

Hudson. *The Romance of Our Colonies.* Pitman & Sons. 1912.

Ker, Alice. *Motherhood: A Book for Every Woman.* Manchester: John Heywood. 1896.*

King Alfred Readers. 8 vols. Edward Arnold. 1900.

King Edward's History Readers. 8 vols. Pitman & Sons. 1901–5.

King Geographical Readers. 3 vols. Moffat and Page. 1901.

Laurie, J.S. *Standard Series.* 4 vols. Marshall. 1871.

Lawson, William. *The Geographical Primer.* Oliver & Boyd. 1889.

Lawson, William. *Holborn Geography Readers.* Book IV. Blackie. n.d.

Lawson, William. *Lawson's Junior Class Geography.* Oliver & Boyd. 1891.

Lawson, William. *Manual of Modern Geography.* Collins. n.d.*

Little Mothers: A Reading Book for Girls in Domestic Economy. Blackie. 1893.

Littlewood, W.E. *Essentials of English History*. Wakefield. 1865.+

Liversey, T. *Granville History Readers*. Burn & Oates. 1902.

Longman's British Empire Readers. 3 vols. Longman, Green & Co. 1905.

Longman's New Geographical Readers. 7 vols. Longman, Green & Co. 1887.

Longman's New Historical Readers. 7 vols. Longman, Green & Co. 1888.

Longman's New Reading Books. 6 vols. Longman, Green & Co. 1885.

Longman's School Geography. Longman, Green & Co. 1887.*

Longman's Shilling Geography. Longman, Green & Co. 1887.*

Longman's 'Ship' Historical Readers. 3 vols. Longman, Green & Co. 1895.

Longman's 'Ship' Literary Readers. 3 vols. Longman, Green & Co. 1903.

MacDougall's The English Homeland. MacDougall's Educational Co. n.d.*

Mackay, Alex. *The Intermediate Geography*. William Blackwood & Sons. 1889.*

Macmillan's Colonial Readers. 4 vols. Macmillan. 1901.

Macmillan's Elementary Geography of British Colonies. 2 vols. Macmillan. 1892, 1904.

Macmillan's Geography Readers. 4 vols. Macmillan. 1897–1900.

Macmillan's New Geography Readers. 3 vols. Macmillan. 1901.

Macmillan's New History Readers. 4 vols. Macmillan. 1901.

Macmillan's New History Readers. Scottish Code. 3 vols. Macmillan. 1905.

Macmillan's Story Readers. 4 vols. Macmillan. 1903.

Malden, H.E. *The Life and Duties of a Citizen*. Methuen. 1894.

Marcus Ward Geography Reading Books. 2 vols. Marcus Ward. 1883.

Marcus Ward School Series: A Short History of England. Marcus Ward. 1897.

Mason, Charlotte M. *London Geographical Readers*. 3 vols. Edward Stanford. 1898.

Meiklejohn, J. *The British Empire: Its Geography, Resources, Commerce, Land-ways, and Water-ways*. Simpkin, Marshall, Hamilton, Kent & Co. 1891.*

Meiklejohn, J. *A New History of the British Empire*. Hughes & Co. 1878.*

Meiklejohn, J. *A School History of England*. Holden. 1901.

Mongan, Roscoe. *Oxford and Cambridge History of England for School Use*. Gill & Sons. 1904.*

Morris, D. *A Class Book of England*. Longman, Green & Co. 1871.

Morris, D. *Historical Readers: History of England*. 4 vols. Wm. Ibister. 1883.

Morris, D. *Senior Standard History Readers*. 3 vols. Longman, Green & Co. 1883.

Morris, Rev. R. *Elementary Lessons in Historical English Grammar*. Macmillan. 1893.

Murche, Vincent. *The Globe Geography Readers*. Vol. 1. Macmillan. 1898.

Nelson's Junior Supplementary Reader. Vol. 1. Nelson & Sons. 1904.

Nelson's Literature Readers. Vol. 1. Nelson & Sons. 1906.

Nelson's Royal School Series. Highroads of Literature. Vol. 1. Nelson & Sons. 1914.

Nelson's Sunday School Series. 2 vols. Nelson & Sons. 1873.

Nelson's World at Home Series. 4 vols. Nelson & Sons. 1905?.

Nestfield, J.C. *English Grammar. Past and Present.* Macmillan & Co. 1898.*

New Era Geography Readers: Our Imperial Heritage. 7 vols. Pitman & Sons. 1901–6.

Newland, H. Osman. *The Model Citizen.* Pitman & Sons. 1907.

Newland. H. Osman. *The Model Citizen.* Scottish edition. Edinburgh: Pitman & Sons. 1910.

Oliver and Boyd's Excelsior Readers. 2 vols. Oliver & Boyd. 1906–7.

Oman, C. *History of England.* Edward Arnold. 1895.*

Oriel Geographical Readers. 2 vols. Marcus Ward. 1886–8.

Oriel Readers. 2 vols. Marcus Ward. 1885.

Oswald, John. *Textbook of Historical and Geographical Terms and Definitions.* Manchester: James Gant & Co. 1886.*

Over Land and Sea: New Geographical Readers. 2 vols. Collins. 1903.

Palgrave, P.T. *The Children's Treasury of English Song.* 2 vols. Macmillan. 1889.

Parrott, J.E. *Waterloo Citizen Reader.* W.H. Allen. 1893.

Patriotic Historical Readers. 5 vols. Collins. 1899.

Piers Plowman Readers. 2 vols. George Philip & Son. 1913.

Pitman's Geography Readers: The Motherland. Book 3. Pitman & Sons. 1913.

Pitman's London Readers. 2 vols. Pitman & Sons. 1906.

Prince Edward Readers. 2 vols. Collins. 1904.

Raleigh Geography Readers. 4 vols. Blackie & Son. 1899–1901.

Raleigh History Readers. 4 vols. Blackie & Son. 1897–9.

Ransome, C. *Elementary History of England.* Rivingtons. 1890, 1900.*

Rice, E. *A Text-Book of Domestic Economy.* Blackie & Son. 1884?.*

Royal School Series. Royal English History Readers. 4 vols. Nelson & Sons. 1880.

Royal School Series. Royal Geographical Readers. 5 vols. Nelson & Sons. 1880.

Royal School Series. High Roads of Geography. 4 vols. Nelson & Sons. 1910.

Royal School Series. Royal Map Books. 3 vols. Nelson & Sons. 1883.

Royal School Series. Royal Osborne Geography Readers. 3 vols. Nelson & Sons. 1899.

Royal School Series. World at Home Readers. Std. I. Nelson & Sons. 1883.

Salmon, David. *Longman's Junior School Grammar.* Longman, Green & Co. 1890.*

The School Board Manuals (in one volume). No. II: English History; No. III: Geography. Charles Griffin. 1873.

Sewell, E.M. *A Catechism of English History*. 1872.

Seymour's Elementary Series: Uncle William's Concise History of England. J.A. Seymour. 1879.

Snowdon, E. *Chambers Story Readers: Stories for Standard I*. Chambers. 1898.

Songs of England's Glory. Ibister & Sons. 1902.

Speight, E.E. *The Temple Reader*. H. Marshall & Son. 1900.

Strachey, Joe St Loe. *The Citizen and the State*. Macmillan. 1913.

Stronach, A.L. *Simple History of English Literature*. Nelson & Sons. 1899.*

Tait, C.W. *Synopsis of History*. Macmillan. 1898.*

Taylor, T.S. *First Principles of Modern History, 1815–1879*. Relfe Brothers. 1880.

Thomas, W.B., ed. *The Citizen Books*. 3 vols. Alston Rivers. 1908.

Tout, T.F. *History of Britain*. Macmillan. 1906.*

Tower History Readers. 5 vols. Pitman. 1907.

Trotter, William Finlayson. *The Citizen and His Duties*. T.C. & E.C. Jack. 1907.

Warwick History Readers. 7 vols. Blackie & Son. 1895–6.

West, A. *English Grammar for Beginners*. Cambridge: University Press. 1903.*

Westminster Reading Books. 6 vols. National Society's Depository. 1891–2.

Whitehall Literary Readers. Std. IV. Gill & Sons. 1889?.

Wyatt, C.H. *The English Citizen: His Life and Duty*. Macmillan. 1894.

Yates, M.T., ed. *Graphic Science and Geography Readers*. 3 vols. Collins. 1900.

Yates, M.T., ed. *Nelson's Royal Star Readers*. Vol. IV. Nelson & Sons. 1887.

Yates, M.T., ed. *New Graphic Readers*. 2 vols. Collins. 1898.

Yates, M.T., ed. *Royal Atlas Readers*. 2 vols. Nelson & Sons. 1895.

Yonge, C.M. *Westminster Historical Reading Books*. 2 vols. National Society's Depository. 1891–2.

York Powell, F., and T. Tout. *History of England*. Longman. 1900.*

Young Britons History Readers. 2 vols. Collins. 1905.

Young, F. *The Class and Home Lesson Book of Geography*. T.J. Allman. 1871.

Young, F. *The Explanatory Reader*. Cassell, Petter & Galpin. 1869.

Index

STUDIES IN GENDER AND HISTORY

General editors: Franca Iacovetta and Karen Dubinsky